Scribe Publications
MEN OF MONT ST QUENTIN

Dr Peter Stanley is director of the Centre for Historical Research at the National Museum of Australia. He was the principal historian at the Australian War Memorial for 20 years, where he worked from 1980 to 2007.

Men of Mont St Quentin is Dr Stanley's twenty-first book. His recent books include *Quinn's Post: Anzac, Gallipoli*; *Invading Australia*; and *A Stout Pair of Boots*. He is well known from media appearances as a leading commentator on Australian history.

For all those
whose lives have been touched
by Mont St Quentin

Men of Mont St Quentin

between victory and death

Peter Stanley

SCRIBE
Melbourne

Scribe Publications Pty Ltd
PO Box 523
Carlton North, Victoria, Australia 3054
Email: info@scribepub.com.au

First published by Scribe 2009

Copyright © Peter Stanley 2009

All rights reserved. Without limiting the rights under copyright reserved above, no part of this publication may be reproduced, stored in or introduced into a retrieval system, or transmitted, in any form or by any means (electronic, mechanical, photocopying, recording or otherwise) without the prior written permission of the publishers of this book.

Maps by Keith Mitchell
Typeset in 11.5/16 pt Janson by the publishers
Printed and bound in Australia by Griffin Press. Only wood grown from sustainable regrowth forests is used in the manufacture of paper found in this book.

National Library of Australia
Cataloguing-in-Publication data

Stanley, Peter, 1956-

Men of Mont St Quentin : between victory and death

9781921215339 (pbk.)

Australia; Infantry Battalion, 21st; 9 Platoon–History; World War, 1914-1918–Regimental histories–Australia; Somme, 2nd Battle of the, France, 1918; World War, 1914-1918–Participation, Australian; Somme (France)–History, Military.

940.435

This project has been assisted by
the Australian Government through
the Australia Council for the Arts,
its arts funding and advisory body.

www.scribepublications.com.au

Contents

Note on sources — vi

Prologue
'The Most Awful Day in Our Lives' — 1

Introduction
Remembering the Great War — 7

Part I: Belonging
The Road to Querrieu — 19

Part II: Fighting
Mont St Quentin, 1 September 1918 — 73

Part III: Grieving
'The War Took Him' — 149

Part IV: Remembering
Shadows of a Battle — 191

Epilogue
The Sound of a Voice So Still — 255

Acknowledgements — 263
Notes — 267
Bibliography — 282
Index — 291

NOTE ON SOURCES

As ever, I have attempted to limit abbreviations and military jargon. The following abbreviations will be found in the notes:

AWM	Australian War Memorial, Canberra
ML	Mitchell Library, Sydney
NAA	National Archives of Australia, Canberra, Melbourne, Perth and Sydney
NAUK	National Archives, United Kingdom, London
NLA	National Library of Australia, Canberra
SLV	State Library of Victoria, Melbourne

Documents in Garry Roberts's Record Books in the State Library of Victoria are identified as, for example, '12/456', meaning folio 456 of Record Book 12.

PROLOGUE

'The Most Awful Day in Our Lives': Melbourne, Friday 13 September 1918

That morning, Garry Roberts rose early. During the week, the Robertses lived at 'Eumana', a small villa in what was then called 'Upper Hawthorn', in Melbourne's eastern suburbs. Garry ate breakfast with his 27-year-old daughter, Gwen, and read the papers: he took both the *Age* and the *Argus*. His wife, Roberta (Berta), was at their weekender, 'Sunnyside', at South Sassafras, twenty-odd miles up the Belgrave line in the Dandenongs, with their youngest child, fifteen-year-old Bert (known as Johnny), who liked to get into the bush and shoot things. Garry and Berta's eldest son, Frank, was away at the war in France—a fact that the Robertses bore with the mixture of pride and fear shared by a million-or-so of their fellow Australians in the fourth year of the most terrible war that humanity had ever known.

The Robertses were a close and happy family, though inclined to overlook Bert and Gwen in admiring Frank's achievements. Garry's job entailed poring over figures—he was the accountant for the Melbourne Municipal Tramways

Trust—but he also dabbled in history as a hobby. He had joined the recently formed Victorian Historical Society, and wrote local histories. Most of all, his family tolerated his diligent, not to say obsessive, desire to document many aspects of their life in the dozens of huge scrapbooks he filled most evenings. It is the existence of Garry's scrapbooks—he called them 'Record Books'—that have made it possible to tell this story.

At breakfast, the postman delivered a letter from Frank, written nearly two months before, in July. Garry shared the letter with Gwen, but then had to leave for the office, in the city. Gathering a bundle of newspapers to post to Frank, he stepped out of Eumana's white picket gate and turned right to walk the couple of hundred yards downhill towards the tram stop on Riversdale Road. There had been a heavy dew that morning, but the early spring day was dry, warm, and mostly sunny.

Garry strode out, secure in the knowledge that, two months before, Frank had been well. Perhaps, as he walked down Hastings Road, a familiar thought struck him: he did not know what had happened since Frank had written, and perhaps the dread surely shared by the loved ones of those in peril rose in his stomach. He caught his usual Hawthorn Tramway Trust electric tram into the city. He probably arrived with seconds to spare, knowing the timetables backwards, and travelled free, probably greeting the driver and conductor by name as he climbed aboard the French grey-painted car. Aboard the tram he saw W.C. Hart, the treasurer of the Sailors and Soldiers' Fathers' Association (which he had joined a year before), and another friend, Guy Innes, the editor of the *Herald*. A great mixer, Garry introduced the two to each other.

Their journey through Hawthorn and Richmond would have pointed to a country and community at war. Many passengers would have worn badges testifying to the way that the war had impinged on their lives. Women wore 'sweetheart' brooches, often in the form of miniature colour patches of their loved one's unit. Others wore 'female relative' badges, indicating that their men were at the war. Some women would be dressed in black; some men would be wearing black armbands. On the roadside, patriotic posters vied with equally vivid hoardings advertising boot blacking, gravy, and soap powder—Norman Lindsay's most lurid propaganda posters had been released about this time.

After a twenty-minute journey and a change onto the cable tram at Princes Bridge, Garry's tram clattered to a halt at the terminus outside the red-brick Victorian Italianate Tramways Building at the west end of Bourke Street shortly before ten o'clock. Garry went, as usual, to his office, and chatted to one of his staff for a while before noticing a buff telegram envelope on his desk. He opened the envelope and read:

I regret to inform you that London advises your cablegram of the 14th August addressed to 6874 Roberts as being undeliverable owing to the addressee being killed in action.

Garry Roberts had learned from this banal and routine message that his son was dead.

We know what Garry did and thought from his own account of that day, preserved in a distracted scrawl in his bulky 'Australia' 1918 diary. He immediately left work and made his way to the Red Cross Enquiry Office, a couple of blocks away in Market Street. He knew what to do from talks with other bereaved members of the Fathers' Association: he *must* have foreseen this moment. The Red Cross's office knew nothing—'Base Records' at Victoria Barracks only sent lists of casualties after informing families—but Garry filled out a form asking the Red Cross to enquire about and report on

Frank. Then he went to Victoria Barracks in St Kilda Road where, he wrote, he had his 'fears confirmed'. Frank had been reported as 'killed' in the latest casualty list transmitted from London. He returned to the Red Cross enquiry office, where he gave the sizeable donation of a guinea to have them cable the Australian Imperial Force records office in London for further 'particulars'—a word that recurs throughout Garry's long search for more and more detail of Frank's death. (Did he distractedly pull a sovereign and a shilling from his coin pocket? Was the sizeable donation, about half the basic weekly wage, somehow proportional to the urgency of his need? Later, he pasted the receipt for it into the Record Book as well.)

Back at the office, he met his brother Will, who had lost his own son, Lennard, on Gallipoli three years before. Will had heard the news from Gwen, who had opened the door at Eumana to see what every civilian with a loved one at the war dreaded: a clergyman on the doorstep. Fortunately, a friend was visiting—Edie Eastaugh, a teacher on holiday. (Edie had taught Frank at the South Melbourne College a decade before, and had become a friend of the family.) Edie stayed with Gwen, and later that morning seems to have seen her onto the train for the Dandenongs to join her mother. Garry thought of Frank's wife, Ruby, and telephoned her father, George, at 'Warwick Farm', also in the Dandenongs. It was George who told Ruby that she was now a widow. Soon after, Berta happened to walk over from Sunnyside to Warwick Farm, and she learned from Ruby that her son had been killed. When she returned to Sunnyside, probably on the Warwick Farm cart, Berta told Bert that his elder brother had been killed.

Garry caught a tram back to Eumana soon after noon. In his diary, he recorded that he took the 6.58 train from Hawthorn to the Dandenongs. What did he do in that empty house between, say, 12.30 and about 6.30? His diary is silent, though he did describe feeling 'sick with grief'. It's likely that, for Garry, these were the blackest hours of his life. With the realisation of Frank's death sinking in, perhaps he simply gave in to weeping for those solitary hours. Later that afternoon, he regained his customary self-discipline and set out for Camberwell station. He needed to reach Sunnyside, to be with Berta and his family. His tread down the street was surely less jaunty than it had been that morning.

Alighting from the train at Belgrave, Garry took the familiar route up the long, steady slope toward South Sassafras. The road ran through a tall forest echoing with bird calls, the white gravel illuminating his path in the gathering dusk. Half an hour later, Berta met him on the steps of Sunnyside. She had been hoping that the news was mistaken, but Garry had to confirm its truth. Garry had to tell 'my brave son's brave mother that our first born had died a hero's death'. The only consolation he could offer was that Frank had died 'to help to save mankind'.

'She was distressed …' he began, then crossed it out and wrote, 'We were both distressed.' Dinner must have been a strained, silent, and sad affair. After Gwen and Johnny had gone tearfully to bed, Garry and Berta sat and talked about Frank, how proud they were of him, and 'what a fine dear son he had been'. Not for another six days was Garry able to take out his diary and write a long account of what he called 'the most awful day in our lives'. Soon after, he pasted the telegram into one of the Record Books that would become Frank's memorial. As he recorded what had happened on that day, Garry began the search for an understanding of what happened to Frank. It became a search that made this book possible.[1]

INTRODUCTION

Remembering the Great War

Two weeks before the most awful day in the Robertses' lives, Australian soldiers had attacked a strongly fortified German position on a hill overlooking the town of Péronne in northern France. They captured the hill, Mont St Quentin, after two days of hard fighting in which about 500 Australians and as many Germans died. The Australian success helped to drive the Germans out of the vital 'Somme bend' at Péronne, a further push in the 'hundred days' of the Allied offensive that at last brought fighting to a close on the Western Front two months later, on 11 November.

The capture of Mont St Quentin has been celebrated as 'the most brilliant achievement' of the Australian Imperial Force; a triumph for its most senior general, Sir John Monash; and a symbol of the disproportionate influence that the Australian Corps exerted in the final months of the Great War.[1] And perhaps it was, although this book presents a more critical view of the dramatic and decisive action. This book began as a study of the 'Battle of Mont St Quentin'. While it still tells the story of some of the Australians who entered this action, it does not attempt to tell the whole story of the battle in detail, nor does it end with the capture of the Mont. In the course of research, my interest in Mont St Quentin shifted: an early encounter with previously unused sources decisively changed its focus. I now use the experience of just one platoon in this one action to explore the relationship between the Australian Imperial Force (AIF) and the society that created and sustained it, and to ponder on that war's impact upon its people in the decades that followed.

Mont St Quentin was a most unusual battle for the AIF in the Great War. It does not connect with the popular image of that war: it did not involve costly trench-to-trench assaults, slogging, futile attacks, and mud; instead, it was a short battle of rapid movement and quick decisions made by many commanders, often acting on their own initiative. I became interested in this action partly because it challenged the conventional view of the Great War, and partly because it allowed me to say something about the Australian experience of the Great War at its end—just as an earlier book enabled me to explore one of the earliest Australian experiences of the war.[2] But, more importantly, it has allowed me to examine the relationship between Australia and the first AIF. Exploring the lives of the men of Nine Platoon, C Company of the 21st Battalion, who took part in the final assault on the summit of the Mont on the afternoon of 1 September, allowed me to do this. I began to investigate this battle not in the usual way—that is, not by tracing the results of commanders' decisions (which has been the model for military history since Thucydides wrote about the Peloponnesian War)—but to begin with the soldiers' experience and, most unusually, with their detailed descriptions of it.

Nine Platoon included Garry Roberts's son, Frank, a 'Number Two' on one of its two Lewis guns. Almost at the moment of victory, Frank was killed: some thought he was hit by a bomb fragment; others, by a bullet in the chest. A couple of days later, the surviving members of his platoon buried him, along with ten other men of the battalion on the Mont. They erected a rough cross over the grave which, in due course, found its way to the Australian War Memorial, where it remains on display. Frank and the Robertses are therefore the focus of the story, but they and their family papers also let us understand what happened to his comrades.

As we have seen, Frank Roberts's family learned of his death twelve days later. Like many bereaved parents, Garry Roberts wanted to know exactly when and how his son had died. He contacted members of Frank's platoon, and badgered, persuaded, and begged them to record their recollections of that day. These detailed accounts provide the route into not just what happened to them on 1 September 1918, but into an understanding of their lives. This book is therefore a 'multiple biography' of a small group of about a dozen men.*

Central to this story are Garry Roberts's papers in the State Library of Victoria. There are also AIF records held by the Australian War Memorial; the personal papers of other members of the units involved in the battle; official records of various kinds, including the AIF personnel and Repatriation Department files in the National Archives of Australia; and various local and family records, including the memories of relatives and friends. Through them, I have been able to explore who these men were and how the Great War affected them and their society.

This is a book about war for readers who may not normally read or may even be uncomfortable with 'military history'.

---

* Let's get this uncertainty out of the way: on 31 August, Nine Platoon had thirteen members. Les Baker was wounded that evening and the platoon entered the actual attack on the Mont twelve men strong. But Les's story is too good to omit.

While it includes a close study of an afternoon of battle, it is not another conventional study of yet another Anzac triumph. It does not assume that the reader knows or cares about Australian military history, the structure and functions of an infantry battalion on the Western Front, or the tactics of war in 1918.

It does begin with the assumption that the Great War became the most important event in the lives of many of the generations who entered it, not all of whom saw the end of it. For some, the war ended lives; for others, it changed them utterly. From 1914, the world was made up of those who went or did not go; those who lost loved ones or welcomed them home; and people who believed that the war was worthwhile or those who became disillusioned with the way that governments and armies had manipulated their lives. For Australians, the Great War became a part of an individual's mental landscape, and their family experience and memory, just as it brought changes to the political and social composition of the nation, and introduced into the physical landscape memorials that have come to symbolise the effects of what remained for most of the Great War.

This is not the first time that Garry Roberts, his dead son, and his family have made an appearance in print. He's not yet the 'hero of a thousand footnotes'—a label given to an unusually articulate tradesman whose diary turns up in every thesis and article written about the working class in Victorian Britain—but he has had several outings. Joy Damousi devoted four pages to the Robertses in her book *The Labour of Loss*, which is a study of bereavement and war in Australia. She told the essential story of the Robertses, drawing on Garry's diary and showing how they created a network of other grieving families to sustain them. Joy mentioned some of the other soldiers who we'll meet in this book—Les Baker and Vic Edwards. She has made a profound contribution to the scholarship in the growing field of grief and remembrance studies, but she couldn't have done justice to their story.

Likewise, Tanja Luckins gives the Robertses' story a dozen pages in her *The Gates of Memory*, a book based on her PhD, looking at the effects of the Great War on bereaved families. Professor Pat Jalland, in her sweeping *Changing Ways of Death in Twentieth Century Australia*, also spends space on Garry Roberts—but it's just a paragraph, because she knows that others had dealt with him, and she had a century of grieving to explain. Professor Bruce Scates touched on the Robertses' story in looking at how bereaved families coped in the absence of a grave they could visit.

This is all to the good.[3] No one would expect any scholar, still less a PhD candidate, to slog their way through the quarry of the Robertses' story; and just as well for me. But all of these fine historical works consider the Robertses' grief from the point of Frank's death, taking that as a given. I look back at Frank's life, but also sideways at his comrades, and forward to the survivors' lives after the war. In short, this book uses Mont St Quentin and the brief life of this platoon as a way of understanding what the Great War did to Australia and its people.

One of the challenges of writing this book has been that the sources relating to the dozen-or-so men at its heart and their families are very uneven. They disclose a great deal about Frank and the Robertses, but almost nothing about other men. Alf Crawford, for example, remains little more than a shadowy presence, while whole decades in other survivors' lives seem to be unrecoverable. The sources reveal a great deal about the events of 1 September 1918, but very little about large and seemingly important stretches of their lives—their upbringing and early adulthood after the war, for instance. As a result, the four parts into which the book is divided have quite different characters. For a time I struggled to try to force the text into the series of coherent blocks that we think of as chapters. But books, like musical works, do not always need to be written consistently. I began to think of the parts as the movements of a symphony, each with its distinctive style, tempo, and tone. Accordingly, the part dealing with the survivors' old age is very different to that on their experiences at Mont St Quentin.

As the product of an historian who has always worked in museums, this book also looks at how Nine Platoon's story intersects with the ways in which the story of Mont St Quentin (and the AIF in the Great War) was shaped by curators, artists, sculptors, writers, and photographers, and at how the story is told through objects as well as documents. It traces the links between Frank Roberts and Charles Bean's telling of the story of the Great War in his mighty official history; how Frank's friend Charles Web Gilbert created both the memorial on Mont St Quentin and the diorama in the Australian War Memorial museum; and the stories told by objects collected for that museum (and objects not donated to it). It touches upon how artists such as Will Dyson and Arthur Streeton and photographer Hubert Wilkins are also part of it. This is not just an account of twelve men on a French hillside: their story stands for the larger epic of the Australian nation in that war, and the way it recorded and celebrated the war and its consequences for decades after.

The book's sub-title, *between victory and death*—a quotation from Homer's *Odyssey* that I picked up from Barbara Tuchman's *The March of Folly*—sums up the two spans of time over which this story is told. One is short and very specific; the other ranges across decades of Australia's twentieth-century history. First, it tells the story of a dozen Australians on a hill in France on the afternoon of 1 September 1918, an attack in which three died and four were wounded—one mortally. The other span traces what happened to the survivors of that group between their victory in 1918 and the time the last man died, 60-odd years later. The first tells us something of what it was like to be a part of that war; the second, what it meant to them, and what it can mean to us. We are now thinking about how we will mark the centenary of the Great War. We recognise that it remains a part of our lives, too. We, too, remain suspended between victory and death: their victory, and our own deaths. Those of us born in the decades after 1918—even those born after the deaths of all of the men whose story this book tells—can never fully escape the weight of knowledge of the great conflicts of the twentieth century, and particularly the one called the Great War.

Why is that war something that Australians should be concerned with? It happened over ninety years ago: more than a lifetime away. We see more clearly as time passes that this war does not go away. Even discounting the hoo-ha that surrounded the death of Alec Campbell, the longest-surviving Australian veteran of Gallipoli, as media-induced frenzy or official hype, there remained a residue of genuine interest, of a yearning for knowledge about a war that shaped the minds and attitudes of Australia for decades.

It's easy to exaggerate this sense that the Great War is still present in early twenty-first century Australia. For example, it is often said that local war memorials are a highly visible reminder in the towns of Australia. I'm not sure that's true any more. If you drive from Melbourne to Sydney, say, you can go from one end of the F5 freeway to the Western Ring Road, and you won't see more than a handful of memorials (the towers at Albury and Goulburn, and the memorials in yet-to-be by-passed towns such as Holbrook and Tarcutta). But you can go for hundreds of kilometres—drive across the width of Victoria—and not see a memorial even accidentally, even when the final stretch takes you past the site of Broadmeadows camp, where Frank Roberts and the members of his platoon trained before embarkation. Even more, much of the population of urban Australia now lives in suburbs that were built after the Great War. You can now traverse vast tracts of outer-suburban eastern Melbourne or western Sydney, and see any number of fast-food outlets, malls, and garden centres, but you'll find hardly any war memorials as we have romanticised them.

And yet the Great War is not slipping out of the consciousness of modern Australia. After a period of apathy coinciding with the Vietnam years (effectively curtailing any large-scale interest in oral history), the Great War became a subject of increasing interest. The Howard government saw the last of the war's survivors die, and a gout of officially sanctioned and inflated hyperbole accompanied their final years and funerals. This veneration fed the mustard gas-inflamed prose of Les Carlyon's *The Great War*, which appeared just as I began research for this book, in 2006. (At 861 pages, Carlyon's book gives the reader a physical sense that the war would never end.) A shelf of other books—some excellent, some potboilers—feed the popular curiosity about this war.

Not all the readers of these books could have been recalcitrant families of the dead of Fromelles seeking a mystical closure. Many had a family connection to Pozières or Bullecourt or Villers-Bretonneux, but many more seemed fascinated with the epic tragedy that afflicted the nation in its formative years, and sought to satisfy that curiosity. It's a connection that Australians generally don't share with other epic aspects of their history—the Great Depression of the 1930s, for example, or the Snowy Mountains Scheme, or the post-war migration story—even though they were just as life-changing for those involved. Not yet anyway. But the Great War still excites the curiosity and engages the emotions of people born a lifetime after it ended. Why that should be so is perhaps partly explained by the story of Nine Platoon in the fight for Mont St Quentin.

PART I
Belonging

The Road to Querrieu

For more than twenty-five years—from 1914 to 1939—the people whose stories this book tells simply called it 'The War'. It dominated all their lives: for some, it ended them. The conflict known to history as the Great War, the '1914–18 War', or, in time, the First World War, became the most important event in the lives of most of those who experienced it. They distinguished sharply between the war and the time 'Before the War'. In the files that the Repatriation Department kept on all the survivors, the period before the war was so commonly invoked that Repat jargon included a standard abbreviation, 'P.T.E.'—'prior to enlistment'. We know only snippets about the lives of Nine Platoon 'P.T.E.', except for one man: Frank Roberts. Frank's life is documented in immense detail, and he inevitably leads us into the story of the platoon with whom he fought and died.

Frank Roberts was better educated and better off than all of the other men in his platoon, and because of his father's dedicated scrapbooking we know a great deal more about him. Four of Garry's massive Record Books (each over 500 pages long) document Frank's life in seemingly compulsive detail. Frank's first scrapbook opens with the receipt for the pram and cot that Garry bought for his firstborn in the winter of 1888. It includes his school reports and clippings that record his sporting career as a lacrosse player.

When he was still an infant, the Robertses moved from Albert Park to 'Eumana' in Hastings Road, Hawthorn. The Robertses were solidly respectable, but Frank's education was public and commercial, rather than the Scotch College and 'Varsity of his cousins. He attended State School No. 888 in Camberwell, sitting in classrooms in old shops across the road, or (when stagnant water was found beneath the shops) in the local Methodist hall. At sixteen, he entered South Melbourne College on a half-scholarship, seemingly destined for a career in finance like his father. He joined the Australasian Bank, sponsored by his uncle Will, a senior stockbroker. But Frank became disillusioned by 'the sedentary life, the tedium and the ... "swank"' expected of even a lowly bank clerk. After five years, he threw in the bank career to start an orchard at South Sassafras, in 1911.[1]

'A FLAMIN' BERRY FARMER, FULL O' TOIL': FRANK ROBERTS'S BACKGROUND

The Robertses became the centre of an artistic and cultural circle. Though untalented himself, except in light comic opera and in dramatic readings, Garry attracted writers, artists, and musicians and their admirers. Robert Croll, one of his oldest friends, recalled the convivial pseudo-Bohemian gatherings at Fasoli's in King Street. Fasoli's, the forerunner of thousands of restaurants in a multicultural Australia, was an outlandish place redolent of potato salad, spaghetti, and salami (supposedly made of horseflesh); Gruyere and Gorgonzola; wine; and what Robert Croll recalled as 'the general flavour of oil and garlic'.[2] The Robertses and their friends sat 'swapping yarns and setting the universe in order' over their exotic dinners. Among the company were the Dysons (Will the cartoonist and Edward the writer), the cartoonist David Low, and the sculptor Charles Web Gilbert. This was no gentleman's club. The diners included the actress Betty Baker; Ruby Lindsay (who married Will Dyson and was to die early); and, often, Berta Roberts, herself a talented watercolourist until marriage imposed other obligations. Robert Croll was honest enough to admit that his fellow diners were mostly tourists in Bohemia. Just as Garry was a responsible accountant, Robert also held down a respectable job as a senior public servant in the Victorian Department of Education.

The Robertses often invited some of their circle to spend weekends at their property in the Dandenong Ranges. The depression of the 1890s had prompted the Victorian government to allow the selection of blocks in the Dandenongs; families took up blocks in the thickly forested hills, and began to clear them to plant fruit trees and gardens. Though close to Melbourne, the district remained poor and isolated, and bushfires occasionally swept over the wooded hills. Early in the new century, though, the middle class of Melbourne began to buy blocks as 'weekenders'. Local historians describe the Robertses as the 'most notable' of these 'invaders'.[3] In 1910, Garry Roberts bought an allotment on Sassafras Creek near Beagley's Bridge, which he transferred to Berta's name. They called the property 'Sunnyside', and it was to have a profound place in the family's history.

The Robertses and their friends went for walks and picnics along bush tracks, outings that were documented by snaps pasted into Garry's huge scrapbooks. Their parties before the war included the artists John Shirlow and Hal Gye (C.J. Dennis's illustrator) and Edie Eastaugh, a brilliant language student at Melbourne University who became a teacher.

Visitors included their neighbour from nearby Monbulk, Jeanie Gunn (known to generations of readers as Mrs Aeneas Gunn, author of *We of the Never-Never*), recently returned from a long European trip. A frequent visitor until he left for Britain in 1914 was the Kyneton-born sculptor Charles Gilbert. Though poorly educated, Gilbert discovered a gift for sculpture at art school in Melbourne in the 1880s. Virtually self-taught—for want of materials, he practised making sugar sculptures as a chef—he forged an Australian reputation. In 1914, the recently divorced Gilbert left Melbourne to make his mark in Britain, as artists before and since have done. The Robertses' Bohemian circle is not just a colourful detail or a distraction: several of its members were to play a part in the telling of the story of Mont St Quentin.

In the spring of 1913, a struggling writer, C.J. Dennis, became drawn into the Sunnyside circle. A gregarious amateur walker, Robert Croll met Dennis living in a 'humpy' in the Dandenongs at Toolangi, and introduced him to Garry and Berta. Dennis remembered this meeting as 'one of the happiest and luckiest events in my life'.[4] He quickly became a part of their literary and artistic set. Garry became a patron to Dennis, paying him a small allowance on the condition that he wrote. Dennis shifted from Toolangi into one of the converted Melbourne horse-bus bodies that Garry had obtained from his employers (and which Frank had hauled up to Sunnyside). There, Dennis wrote the romantic compound of urban folktale and rural idyll that was to seize the imagination of Australia—perhaps because, by the time it appeared, it allowed them to escape from the awful present of 1915.

Dennis dedicated *The Songs of a Sentimental Bloke* to Garry and Berta. Besides keeping him alive, the Robertses made several contributions to Dennis's writing. Over long fireside chats, Garry confided to Dennis his feelings at the birth of his firstborn, Frank, nearly thirty years before. Dennis recalled the essence of Garry's emotions, and transmuted them into the vernacular verse of which he became the acknowledged master. Dennis was, at the time, unmarried and childless, but the gift of an artist is to imagine rather than merely record, and Garry's recollection is said to have inspired the last-but-one of the Bloke's songs, 'The Kid'. Frank Roberts is therefore immortalised at second hand in one of the most moving of Dennis's poems. Frank also told Dennis anecdotes of Dandenong life and of the fruit markets—Dennis published a complicated and not especially funny story about a swindle involving cabbages in *Norman Lindsay's Book No. II*.

Frank formed a shy friendship with 'Den', as they called him (like Frank, he called Garry 'Dad'). The two became friends, though not intimates—Dennis's melancholia kept friends at a remove—but they swapped stories and shared an admiration for Garry. Soon after meeting the Robertses, Dennis travelled with Frank on the tiring overnight trip carrying fruit from the Dandenongs for sale in the Melbourne markets. Dennis damned Chinese and Italian merchants as 'the dirtiest crowd I ever want to see', claiming to have been turned exclusively carnivorous by the sights he had seen at the markets. On the horse-dray, Dennis got to know Frank. 'A few years ago', Dennis wrote, 'Frank was a bank clerk, but the vocation did not appeal to him'. He chucked in his job, 'went on the land and got his hands dirty', and never regretted it. He became tanned, Dennis wrote, among the 'raspberries, gooseberries, strawberries and currants'. (Garry, accurate to a fault, crossed out 'strawberries' in the article he clipped, because at that time Frank did not grow them.) In writing *The Sentimental Bloke*, Dennis drew on Frank's descriptions of his work in his orchard: he portrayed the reformed, married Bloke as 'a flamin' berry farmer, full o' toil'.[5]

But Frank was no rustic. Stopping for a brew on the journey, Dennis expected Frank to get out a blackened billy, but instead he produced a stainless-steel vacuum flask—and then discussed Bernard Shaw, H.G. Wells, 'Futurism' in art, and 'the higher criticism' in literature.[6] Dennis may have had to work hard to draw out his new friend's views. Though hardly unconfident, Frank seems to have had an innate reserve. In the photographs of the Sunnyside set he often stands to one side, looking like a natural listener rather than a person at the centre of attention. Frank, though, had a flair for leadership. Already secretary of the South Sassafras Progress Association, in August 1914 Frank decided to stand for the Fern Tree Gully Council. He asked Garry to print a flyer, including a photograph of him as a pipe-smoking besuited candidate, presumably because he was anxious to convey an impression of reliability and a responsible attitude towards keeping rates down and roads up, and encouraging development. By the time the election had been held—Frank was unsuccessful—the long-expected Great War had broken out with paradoxical suddenness.

'GOODBYE, SWEETHEART': FRANK GOES TO WAR

While the Robertses loyally supported the empire's war, they did not at first see a need for Frank to volunteer. There seemed to be enough younger men willing to volunteer; besides, Frank had his orchard to develop, and growing ties. By the middle of 1915, Frank had what he called a 'sweetheart', Ruby Barratt. Her father, George, had opened up 'Warwick Farm', between Sassafras and Perrin's Creeks, in 1907, growing berries, while her mother, Mary Ann, let rooms to holidaying Melburnians. The Barratt boys, Ted and Percy, had helped build Sunnyside in 1910–11; presumably, Ruby and Frank had known each other for several years, and the two could easily have walked to see each other along the forest road by Beagley's Bridge in about half an hour. Ruby was certainly another peripheral member of the Sunnyside circle before the war—Den wrote an original verse lampooning the 'Hun' in her autograph book in 1914. Perhaps she and Frank drew together in reaction to Garry's more ebullient Bohemian friends. By the following year, some of Frank's friends and his cousin Lennard had enlisted. He pondered in letters to Garry (who lived at Eumana during the week) whether he should, too. Soon after the landing on Gallipoli, he admitted that he was disinclined: 'I reckon we've too much to lose at present.' But he decided that, 'should the casualty list reach terrible proportions ... I guess I'll go'.[7]

By the time that the casualty lists from Gallipoli began to appear, the war had come to dominate Australian life and the Sunnyside set. David Low's cartoons portrayed the 'Hun' as bestial; the *School Paper*, published by Robert Croll's Victorian Education Department, disseminated nothing but war stories, poems and—frankly—propaganda in the state's classrooms. Den got a job with the Navy Office; in Britain, Web Gilbert began to receive commissions for memorials to the dead.

At last, the pressure of casualty lists (including Lennard's name appearing among the dead of Gallipoli), of public appeals, and of conscience persuaded Frank that it was time for him to do what he saw as his duty. He volunteered for the AIF on 23 February 1916, but was to spend more than a year in Australia, training at Broadmeadows and passing an officer cadet course at the Royal Military College at Duntroon, near Canberra. Frank and Ruby married at Olinda in September 1916. For a time, Ruby moved into a room in Parkville, in inner Melbourne, down Sydney Road from the Broadmeadows camp. It was their only marital home, and where Ruby became pregnant early in 1917. Soon after, Frank's name appeared on a draft for active service, to leave Melbourne with the 19th reinforcements for the 21st Battalion.

On Frank's final evening at Eumana, he and Ruby, who was five months pregnant, spent most of their time in Frank's room. Garry and Berta hoped to make their farewells at the dockside the next day. At a quarter past eleven, obedient to the tram timetables, Frank had to leave to return to the Broadmeadows camp. At the gate of Eumana, he said goodbye to his father and mother, and to Ruby. She did not feel up to seeing him away at the quayside the next day: this was their last goodbye. Both were in tears; Frank, Garry recorded, was 'crying like a kid'. His final farewell call as he dutifully strode away down Hastings Road — 'Goodbye, sweetheart' — sounded, Garry felt, 'pitiful'. At Broadmeadows, his friend Alf Fox, himself red-eyed, greeted Frank with 'Hello Robby — been crying. It's a bugger, isn't it?'[8]

The next day, 11 May 1917, the reinforcement drafts for several battalions embarked aboard the transport A11, the *Ascanius*. Garry and Berta arrived at New Pier a little before one that afternoon. It was a cool, breezy day, warming as sailing time approached. Photographs of the event show crowds of civilians mingling with soldiers; even the governor-general turned up to wave goodbye. Despite the throng of relatives and friends, Garry and Berta found Frank, and Garry was able to shake hands with him, in what was to be their last contact. Garry had brought a kit-bag of comforts — shoelaces, razor blades, cigars, and lollies, and a parcel of newspapers for the men of Frank's platoon — and he gave Frank half-a-crown as a sweetener to the steward to allow it aboard. So many crowded the wharf that women and children were pushed down in the crush and, Garry noted in his diary, 'a good many women fainted'.

The ship pulled away from the wharf at about twenty past one among the customary fluttering of paper streamers as the troops cheered and sang, and as friends and families waved and wept. Garry and Berta waved little paper flags—probably union jacks. Garry reflected that 'many hearts were sore and many minds were wondering would they see their dear ones back again'. Of the 154 men of the reinforcement draft, fifteen would not return. 'And so my son sailed away to take his part in the Great War', Garry ended his record of that day.

The *Ascanius* reached Britain after a slow, 69-day voyage by way of Fremantle, Durban, Cape Town, and Freetown. The ship's 1600 passengers ate heavy meals of roast or boiled beef, mutton and stewed rabbit, followed by rice pudding, topped off with biscuit and cheese for supper. The days passed with lectures, signalling, and medical training, concerts and sports, and a good deal of dozing in hammocks, though in the tropics the men escaped the stuffy troop-decks to sleep in the open air. The voyage was uneventful, except that at Cape Town, while drinking and dancing with 'native women' in the 'native quarter', a member of the 22nd Battalion knocked down a man who later died on board. The 21st's draft was the first off the ship at Plymouth, 'entraining' (as the army called it) for the depot at Amesbury, in the midst of the Australian camps spread around Wiltshire. Frank, a temporary sergeant on the voyage, went off on yet another officers' training course, at nearby Tidworth.

In Britain, Frank made the most of the opportunity to travel to see the places that Garry (and most other Australians of his generation) called 'home' ('did Stonehenge', he recorded in his diary). Garry's Record Books 3 and 4 are full of postcards and souvenirs of Frank's visits to Salisbury, London, and Ireland. Postcards and coloured illustrations of historic and tourist sites are labelled 'Frank here'. Garry's artistic and cultural networks penetrated even to London. Accompanying a drawing of The Monument by the artist Stanley Anderson is the annotation 'Frank met Stanley Anderson at Web Gilbert's'. In September 1917, he twice visited Gilbert at his studio, meeting Mabel, 'the new Mrs Web Gilbert', and Gilbert's twin infant sons, reporting that 'Web Gilbert has a hell of a fine opinion of you, Dad'. While there, Gilbert sketched Frank, with consequences that became apparent a year later. Much of Frank's Australian mail (from C.J. Dennis, Robert Croll, and Jeannie Gunn, as well as from the family) came via Gilbert, and Frank left many items with him for safekeeping. In October, Frank travelled to Ireland to stay with Garry's maiden cousins Lucy and Emily at Enniscorthy, in Wexford. Lucy and Emily, he reported, were 'old maids but fine sports'. Garry accordingly pasted in the many cards and maps that Frank collected, as well as entire guidebooks, and clipped newspaper stories about the Irish Question, Home Rule, and the 1916 Dublin rising.

The three months he spent in training in Britain gave Frank further skills that he would need at the front. A lecture on the 'spirit of the bayonet' appalled him—'really it was a talk on how to kill, Dad, and keep on doing it'.[9] While the AIF gave him these uncongenial skills, war service confirmed his democratic principles ('Damn all Dukes, say I', Frank wrote after an inspection by an aged royal duke) and his pride as an Australian ('thank heaven I am an Australian and come from a democratic country where a man is judged on what he is').[10] Regarding enlistment as a manly duty, he still disliked military life. As a 'reinforcement sergeant', Frank was bullied by his first platoon sergeant. 'How I love the Army; bastards', Frank wrote sarcastically to Ruby on Christmas Day, confirming his confession that he swore more than he had before.[11]

Having completed two officer cadet courses, both with high marks, Frank expected to become an officer after a further course at Oxford. Garry wanted to lobby Major-General John Monash (whom Frank called 'your friend'), but Frank told him firmly that he wanted to earn promotion.[12] (In any case, appealing to Monash would not have succeeded: the surplus of experienced NCOs already in France made a commission impossible.) Eventually, Frank accepted philosophically that he was 'doomed to be a private to the end of this war'.[13] Had he enlisted or embarked sooner, he may have been commissioned—and would probably have been killed all the sooner rather than at Mont St Quentin.

Frank warned Garry early in November that he was about to embark for the battalion, asking him to tell Ruby so as not to alarm her. Frank arrived in France with a draft for the battalion on 6 November 1917, just in time to miss the muddy end of the third battle of Ypres, in which the 21st had lost about 350 men—more than a third of its strength; even so, men said that 'the 21st has always been a lucky battalion'.[14] By mid-November he was a rifle grenadier in Nine Platoon, C Company, his home for the rest of his life.

Throughout his service overseas, Frank expected to survive. On 1 September 1917, exactly a year before his death, Frank re-read a letter he had begun a few days before, and continued. 'My word, Girlie, what a bright future lies before us'.[15] He never ceased dreaming of and planning his life with Ruby and his baby after the war. His dreams centred on the property at Warburton that he wanted to call 'St Yves', where he had been, near Ploegsteert Wood, when he had finally heard of his daughter's birth. 'When our apple trees at Warburton are grown', he wrote, 'we will make our own cider Darl …'[16] He looked forward to working with his younger brother, Johnny: 'Oh, I have so many great plans in my head'.[17] Would they, he wondered, remain 'dreams on the wind'?[18]

'BROTHER FRANKIE WAS AWAY': NANCY

By the time he reached France, Frank had become a father, though he did not find out immediately. As Frank had predicted,

Ruby had given birth to a daughter (Nancy) at the Redan Street Maternity Hospital, Prahran, a couple of days before he left on a draft for the front. Garry's telegram — 'Ruby, daughter well Congratulations Love "Grandad"' — reached him a month later, forwarded from Britain by the dilatory AIF postal service as a letter. Ruby and Nancy lived with her parents at Warwick Farm. Everyone yearned for Frank's letters, and both Ruby and Frank's parents shared theirs with each other.

Nancy's arrival stirred Johnny to the Dennisesque-verse for which had a flair. He sent Frank a poem, 'My Niece':

Who was it came on Flower Day?
While brother Frankie was away;
Who could it be but Nancy May,
My niece
Who is it will so happy be
When father Frankie o'er the sea
Comes safely home, in haste to see?
My niece[19]

When she was still a couple of months old, Frank wrote a moving letter to his 'dear little daughter'— the only direct communication she would ever receive from her father. 'Hullo! Little stranger', it began, 'we haven't been introduced'. He went on to tell her 'how pleased and happy I am to know that you left the "other world" to come down to this old earth to be company to little Mother Ruby—my beloved wife ...' Frank hoped that 'this terrible war will soon be over so that I can come home to you and Mother: won't we have high times then?' He urged her not to cry 'too much'—'poor little Mother has quite enough to worry her now. But between you and me, Nance,' he reassured her, 'Mother is glad that I've taken a place in the ranks of the A.I.F. where the *men* of

Australia are at present and she wouldn't want me home now as a civilian on any account.'

> Years hence, when you will be getting a big girl and perhaps worrying Mother because you have so many sweethearts (as she did the pretty rascal) Mother will be pleased and glad she will be able to tell you how "Dad" played his little part—irksome though it was—in the world war, and that as a volunteer not as a conscript.
>
> Now little daughter "clap hands" because Daddy feels he will soon be coming home and then Mother will show me "our" little girl …[20]

Unknown to Frank, his family was having a dramatic time while he was composing this letter. Johnny, out shooting rabbits, as usual, caught the trigger of his gun as he climbed through a wire fence, and the gun went off, mangling his right hand dreadfully. The next day he went into hospital, where a doctor had to amputate his thumb, forefinger, and middle finger. As he was about to go under the chloroform, Johnny said, 'I hope I've got Frank's knock instead of him.'[21]

'NO 9 PLATOON': FRANK'S COMRADES

If we could stand downwind of them, we would probably smell them before we saw them approaching around a bend in the summer heat. We would sniff a compound of sweat-stained serge uniforms, with a pall of blue Woodbine Virginia tobacco smoke hanging over them at each halt. Who were they? In the statement he would write for Garry Roberts, Jack Castle mentioned being a member of 'No 9 Platoon Machine-gun Section'. This is the only reference in the entire 17 pages of testimony that one of Frank's comrades mentions the particular sub-unit to which they belonged, but its dozen members are the subject of this book: Nine Platoon.

For all the casual demeanour of its fighting men, their celebrated informality in and out of action, and their famous larrikinism, Australia's army is documented much more thoroughly than their British allies or German enemies. The quantity of records available is staggering. Not only does the individual file of every serviceman survive (digitised on the internet), but the war diary of almost every unit is also available digitally. Beyond that, a mass of official records is open, as are hundreds of private records such as collections of letters, diaries, and memoirs. This vast lode of records, as we will see, reveals a great deal. But the one thing that none of these documents disclose is the exact composition of Nine Platoon at Mont St Quentin. A section was notionally about ten men; a platoon, 30-40 strong; and a company, up to 200 men. By mid-August 1918, though, C Company of the 21st Battalion was, in fact, only 27 men strong. The 'platoon' was the size of a section. This is something that no one involved bothered to explain (at least on paper), even to Garry Roberts, who desperately wanted to know. Fortunately, its composition can be inferred from Frank's diary and from the survivors' accounts of Mont St Quentin.

On 31 August 1918, Nine Platoon comprised only thirteen members, one of whom did not see the Mont. They had joined the Australian Imperial Force between March 1915 and May 1917. First to enlist was Godfrey Dobson, a lithographer from Albert Park. A month later, Vic Edwards, a 26-year-old labourer from Launceston, Tasmania, joined. Godfrey and Vic were to serve on Gallipoli, and both survived the torpedoing of their transport, the *Southland*. Godfrey Dobson fell so seriously ill with enteric fever that he was sent home to Australia and discharged early in 1916. He must have been a strong young man, because within three months he embarked again. By then, four others had joined the AIF: Les Baker, a casual painter with five children; Tom Wignall, a recent British migrant (a Lancashire 'vanman' who worked as a 'gardiner' in Melbourne after his arrival in March 1914); Jack Castle, a Prahran labourer; and Frank Roberts, about whom we know more than all the others put together.

In 1916, six other men joined. In June, Charlie Tognella (or Tognulla — neither Charlie nor the army ever managed to spell his name straight twice in a row), a woodcutter from Graytown in north-central Victoria, and Ted Heath, a coach driver from Curdies River, inland from Port Campbell in Victoria's Western District, both enlisted. In September, Bill Rabling, a despatch clerk from Brunswick just turned eighteen, volunteered as soon as he could, followed by Noble Norwood, a bookseller who had returned to Melbourne from Perth to enlist. Alf Crawford, a New South Welshman from Delegate, just over the Gippsland border in the high country, enlisted in October while working around Orbost in Victoria. In November, Roy Smerdon, a labourer from the north-west of Victoria joined up, along with his elder bother Cliff.

Finally, in May 1917, the oldest member of the platoon volunteered, a 39-year-old 'agent', Albert Kelly, a big, barrel-chested man, married with two children, who wore the orange-and-black ribbon of the South Africa Medal on his chest. Albert seems to have been something of an adventurer. He enlisted for South Africa while in Western Australia, and returned to serve with another mounted infantry contingent. After the war he spent time in South Africa, but ended up in Canada around 1905. There he met and married Isabel Robinson, of an Ottawa clerical family — like Albert, Methodist. By 1908 the Kellys were back in Victoria, but living variously in Essendon and Frankston, where their two children, Grace and Albert, were born.

Nine Platoon's members on 31 August 1918 do not correspond to the under-age boys of popular memory. At enlistment they ranged in age between 18 and 39, with an average age of almost exactly 25; as the entered the battle they were about 27. We know very little about these men's lives before they took up the Bible and swore an oath to 'resist His Majesty's enemies'. We know something of their families, where some of them went to school and whether some were cadets, but very little more. Disproportionate effort would disclose more details, but little of substance. We must generalise from others' experience. In the late 1960s, historian Lloyd Robson had Nicholas Dawes collect and collate the writing of just over 200 former members of the AIF. The result, their book *Citizen to Soldier*, gives many individual but anonymous answers to the question, 'Why did you volunteer for that war?' A sample of their replies suggests the range of reasons:

- 'I was a bit curious and … [a] member of a rifle club [so] I thought I would give it a go'
- 'had enough of the missus'
- 'always wanted to be in something more than just earning a living'
- 'to elevate me to a complete and Satisfying Manhood'
- 'a desire to test myself out to which was added a little patriotism'
- 'A TRIP OVERSEAS'
- 'at least 90% of us were conscripted by our consciences'
- 'I read many war books, The Boer War, Deeds That Won the Empire'
- 'I thought it was my duty'
- 'I don't know'.[22]

'THEIR STRANGE HISTORIES': NINE PLATOON'S MEMBERS

Ultimately, indeed, we do not know why the men of Nine Platoon enlisted, but they probably shared these reasons. It is perhaps significant that four men 'volunteered' in the spring of 1916, in advance of the conscription that most Australians expected would be introduced.

Roy Smerdon came from north-west Victoria. From 1909, the Victorian government opened to settlement half a million acres of the Mallee. Men cut and cleared the scrub using rollers drawn by horse teams, cutting out wheat farms in the dry, sandy country. The new Ouyen–Pinnaroo railway line extended westwards from Ouyen from 1909 to 1912, bringing new settlers to a harsh frontier. Surveyors opened blocks in Duddo Parish for sub-division in 1909, and Roy's parents, John and Ann, occupied land around late 1911, a dozen-or-so kilometres north of the new settlement of Murrayville, named after the Victorian premier. The Smerdons had shifted from around Ballarat: John was the son of a Devonshire man who had become a butcher on the goldfields.

Surveyors laid out Murrayville itself in 1911, a few corrugated iron-and-weatherboard houses and shops, lit by kerosene lamps. The new country sounded unpromising. A pioneer described it as 'a vast tract of sandy country, thinly grassed', with 'numerous salt bush flats and sandhills'.[23] Government and private bores tapped artesian water, allowing settlers to plant crops and run sheep and cattle, but the country was devoted to wheat. The railway hauled away the bags of wheat produced by the new settlers, and the district's volunteers travelled on it to Melbourne and Broadmeadows camp.

Between 1884 and 1909, John and Ann had twelve children. Two (both named Florence Emily) died in infancy. In 1915, their seven boys were aged between 13 and 30, most still living and working on the family's new wheat farm. It seems that, like many farming families, the Smerdons decided that some could go to the war and that some had to stay. Roy and Cliff Smerdon took the train to Ouyen and Melbourne, enlisted on the same day in October 1916, and steamed off with the 18th reinforcements for the 21st. Their 'eligible' brothers (Harry, John, and Arthur) stayed at home.

Nineteen-year-old Charlie Tognella, the woodcutter from Chiltern, in north-eastern Victoria, also enlisted with his older brother: Albert and he signed up in June 1916. The sons of an Italian migrant, the Tognella boys were oddities in Anglo-Celtic Australia. Charlie was Nine Platoon's only Catholic. Of its other members, eight were nominally Anglican and four were Methodist. About 40 per cent of Australians, though making up fewer than a quarter of the 21st Battalion, were Catholic (including its colonel, Bernard Duggan). Nine Platoon was, perhaps, a statistical anomaly. Charlie was a restless soldier, twice charged with going absent and with disorderly conduct on parade. The war would, perhaps, change Charlie's life forever.

Twenty-four-year-old Godfrey Dobson was not, as an entry in the Embarkation Rolls suggested, merely a lithographer. He was also a Methodist Home Missionary. In February 1917 he became the only member of Nine Platoon to come before a court martial. A district court martial was—and was meant to be—an intimidating business.[24] Armed guards marched Godfrey into a hut at the camp at Perham Downs, in Wiltshire. With much stamping and shouting, Godfrey—hatless and beltless—stood at attention before four officers. The president of the court, a Major Richard Holman, convened the court and a clerk read out the charge sheet. While on leave in London, Godfrey had been charged with 'an offence of a fraudulent nature'. On Australia Day, 26 January 1917, he had altered his pay book, with a stroke turning three pounds into thirteen pounds. He pleaded 'not guilty', but a corporal from the pay office at the AIF's Horseferry Road depot testified that he had noticed Godfrey's attempt to gain an extra ten pounds. Challenged, Godfrey admitted to altering his pay book. He explained that he had wanted to go to Scotland on leave but, thinking he would be short of funds, altered his pay book. 'I did not ... realize the gravity of the offence', he explained. 'I thought the alteration would be adjusted when a periodical check of my account took place.'

Proceedings moved along briskly. Holman, who had been wounded on Gallipoli and at Fromelles, was awaiting repatriation to Australia and was in no mood to mess about with inept petty thieves, however impulsively they had acted. The court sentenced Godfrey to six months' imprisonment with hard labour and, with more stamping and shouting, the guard marched him off. Godfrey went to a detention barracks. It may seem curious that at the end of the Somme fighting of 1916 such an infraction could put a man in prison for six months.

Arthur Baker, known to everyone as Les, had been a 'contractor', a jobbing painter, working around the little towns and villages straggling into the foothills of the Dandenongs. He had enlisted at the age of 32, already the father of five children who had been born every second year since he and Agnes had married in 1907; the youngest was either not yet born or an infant. Les Baker's decision to enlist may have been economic. He could have calculated that his steady army pay and the dependents' allowance paid to his wife, Agnes, were better than unreliable employment. Or had Les 'had enough of the missus'? Les's AIF pay did not go far—not as far as Ringwood, anyway. As the winter of 1917 approached, Agnes wrote to the State War Council seeking assistance. She owed money, mainly to the grocer, and her five children, aged two, four, six, eight, and ten, were 'in urgent need of warm clothes and blankets'.[25] Life would never be very easy for the Bakers.

These individual stories can be gleaned from the records. Except for Frank's diary and his letters, we have no intimate record of Nine Platoon's life, though almost every one of the men who fought with him at Mont St Quentin are mentioned in it. The sources give out a few tantalising clues to the friendships that connected its members. Frank recorded that he had gained a name as a scribe, because he had 'extricated [a comrade] from a business difficulty with Horseferry Road & the Commonwealth bank'. It seems that Frank had saved Godfrey Dobson from another spell in the detention barracks.

But, apart from shafts of illumination from Frank's diary and occasional mentions in other records, we have few other insights on who made up Nine Platoon. For example, Frank wrote of how he admired one man of his platoon—'I've seen that man calmly walk along through a hail of shells while the rest of us are scuttling along like rabbits'—but he does not name him.[26] He also mentioned men who were not members of the platoon at Mont St Quentin, but who were to play a part in its story. They included Alf Fox, a cork cutter from suburban Parkville, and Phil Starr who, like Frank, had given up a clerical job in a lawyer's office to go on the land, and travelled to war aboard the *Ascanius*. Oswald Green, a Dandenong blacksmith, had been a drill instructor in the Militia, oddly rejected as 'physically unfit', but at last allowed to transfer to the AIF. He, too, had left Melbourne on the *Ascanius*.

Frank wrote of the men to whom he became particularly close—Noble Norwood and Ted Heath. Norwood ('known as Norrie') was, Frank thought, 'a fine chap with literary tastes the same as mine'.[27] As clerk to C Company, Norrie put several jobs Frank's way, including three trips collecting and escorting re-captured absentees. In this way, he saw Rouen as well as 'miles of pretty country and countless little villages untouched by war'.[28] Frank admired Ted Heath as 'a hard doer, an old soldier [though he too had enlisted in 1916] and a souvenir king of exceptional qualities'; like many Australians, Ted and Frank 'ratted' prisoners, robbing them of their valuables. Frank thought of Heath as 'one of the best—no ducking and diving with him'. He relied on Ted's 'coolness and lack of wind up': 'he'll do me', he wrote.[29] Perhaps it was Ted who walked calmly through shell-fire. Australians call this 'mateship', and often talk as if they had copyright on comradeship. Inspired by 'Den', Frank thought of writing a piece for the soldiers' magazine *Aussie*, which would be 'a study of some of the chaps of the platoon'. He was making notes on 'their strange history … they come from all walks of life and are real good stuff for a writer'.[30] Sadly, he did not publish a piece in *Aussie*.

Frank detested the discomfort and boredom of life at the front, and thought military formality 'rot'. Through the winter of 1917–18, the 21st lived in underground barracks at the 'Catacombs' near St Yves, in Belgium. Everyone was cold, hungry, and lousy, fed up with endless fatigues, and famished for mail and news of home. 'Do you savvy *now* why the majority of soldiers vote *NO* on conscription?', Frank asked his father (though he had voted Yes).[31] The No vote, Frank thought, would mean an easier time for the AIF. He predicted (wrongly) to Ruby that 'we won't get so much or dangerous work as before'.[32]

'BLACK AND RED DIAMOND': THE 21ST BATTALION

A soldier's home was his unit. For most of the AIF, and for all the men whose story this book tells, that meant a battalion. The 21st was commanded by Lieutenant Colonel Bernard Duggan, a 31-year-old farmer from St Arnaud in Victoria. Most battalions had some idiosyncrasy about them. The 21st's included the fact that the *Southland* carrying it to Gallipoli had been torpedoed in the Aegean, and the ordeal had given it an individuality. (*Southland* survivors formed an association that lasted almost as long as the battalion association.) The 21st claimed several other 'firsts': the first battalion formed in the brigade, and the first Australian battalion to enter the trenches in France (although the latter claim was not supported by Charles Bean's official history). It also boasted 'Nap', its monkey mascot, who lived with the battalion's 'left out of battle' party.

Bernard Duggan's was one of sixty Australian infantry battalions in the Great War. All dressed in the pea-soup-green uniforms, they seem alike, except for the bright colour patches worn on each man's upper arm. These patches became one of the symbols of a battalion's identity. It seems hard to understand how a simple numeral and a red-and-black diamond-shaped colour patch could command such loyalty. In fact, the number and the patch only represented an aggregation of human bonds. A battalion was fewer than a thousand strong at any time. It was what sociologists would later describe as a 'total institution': a group that men lived among for months without mixing much outside it.

The shape and colour of the patch told the AIF's members everything they needed to know to place it in the force's hierarchy. The 21st's patch was diamond-shaped, as were all of the 2nd Division's. Its bottom half was red, the colour of the 6th Brigade. The senior of the four battalions of the brigade, the 21st's was therefore a black-over-red diamond. It gave some men a badge that they wore for the rest of their lives.

Brigadier-General James Robertson, a Toowoomba stockbroker, commanded the 6th Brigade. Robertson had been wounded in the landing on Gallipoli, and had commanded a battalion on the Somme and a brigade at Ypres. After taking leave in Australia, he returned to France and, in July 1918, took over command of the 6th Brigade from John Gellibrand, whom Charles Bean idolised. Like many Great War generals, Robertson looks crusty in his portrait, but he had just turned forty: it must be the uniform and moustache that does it. Competent and undeniably effective—he ordered his battalion into the attack eight times on the Somme in 1916—he remains strangely colourless, oddly ignored by Bean's official history. Bean found him stubborn: he 'would never admit argument' about his orders, 'as Gelly would'.[33] Robertson's brigade comprised the 21st, 22nd, 23rd, and 24th Battalions, all raised in Victoria.

The 6th Brigade was one of the three infantry brigades in Major-General Charles Rosenthal's 2nd Division, of which he took command in May 1918. Rosenthal was in his early forties, an architect in civil life, a generous spirit. As a musician, he attracted the esteem of the Methodist congregations of Coolgardie and Perth. Bankrupt and recovering from typhoid, he bicycled back east to Melbourne, crossing the Nullarbor in summer heat while his wife went by ship. In Sydney, he re-built his architectural career and, no less active as a musician, became a militia artillery officer. (Architects and engineers seem to have had a head for the sums inescapable in gunnery—his fellow gunners included Talbot Hobbs, another Perth architect who commanded the 5th Division in the larger battle of Mont St Quentin, and Monash himself.)

On Gallipoli, Rosenthal had commanded a field artillery brigade. His tunic, peppered by Turkish shrapnel, is on display in the Australian War Memorial. It shows that he was a big man in several senses. Lying on the deck of a hospital carrier, Rosenthal kept up the spirits of his fellow wounded by singing 'Arm, arm ye brave' from Handel's *Judas Maccabeus*. (Rosenthal, of Danish origins, was a staunch non-conformist.) He was no chateau general, becoming as popular in the 4th Division as Pompey Elliott was in the 5th. He got so close to the front line during the Third Ypres offensive that he was gassed at Passchendaele, and he captured Germans in no-man's-land in 1918. Wounded for a fourth time, soon after his promotion to command the 2nd Division in the spring of 1918, he was back in command in time for the great attack of 8 August.

Rosenthal's new division had taken part in the ordeals of I Anzac Corps: Pozières and Mouquet Farm; the notorious 'Somme Winter' of 1916–17; the pursuit to the Hindenburg Line; and the second battle of Bullecourt. After a long rest in the summer of 1917, the five Australian divisions entered the protracted offensive known to history as the Third Battle of Ypres. They took part in all five of the great assaults made by the AIF: the Menin Road, Polygon Wood, Broodseinde, Poelcapelle and, finally, Passchendaele. Late in 1917, the five divisions were combined to form the Australian Corps, the largest in the British Expeditionary Force. A miniature Australian army, from 30 May 1918 it was commanded by Lieutenant-General John Monash.

'THEIR LONG SUIT IS ANNIHILATION': THE LEWIS GUN

John Monash towers over the history of the AIF on the Western Front in 1918. Its triumphs became his; his reputation bolstered its. For more than twenty years, Monash's own account of *The Australian Victories in France* shaped and dominated Australians' understanding of their part in the war's victorious battles. Charles Bean's official history, so influential and pervasive for Gallipoli, appeared long after the Monash version of 1918 had set. Even now, Monash's reputation is inflated (as a recent book puts it, as *The Outsider Who Won a War*). It is hard to contest this pervasive influence, but it is necessary if we are to understand—free of myths and assumptions—Australia's war in 1918.

Monash inspected the 21st at Querrieu on 23 June 1918, the closest that Nine Platoon's members would come to the man who in part determined their destinies. Frank, detailed to guard duty, missed the parade: 'so sorry', he noted sarcastically in his diary.[34] As he strode or rode past the battalion, which was standing to attention in ranks, platoon-by-platoon, Monash would have noted with approval the number of Lewis guns carried by them. He famously declared of his infantry battalions that 'so long as they have 30 Lewis guns it doesn't matter what else they have'.[35] What was this weapon?

Two days before Monash inspected the battalion, falling numbers compelled Lieutenant-Colonel Bernard Duggan to re-organise it yet again. Nine Platoon was re-constituted as a double Lewis Gun section, though misleadingly still called a platoon, little more than a dozen strong. Indeed, by 26 July there were only ten men left in it.[36] The platoon remained a viable force in battle because of its weapon.

Introduced in 1915 to meet a shortage of the heavier Vickers and Maxim guns, the American-designed, British-made Lewis gun vastly increased the infantry platoon's killing power. At 28½ pounds [13 kilograms], the Lewis gun hardly seems like a 'light' machine-gun, but it was portable enough to be useful in trench warfare. The Lewis could fire at a nominal rate of 500 rounds a minute although, because it used a circular 'pan' magazine holding only 47 rounds, Lewis gunners fired in short bursts of half-a-dozen-or-so rounds at a time. Because it was air-cooled (the barrels of heavier machine-guns were water-cooled, and therefore immobile) it could not fire for long before the metal jacket enclosing the barrel became unbearably hot.

Frank Roberts first encountered the Lewis gun almost exactly a year to the day before his death, when he 'sneaked into a Lewis gun class' while at the 6th Brigade's training battalion at Rollestone in Wiltshire.[37] He learned that machine-guns were useful in defence, but gunnery instructors emphasised their value in the attack. 'After an assault', they stressed, 'the Lewis Gun must rush forward in time to annihilate any formed bodies of the retreating enemy'. If they could kill disorganised defenders withdrawing to the next trench or strong-post, 'the next position is half won'. The instructors dwelt on the Lewis's portable killing power in giving infantrymen the confidence to attack. These guns would help them to kill Germans, and to take and hold their trenches: 'their long suit is *annihilation*'.[38]

But the instructors also taught that the Lewis was 'a lady of moods'. It was demanding to maintain and fire. Learning to fire it well, they said, was 'very much like learning to play the piano'. Learning the notes was easier than putting them together, and much of the training dealt with maintaining the gun and coping with stoppages. Keeping a gun supplied with ammunition pans demanded a team of men, all with particular tasks, though all of them shared the dull but essential chore of loading bullets into the pans and lugging about the gun, magazines, and tools.

A Lewis gun team usually comprised four or more men, each performing a numbered job. The Number 1 fired the gun. He needed to be 'the best shot and mechanic combined', and with the Number 2 carried a bag of tools and parts, including a spare barrel. The Number 2, also 'a first rate shot and mechanic', lay or knelt alongside the Number 1, repeating commands from the section leader and calling up magazines from the other numbers. Both men carried revolvers rather than rifles (the instructors urged them to practise with the revolvers 'so ... they are a greater danger to the enemy than to their friends'.[39]) Numbers 3 and 4 (and 5 and 6 if available) each carried half-a-dozen magazines in webbing panniers slung over their shoulders, keeping up with the firing team but not offering a target. Ideally, all the men were trained to do each others' jobs, and they drilled endlessly out of the line so that in the stress of battle their responses would be automatic.

In the summer of 1918, the Australian Corps entered an ordeal that would bring its members among their greatest ordeals and crippling losses, but also its greatest triumph. Frank Brewer, a Queensland journalist who joined the 20th Battalion and was to play a small and overlooked part in the story of Mont St Quentin, made notes in his diary in July when the 21st Battalion relieved his battalion. He described his own company as 'physical wrecks … exhausted by fatigue, trembling and feverish through lack of sleep'. Tormented by lice and a monotonous, nutritionally inadequate diet, Brewer's own body was 'a mass of running sores', and he was evacuated to hospital with 'hysteria'.[40] Every Australian infantry battalion was in as poor shape. The paradoxical wonder is that the AIF made its greatest contribution to winning the war as it reached the limits of its physical endurance.

At its most brutal, men had been killed and wounded and not replaced. Frank told his daughter of his pride in serving as 'a volunteer, not as a conscript', but in Australia too few volunteers came forward to keep up the rate of replenishment. The Somme, Bullecourt, Third Ypres, and the continuous action from the spring of 1918 had inflicted gaps that could not be filled. The British army, suffering the effects of four years of losses, had already begun to reduce divisions from twelve battalions to nine. By August 1918, Monash's Australian Corps had also become increasingly short of men and had begun to disband some of its infantry battalions. Monash admitted that he was 15,000 men short—nearly the equivalent of an entire division at full strength. But he resisted advice to disband more battalions and re-distribute men to make fewer but stronger units. Everyone expected the war to continue into 1919, and Monash wanted to defer the decision to the following winter. But even as the arguments went back and forth between the War Office, Douglas Haig's British Expeditionary Force General Headquarters, the AIF, and Australian Corps headquarters, the unrelenting pace of operations drove numbers down—from an average of 706 in mid-August, to 695 a week later, to 653 a week after that.[41]

As the AIF's numbers dwindled in 1918, the battalions came to rely upon the Lewis's firepower as a substitute for reinforcements. But having thirty Lewis guns did not make the effort demanded of them much easier. In action, smaller battalions could not cover as great a frontage or send men in adequate numbers to reinforce success or prevent failure. A battalion top-heavy with Lewis guns still needed men to do fatigues, and to provide gas and anti-aircraft guards, stretcher-bearers, runners, and orderlies; it still needed men to carry rations, care for horses, hump stores, and cart water and ammunition. The result was that men did more work than before, and became more tired than ever.

Between his triumphs of Hamel and Amiens, Monash had acknowledged (to Brigadier-General Charles Brand) that 'many units are suffering, not only physically but morally and mentally'. The strain, he admitted even before the opening of the Amiens offensive, was 'severe'. But he ruthlessly suppressed this knowledge, refusing to admit that his corps was feeling the strain. The gamble of pushing his men hard paid off: Monash was a lucky general.

'CARRY ON!': THE ROBERTSES AT WAR

As Australian patriots and empire loyalists, the Robertses never doubted the justness of the cause Frank that served. Though proud that Frank had volunteered, Garry and Berta had twice voted Yes to conscription. Garry thought that 'any person who votes No is a traitor to the soldiers who have gone; to the country and the empire'.[42] Garry pasted into his Record Book a clipping that made clear his feeling that those who refused to enlist were 'shirkers'. A sarcastic verse Garry clipped from the *Herald* in February 1917 leaves no doubt about his feelings about 'eligibles' failing to enlist:

> Our brothers they left us their blessings,
> > Our cousins set sail for the front,
> But we stayed at home with the women
> > To help them in bearing the brunt
> > > (Dear girls!)
> They might be distressed by the brunt![43]

Shortly before Frank arrived on the Western Front, Australians had voted in the second of the conscription referenda. It, too, was lost. Garry was naturally 'disgusted' with the result. 'A lot of traitors in Australia', he confided to his diary.[44] Even to this day, the troops' vote has been the subject of widespread misunderstanding. Many writers have assumed that the soldiers voted overwhelmingly for conscription. The AIF, however, voted only narrowly but decisively against conscription: many soldiers in the depots in Britain voted in favour. One of the catchphrases that Frank collected explains the troops' view. In the middle of a particularly wearisome fatigue, or even in a lull in a bombardment, a man could be heard to say, 'Dear Bill'. To the troops, Frank explained to Garry, it was short for 'Dear Bill, this is a bastard — don't come'.[45] Many front-line soldiers did not think that men should be compelled to share the fate they had unknowingly chosen.

Frank's letters confirm that he was collecting soldiers' slang from January 1918, inspired by his friendship with C.J. Dennis. A letter from Dennis, who was writing *Digger Smith*, just after news of Frank's death reached Melbourne, confirms that Garry gave Dennis a 'list of slang words sent by Frank from the front'.[46] Garry must have forwarded an original list—his exhaustive scrapbooks contains no glossary. But the glossary in *Digger Smith* mostly contains larrikin slang, with very few specifically AIF words, which were already well known—such as 'Digger' (a nickname coined in 1916) and 'Blighty' (army-Hindustani slang for 'Britain').

In March 1918, Frank and 'Norrie' Norwood went to Paris on leave. They stayed in a hotel and were shown around the city by Miss Edith Alston, an Australian woman, an artist, and a friend of another of the Robertses' circle—this time, a friend of Berta's, in a reminder of the artistic life she had given up to be a mother. She 'treated us like small brothers', Frank told his family. He described how they had seen all the sights: the Eiffel tower, St-Germain-de-Prés, the Panthéon, Notre Dame, and Les Invalides, though Napoleon's tomb was closed, sandbagged as a precaution against bombing. Bathed and changed, with a haircut and a fresh uniform, Frank had a photograph taken—his last. Garry was to paste dozens of prints of it into the scrapbooks he created in Frank's memory. (Oswald Green, the Dandenong blacksmith, travelled to Paris with them, but his tastes differed from Frank and Noble's, and he stayed elsewhere.)

At home, Garry had begun to take a strong interest in the recently formed Sailors and Soldiers' Fathers' Association. It attracted 3000 members in Victoria within a few months of starting, and over 140 fathers a week were joining by the time of Mont St Quentin. Mainly a middle-class organisation, the association provided what would today be described as a support group for those sharing the worry of having a son at the front, or the burden of having lost one to the war. Its meetings provided a place where men could be with others in the same situation, though not necessarily to talk. 'Men bereaved are not prone to words' an *Age* reporter noticed, 'but a tactful question, a nod in reply ... and a handgrip, convey much'.[47]

The association's magazine, *Our Empire*, published in its May 1918 issue a poem, 'Carry On!', that became the mantra for the rest of Garry's life. It began in Kiplingesque style, 'You can hear the big battalion coming up the crowded ramp ...' Garry felt he was a part of it, but it was not a battalion of soldiers like the 21st:

> [T]hey aren't clothed in khaki, and they haven't got a band ...
> but they prove that all the heroes haven't gone from out the land —
> They're the fathers who were left to carry on!
> 'There are some who march together in a loud, loquacious troop —
> There are some who walk a little way apart.
> For it's "Poor old Jones; I'm sorry; he's just told me in the train,"
> Or "Yes, and now his youngest boy is gone" ...[48]

Not surprisingly, it turned out to be a respectful parody of Kipling's 'The Lost Legion'. 'Carry On' became the Association's motto. Frank picked it up, too, and used it in his letters home. Garry, Berta, Ruby, Bert, and Gwen 'carried on' as best they could. The irregularity of postal deliveries concerned Ruby particularly. Frank sent occasional, expensive cables, but letters took a long time—as much as six or even eight weeks. Frank reassured Ruby that 'non-arrival of letters should not put the "wind up" you'. He urged Ruby to 'look up at our star and wink back at him and whisper to little Nance that Daddie will soon be home'.[49] After evading shellfire in Belgium, he assured Ruby that 'I'm immune now'.[50] In May, he predicted that the war would be over by September: for him, it was.

'THE SMALL WORLD': BREWERY FARM, QUERRIEU

Australia's understanding of the Great War cannot be separated from the ways in which the story of their troops' part in it was recorded and conveyed. At the war's outset, the Australian government commissioned an official correspondent to travel to the war with the Australian Imperial Force. Charles Bean, a 34-year-old journalist, narrowly won a ballot held among members of his trade union, the Australian Journalists' Association. Already conscious of the desire to document a national achievement, Bean soon saw the need to collect and create records of the war. He lobbied to have photographers and artists appointed and to establish an Australian War Records Section to collect documents, such as unit war diaries, and the trophies and souvenirs that he called 'relics'. By 1918, a small artistic colony lived among the Australian Corps, mainly at formation headquarters. Much of what we know about the Australian Corps' part in the last year of the war comes directly from what they wrote, painted, photographed, or gathered.

The correspondents included Bean, Gordon Gilmour, and Keith Murdoch (when he wasn't playing king-maker in London during Billy Hughes's visit to Britain). The premier expatriate figures in Australian art became a part of the war art programme, and artists such as A. Henry Fullwood, Will Dyson (whom Garry probably met in Fasoli's restaurant), Arthur Streeton, and Will Longstaff moved about the Australian divisions' rear areas, often sharing billets with the writers and the photographers. The photographers included Hubert Wilkins and Frank Hurley, veterans of Polar exploration who emerged from the planet's frozen wastes to enter the madness of war.

Wilkins was to be closely associated with the attack on Mont St Quentin. A colourblind cinematographer from rural South Australia, he had arrived on the Western Front in 1917 to work for John Treloar's War Records Section. Wilkins took extraordinary risks to capture combat with his camera—he was twice awarded the Military Cross. His biographer claims that Monash called him 'the bravest soldier in his army'; although, with such a galaxy of gallantry to choose from, it sounds unlikely. Charles Bean, another admirer, recorded how he had tried to take photographs of the Germans retreating late in August. Wilkins brushed aside Bean's alarm, explaining blandly that 'you only had to dodge the machine-guns for about 50 yards'.[51]

Several of these men, among the most important chroniclers of the emerging Anzac legend, gathered in the village of Querrieu in the spring of 1918. In their billet at Brewery Farm there occurred some of the most significant conversations in Australian military history. There, Bean, Dyson, and Murdoch colluded to try, unsuccessfully, to prevent Monash being given command of the Australian Corps. (Tainted by the common anti-Semitism of the day, they disliked him as an ambitious, albeit successful, Jew, and later acknowledged their error.) Bean, Dyson, and Wilkins sat about after dinner discussing how the sacrifices and achievements of the war could best be remembered. They had already conceived the idea of a war memorial museum, but wondered what 'the most interesting kind of exhibit' should be.[52] Someone—probably Bean—suggested battlefield models, like those in the United Services Institution in London. Dyson certainly suggested that these models be created by 'first rate artists and sculptors'. The first of the picture models they conceived would depict the attack on Mont St Quentin, and the 21st Battalion would have a part in it, too. And in the yard at Brewery Farm, Charles Bean finally decided to take an interest in the men to whom he devoted his life, beginning with Nine Platoon's comrades of the 21st Battalion.

Querrieu, the first village on the road from Amiens to Albert, was filled with Australians in the spring and summer of 1918. Brigades in reserve were billeted there, one after the other, for three or four days apiece. The village straggled up from a shallow stream, the Hallue, and its surviving houses, cellars, and barns became home to thousands of Australians, who were successors to a London division. The village, a passing journalist noted, 'has not many street corners', but he noticed nearly two years after the war that each of them still bore the name of a famous London street. The main street was Oxford Street, and off it to the right and left was Shaftsbury Avenue, Lombard Street, or Finsbury Circus.[53] The street names helped billeting officers to direct the parties of troops, including the 21st Battalion, who streamed into the village a couple of times a week.

Henry Fullwood painted a watercolour, *Road to Querrieu*, depicting lorries rumbling along the dusty pavé towards the front. Fullwood's painting forms a metaphor for the journey that brought men of the 21st Battalion to this place, where Charles Bean would at last notice them.

At Querrieu, Bean dined with Edwin Brissenden, a middle-aged Sydney lawyer who famously passed up a judgeship to become a second lieutenant in the AIF. Brissenden 'tackled' Bean with 'never having written up the life of the soldier'. Fair-mindedly, Bean conceded the point and acknowledged, at least in his diary, that 'I have been shy of these men', doing his work 'as a staff officer, as it were'. He admitted, too, that he had become unpopular in Egypt, before the embarkation for Gallipoli, when he sent home an article damning men who had caught VD from prostitutes in Cairo. It was true, but many soldiers resented the slur on their characters—or that Bean had let out of the bag in articles read by their families the fact that men visited brothels. Despite spending most of 1915 in a dugout on Gallipoli, and sharing many of the risks of the front line on the Western Front, Bean admitted privately that he shrank from living among the men: he was 'too selfconscious to mix well'.

Spurred by Brissenden, he now resolved to change this. But rather than 'mixing' with 'the men', he lived beside a group of them, as would an admiring anthropologist. He sat in the window of Brewery Farm, looking out onto the yard, and wrote what he saw and what he overheard. The result is one of the most intriguing passages in all of Bean's thick volumes.

Early in May, the 21st found billets at Querrieu. The halting of the German offensive, the spring weather, and a few days' rest moved the men to optimism. Frank caught up on his correspondence, writing to tell Ruby that all his mates reckoned that the war would be over by September. 'We're winning', he told Miss Alston (who kept up with Norrie and Frank): 'the end is not far off'.[54] In a letter to his mother—did she surrender all her letters to Garry's scrapbooks?—Frank allowed himself to look forward to life with his family in the Dandenongs 'when this "stoush" is all over … Lord! what good times are ahead of us'. But he reassured his mother that, though far from his own family, he was 'not lonely with the boys'. With his platoon, he felt 'one of the "Aussie" family over here'.[55] (Absence from home deepened their sense of being Australian. About this time, Roy Smerdon sent a postcard to his sister Emily, in which he reported that the flowers were out in France, 'but there [sic] not as pretty as they are over home'.[56])

Charles Bean was now to capture the spirit of that 'Aussie' family at this very place and among the 21st Battalion. Sitting at the window of the farmhouse, Bean watched and noted. He recorded what he called 'the small world' in which the company lived and moved. Drawn from life, his account is both realistic and romantic. His description begins with the company cooks, waking before dawn to chop firewood and prepare breakfast, and takes the reader through the company's day: from the time that the first of the men emerge in undershirts and breeches to bathe in the cold, tumbling stream of the Hallue, to teatime, when the cook-house orderlies distributed bread, biscuit, jam, and chocolate. Bean watched the public life of the company in the farm yard—he describes one group playing cards in a barn doorway as like a stage set or a Rembrandt painting—but he did not follow Hubert Wilkins into the billets to photograph them at play and rest.

Bean saw the billet as 'a world of strong, independent, determined individuals'. He admired them as men whose 'every statement is downright, unhesitating, ripped out without the slightest doubt'—men so unlike himself, with the historian's awareness of the slippery nature of evidence and interpretation. 'You never hear any sort of qualification', he wrote; 'if a man wants to deny a statement he simply says "No" or "No he did not"'. He described them playing two-up, entertained by the 21st's band (Frank Roberts listened, too), sewing sandbag covers onto their steel helmets, and parading to march across the stream to drill in the willow-fringed meadow. (Another thing he did not do was watch them practise their bayonet or outpost drill or the rifle-grenade and Lewis gun drills that formed part of the foundation of their battlefield expertise.) But he noted fragments of dialogue that floated up to his window, many conforming to the larrikin image that Bean came to deplore. Once, when a nearby British heavy gun fired, a man exclaimed, 'Oh Jesus! Cut it out!'—a suppressed sign of the tension they all felt to some degree.

Bean projected his idealism onto these men. In his notebook, they are 'diggers'; but, by the time he wrote the chapter of the history, twenty years later, they had become 'Diggers'. His account is both closely observed and highly stylised, as if the men are stage characters impersonating the typical 'Digger'. Here were 'big confident men': the grinning larrikin, the two-up king, the independent-minded private, the confident NCO. Bean's admiration for the men of the AIF blossomed in the summer of 1918. Just before the attack on Mont St Quentin, he described in his diary citizen volunteers-turned-skilled fighters as 'exceedingly workmanlike — as if each knew exactly what to do and where to go … as if it were the only profession they ever had in life'.[57] For many, of course, soldiering became the last profession; for some, the only profession they had in life.

'THE BIG ADVANCE': HAMEL AND AMIENS

Inevitably, the holiday at Querrieu ended. On Thursday 9 May, Bean watched the 21st Battalion form up company-by-company and march off back to the line, holding trenches on the 'Bloody Triangle' between the Somme and the Ancre. Among the column were Frank Roberts and the rest of Nine Platoon, assembling at Tom Wignall's command in C Company's ranks.

The 21st Battalion took part in the first offensive moves after the great German spring offensive had been halted, an attack with the three other battalions of the 6th Brigade against the village of Ville-sur-Ancre and the 'Caterpillar' position on 19 May. This, which Frank described as 'the neatest little action' the battalion had fought, cost relatively few casualties, and introduced Frank to what battle meant. He and Ted Heath volunteered to work as stretcher-bearers after this 'stunt'. Carrying badly wounded men back, he told Ruby, 'I saw "War" for the first time'. Shaken, he described 'the sight at the dressing station I'll never forget', with wounded Australians and Germans lying about, some comatose, others 'smiling and smoking', glad to be out of it, many 'taking no notice of ghastly wounds'.

'Oh, sweetie', he wrote, 'I was proud to be one of the boys that morning', because 'they took their wounds so well'.[58] From their billet in Querrieu, Charles Bean and Will Dyson followed the troops into action. In his diary, Bean described the taking of Ville-sur-Ancre as 'a magnificent little success'.[59] Will Dyson haunted the area, drawing darker impressions of the troops' ordeal. His 'cartoon', 'Company awaiting relief: the Caterpillar, Ville-sur-Ancre', shows men (perhaps of the 21st Battalion) worn down by the demands of taking their turn in the trenches.

On 4 July, the 21st took a part on the right flank of the attack at Hamel, one of the set-piece attacks Monash ordered to refine his methodical approach to offensive warfare. Though enduring a cold and anxious night before the 'hop-over' ('all rather 'screwed up' … *not* "funky"'), he looked up to see 'our lucky star winking away at me'. He remained optimistic, daydreaming in letters to Ruby about their life to come, when Nancy was demanding that Frank leave his fireside to take her to dances, and teasing that, like her mother, she would be a 'a born flirt—*Was*, Dear, I mean *Was*!'[60] Towards dawn, feeling 'brightened', Frank and Nine Platoon advanced with C Company in the second wave, 'an easy walk over'. Advancing with his rifle slung, he met no Germans until C Company reached the final objective. There, he saw a German and 'spared his life to rat him'. (That is, to rob him of souvenirs: Frank was known as a 'souvenir king'.)

The great novelty in later July was the arrival among the battalion of Americans—'Goddamns', as Frank and his friends called them, from their favourite (repeatable) expletive. They spent some days gaining front-line experience at a relatively quiet time, though they were 'badly scared' by shelling.[61] Frank was now a veteran. The Goddamns impressed the Australians as friendly and willing to learn, even though they were still 'green' and liable to make many costly mistakes in the fighting to come. (Its troops fought on the Western Front for five months, from July 1918, but the United States lost as many dead as did Australia in the entire war.) Ten Americans restored the platoon to its nominal strength late in July. Australians enjoyed many jokes at the Americans' expense, such as affecting to think that the Yanks called themselves 'Shark Troops'—explaining that they meant 'shock troops'.

The first great counter-attack of the hundred days opened with a British, Australian, and Canadian attack on 8 August, known as the battle of Amiens. The 21st took a small part in this big attack, on the far Australian right flank, beside the Canadians at Marcelcave. It remained in support or reserve throughout the celebrated 93-minute advance. The 21st lost only two men killed on 8 August. Frank's account of the battle was laconic: 'We hopped over behind our barrage and Fritz promptly evacuated the territory we were after without a fight.' This was hardly true—the victory at Amiens cost 6000 Australian casualties, most in the days following as German resistance hardened. General Erich Ludendorff, the real commander of Germany's armies, called it 'the black day of the German Army', the point at which he accepted that Germany could not win the war.[62]

For the 21st Battalion, August was to be an easy month, mostly spent in reserve or support. Besides the two killed at Amiens, it lost only 28 wounded, and one man drowned accidentally while boating in the Somme. It saw little action when, towards month's end, it played its part in the 'peaceful penetration', shoving the Germans back across the plateau south of the Somme. This was no cake-walk—the brigade report on this period describes the 21st as being 'worn out' after 36 hours of continuous action. While suffering 'slight casualties', it lost men to gas shelling, and the burden of being under-manned gave everyone more to do.

Frank continued to take an interest in the slang of the AIF. He sent examples to Garry of the Franglais spoken by the battalion: 'Toot sweet'; 'damn quick'; 'Bon' (and, conversely, 'no bloody bon') and 'bookoo' (beaucoup)—'plenty to spare'.[63] He asked Garry to forward them to C.J. Dennis. In describing the company of the 21st Battalion at Brewery Farm, Charles Bean made his only commentary on the AIF's command of pig-French. It is tempting to wonder whether the quiet soldier with an interest in slang, and the self-effacing journalist with the interest in soldiers, swapped notes one day in Querrieu. The 21st's other companies were, after all, not far from A Company's billet. Frank continued to collect examples that would interest his father and (incidentally) inform later generations of the humour that helps to explain how they endured the discomfort, danger, and misery of a war that was about to enter its fourth year.

Gradually, inevitably, Nine Platoon became whittled down. Oswald Green, the Dandenong blacksmith, died of wounds at Hamel on 4 July. Alf Fox was evacuated, having been gassed on 23 July. For a time in late July, the platoon numbered just six men and a corporal. Men returning from leave and hospital helped to boost its strength, but at the end of August just thirteen men marched along the Somme canal bank towards Mont St Quentin. They were the platoon's two sergeants, Tom Wignall and Vic Edwards, and, in alphabetical order, Les Baker, Jack Castle, Alf Crawford, Godfrey Dobson, Albert Kelly, Noble Norwood, Bill Rabling, Frank Roberts, Roy Smerdon, and the Catholic woodcutter, Charlie Tognella. Frank had mentioned them in his diary or letters over the preceding six months. He had walked to the celebrated 'catacombs' at 'Hyde Park Corner' with Bill, repaired a dugout with Vic, farewelled Les on Blighty leave, visited Paris with Noble, dug trenches with Ted and Godfrey, chummed Alf as Number 2 on a Lewis gun, and joined Roy and Charlie at a forward post.

Frank told Ruby that he expected to miss 'the next stunt'—he thought he would be posted to the battalion 'left-out-of-battle party', comprising men from each company who could provide a basis for re-building the unit should it suffer catastrophic losses, as had happened before. A letter written on 24 August (the last letter that Ruby would receive from him) was chatty and positive. He ended lovingly:

> Kiss our little darling Nancy for me & for your own dear self take all the love & kisses you want in imagination & I will repay you later.
>   For a little while beloved adieu
>
> From your ever true & loving husband
> Frank
>
> XO for Nancy

Garry pasted this letter into his Record Book and later added the note, 'and so ends the dear old chap's last letter'.[64] On Friday 30 August, Frank sat in the sun catching up on his diary. The last words he wrote in it were to note that the 5th Brigade had taken over the advance. 'We hear they are around Péronne which however has not fallen to us yet.'[65]

'WE'RE WINNING, SWEETHEART': ADVANCING TO VICTORY

In the popular memory, the Great War remains a wearying succession of mud-bound offensives bound to fail amid machine-gun and shell fire. But the war's final summer was not like that. Allied armies returned to the attack, and in a series of offensives began the final advance to victory. The war remained costly—5000 more Australians were killed and 25,000 wounded in the war's last six months—but it became a war of movement and of successes. General Sir Henry Rawlinson's Fourth Army, and within it Lieutenant-General Sir John Monash's Australian Corps, made slow, jerky advances from August. After the victory of Amiens, Australian troops enjoyed the novel sensation of finding the front shifting further and further eastwards as German resistance gave way. By late August, Rawlinson's divisions were moving toward the Somme bend, where at Péronne the river swings from a northward to a westward course. The British commander-in-chief, Sir Douglas Haig, now recognised that the time had come to break the habit of the methodical advance, hoping that the long-dreamed-of breakthrough could be achieved by his commanders driving for 'distant objectives'. He told them that they should use their 'initiative and power of manoeuvre'. At the same time, Rawlinson's was only one of five great British armies, and even the Allies' growing material superiority could not sustain strong advances everywhere. On 23 August, Haig told Rawlinson that he would transfer his main thrust northwards to the Third Army advancing toward Bapaume, a few miles to the north. Rawlinson, in turn, told Monash to 'mark time', to not rush to seize the Somme crossings.

Monash, a supremely ambitious commander, confident of the power of his corps, even though it was visibly losing strength, did not accept this decision. He issued an order to his divisional commanders directing that he would continue his offensive policy, taking advantage of 'any opportunity to seize the enemy's position'. In the last days of August, he saw such an opportunity arise as the tired AIF battalions pushed on into the Somme bend. He would take Mont St Quentin, and with it Péronne and the river crossings, by a swift manoeuvre such as had not been seen on the Western Front since 1914. Or so he planned. In his memoir, *The Australian Victories in France*, Monash represents himself as the commander whose daring would bring victory. He described how, when he told Rawlinson of his plan on the afternoon of 30 August, his British superior responded 'satirically'. Rawlinson is supposed to have said:

> [S]o you think you're going to take Mont St Quentin with three battalions! What presumption! However, I don't think I ought to stop you! So, go ahead and try! — and I wish you luck![66]

Other officers doubted whether the Australian Corps should be committed to further operations. Monash told Keith Murdoch that, after Amiens, he thought that the Germans were retiring, and likely to retreat 'if pushed'. This, Charles Bean thought, meant that 'we're going to put in at least 3 of our divisions again straight away'. James Robertson, commanding the 6th Brigade, expressed a concern among those closer to the troops. Observing how all the troops were tiring in the long, hot, exhausting summer campaign, 'hadn't we better chuck it', he asked, 'if ... other people can't go on'?[67] Almost everyone (though not Charles Bean) expected the war to last into 1919.

Was Mont St Quentin Monash's greatest triumph, or did the battle acquire a momentum of its own? Did Monash direct it masterfully, or did he preside over a battle directed by his subordinates? So improvised was the fight for Mont St Quentin that it is not even mentioned in the Fourth Army headquarters' intelligence reports and planning documents until the very last day of August, by which time the first units were climbing its slopes. Monash certainly conceived the broad outline for the

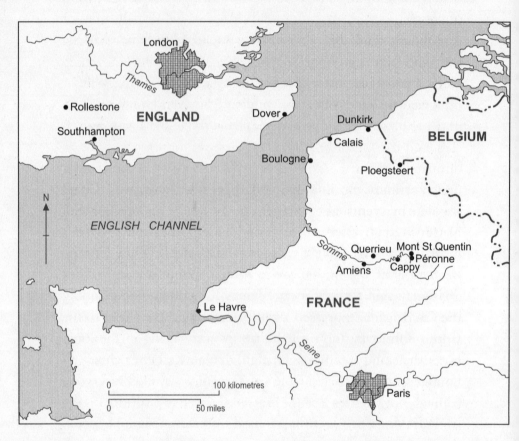

Southern Britain and northern France, showing Mont St Quentin and places significant to Nine Platoon's story

operations that resulted in the seizure of Péronne. On the afternoon of 29 August, he met his divisional commanders at the 5th Division's headquarters near Morcourt. Monash decided that, 'as a result of Army policy', his corps would advance not easterly, directly for the Somme bend, but north-easterly, aiming to seize Péronne by a turning movement from the north.[68]

Monash and his divisional and brigade commanders, shuttling from conference to conference in dugouts and ruined barns, barely kept up with a fast-moving battle. They brought off a victory, operating at the limits of the technology of 1918, drawing on aerial reconnaissance, racing to conferences in staff cars, and passing orders by telephone and motorcycle, though ultimately reliant on the speed of marching men and horse-drawn artillery. Both orders and reports were often rendered obsolete by events. But they managed to retain enough control, blessed with good luck, to bring off a battle unique in the AIF's history.

Both sides saw the Mont as a priceless tactical asset. Its face and summit pocked with craters, the village on its crown ruined, the wood around it slashed and shattered, the Mont remained a strong-post in the German defences. From its summit, artillery observers could look down across the treeless slopes toward the Somme and, beyond it, westwards. Officers with binoculars, compasses, and maps could plot movement and positions on the Allied side of the line and call down the fire of what had been the finest artillery force in the world. Looking back toward their own lines, they could see signs of the German defenders' tail—roads with wagons, ambulances, and lorries: horse-lines, bivouacs, and camps. Whoever controlled the Mont controlled a great swathe of France north and south of the Somme. Both sides pounded the front and rear areas around the Mont, the devastated front-line village of Cléry, and especially Péronne, with its bridges and railway yard. In late August, they lay in the path of the advancing Australian Corps.

By the summer of 1918, the Australian Corps was growing increasingly weary. Most of its divisions had been in action without a long break since late March, and both units and individuals were feeling the strain. Hubert Wilkins, who followed patrols out into the weedy fields in search of action photographs, told Bean how the infantry were 'very done and were getting rather depressed' by the incessant pace Monash imposed.[69] But unlike the desperate years of 1916 and 1917, with their bloody and unproductive battles, by the war's final summer many men sensed that they had turned a corner. Frank Roberts reflected this optimism. In August, he reprimanded Ruby for simply wanting the war to end. 'My dear girl', Frank rebuked her, 'we don't want peace yet because we have the Hun where we want him ... we want to give him a taste of war in his own country'. A week before his death, Frank affirmed that he felt 'in the best fighting mood and spirits'. 'Why?' he asked rhetorically. 'Because we're winning, sweetheart'.[70] Ruby was to read this letter knowing that Frank was dead.

On the evening of 30 August, the 21st bivouacked on the south bank of the Somme. Someone had found a fish-trap, which they thought had been left behind by the Germans (or was it French, having been there all along?) Arch Green, a handy man, skinned eels and gave them to the company cooks to serve to those fed up with fat ration-bacon. Frank Roberts left his own company's area and went to find his friend Phil Starr in A Company. Phil later described how he and Frank strolled along the bank of the canal, yarning and smoking for a couple of hours. His account of it—written to feed Garry Roberts's consuming need to know—paints a sentimental picture of how they were:

talking of nothing in particular, perhaps exchanging an experience of the last day or so, with an occasional reference to some incident of home life, just as good pals would, satisfied with each other's company, not knowing when we would meet again.

In fact, Phil wrote, 'it was our last yarn together'. That night, they pulled on greatcoats taken from German dugouts to keep out the night's chill, tired by the extra work in their under-strength unit.

Bernard Duggan's 21st Battalion was entering the fight for the Mont in a weakened state, just twenty officers and 421 men strong, much less than half its nominal size. Its four companies were of varying size; C Company was the weakest, with fewer than fifty fighting men; of its three platoons, Nine Platoon was weakest, with just thirteen members.

'Numbers are going down pretty fast', Bean noticed. 'Battalions are going into some of these fights 150 strong … feeling that they have had more than their share of fighting.' He noted that officers and men were predicting that if things went on, 'there won't be any dominion army soon'. Bean hoped that the AIF would be withdrawn and rested, but he thought that neither Haig nor Monash cared, provided that the advance continued.[71] He knew the AIF in and out of the line, mixed with knowledgeable battalion and staff officers, and so knew that Lewis guns could not compensate for weakened battalions. Frank gloomily told Ruby that 'we are double worked'. Indeed, he had 'seen men die because exhaustion undermined them'.[72]

Though weak in numbers, the 21st was an experienced fighting unit. Three of its four company commanders had been awarded the Military Cross. But all were lieutenants—a sign of the severity of the AIF's manpower shortage. Commanding

C Company was Lieutenant William Emlyn Hardwick. As his middle name hints, Hardwick was a Welshman, from Brecon. A carpenter by trade, he had emigrated to Gippsland, where he had cousins, and became a member of the Leongatha Rifle Club. He had enlisted, aged 29, in January 1915, had been promoted to company sergeant-major, and was commissioned after Pozières. Hardwick was a leader, wounded while charging and capturing a machine-gun at Bullecourt—a feat that gained him a Military Cross. The 'severe' gunshot wound to his right arm and concussion kept him convalescent in Britain for fifteen months. But, despite still suffering from a suppurating discharge from the ears, chronic headaches, and tinnitus (aggravated by loud noises), he soon returned to the 21st. Late in August, Duggan gave him command of C Company, which had lost two commanding officers in the course of August.[73]

C Company's other officers were Willie McConnochie, a twice-wounded Footscray carpenter who embodied the AIF's tendency to promote leaders regardless of their background. George Dearden, a former light-horse signaller commissioned into the 21st in 1917, led Number Ten Platoon in the attack on the Mont. The company's most junior officer was Lieutenant Alfred Sennitt, a Melbourne clerk. Sennitt had enlisted early in 1916, shortly before Frank Roberts, but had seen more active service. Nine Platoon, under Sergeant Tom Wignall, had no officer to lead it.

On the afternoon of the 31st, the 6th Brigade crossed the Somme over the smouldering remains of a bridge (re-built and re-named Duggan Bridge, in honour of the 21st's commanding officer). Moving in single file, platoon-by-platoon, the 21st marched northward across the channel, a maze of islands and banks fringed by reeds. Just downstream of Hem, they turned right to follow a path between the river and steep hillsides. As they neared the rubble of Cléry, on the north bank of the river,

German shells began to crash down and fall into the river, sending up geysers of water fifty feet into the air. Tom Wignall, the Lancastrian gardener, had obviously picked up Australian slang in the AIF. He described this as 'a bonzer exhibition of water splashing'. Major Donald Coutts, the medical officer of the neighbouring 24th Battalion, watched parties cross for an hour, with shells falling every fifteen seconds but causing no casualties. Around lunchtime, the column halted on the railway line in the narrow corridor between the river and the high banks. Shells splashed into the Somme, spraying the troops with water. Coutts and many others chewed on bread and jam as they waited for the shelling to ease.

Tom Wignall's Lewis gunners carried rifles, but nothing heavier—the guns had been loaded onto horse-drawn limbers. Not until teatime were the guns and their teams reunited, and after dinner they retrieved them and spent the last hours of daylight cleaning and re-assembling their weapons. German shells continued to fall around them, but hardly often enough to disturb men who knew the worst of war on the Western Front. Coutts, who had served at Ypres with a field ambulance, had dressed many men mutilated by shell splinters, and had a wary respect for German artillery. He had no compunction in running from shell bursts, reasoning that, where one fell, others would follow. But it seemed that the German gunners had lost their edge. Disrupted by their retreat, they were unable to find the range of the narrow riverside path. The marching men passed on rumours and reports from the head of the column. They heard that the 5th Brigade had attacked the Mont but had been driven back—some reports said, almost back to the river. Late that afternoon, they reached 'Lost Ravine'.

French canal engineers had begun cutting the channel of the new Canal du Nord before the war. It had stopped construction, but the deep cutting—named 'Lost Ravine' on

British maps—provided shelter from shelling. Men of the 6th Brigade crowded into it. Many entered the dugouts that the Germans had excavated in the western face of the canal. The 6th Brigade's battalion headquarters and regimental aid posts moved into the big dugouts, leaving their men to find or scrape 'pozzies' in the banks. Huddled in these holes in the chalky soil, they sat out the shells bursting around the ravine into the evening.

Robertson and his battalion commanders met at the 23rd Battalion's headquarters on the evening of the 31st to plan the attack on the Mont that they were to make the following morning. John McColl, a staff officer, told Bean that Robertson did not try to diminish how hard their task would be. 'The job', he told them, 'was very big—tremendous front and Germans so strong'.[74]

That evening, as 21st Battalion men gathered for their meal in a chalk pit by the canal, German shells continued to fall around them. Tom Wignall, the platoon sergeant, who had been 'greatly interested in' the shelling, happened to be sitting with a group of his men—Frank Roberts, Roy Smerdon, Jack Castle, and Les Baker—when 'a stray shell lobbed fair among my platoon'. It showered them with dirt, but wounded only Les Baker. Wignall admired his wound as 'a nice Blighty one'—a wound that would see him evacuated to Britain (*belait* in army Hindustani).[75] Stretcher-bearers carried Baker to Captain Harris Mendelsohn's aid post in Lost Ravine, and he was soon evacuated to the west. (Mendelsohn, a newly qualified Melbourne GP, had volunteered in 1916, and had been wounded serving with a field ambulance earlier in the year on the Somme. He joined the battalion late in August and stayed only a month, so his only time with the 21st was at Mont St Quentin.) Nine Platoon had suffered its first casualty at Mont St Quentin.

Major Coutts dressed men of the 5th Brigade and those hit by splinters from the exploding shells. He amputated the shattered limbs of two men; at the same time, one of his orderlies fell with a shrapnel splinter in his back as he dressed wounded men. As Coutts worked away with splints and bandages (for five hours wearing his gas respirator), he noticed that the stretcher-bearers were bringing in more German wounded. They confirmed the rumours, washing back from the front in the dark, that the 5th Brigade had taken the summit of the Mont. Donald Coutts treated his wounded for 52 hours without a break.

The German shelling, Godfrey Dobson recalled, caused some 'very anxious moments'. That night, Wignall's men were moved from their pozzies in Lost Ravine and made to shift back a hundred yards to an old trench. This caused 'a high outburst of language'. They had to sleep in the open, and when it began to rain 'we all got pretty wet'. (As a Lancastrian, Wignall knew rain when he felt it.)

With Les Baker carried away to hospital, Nine Platoon would enter its last battle a dozen men strong. As the misty dawn of 1 September spread its dull light, men could see on the south-eastern skyline the low bulk of a hill that they probably now knew to be Mont St Quentin. Nine Platoon had come together on the road to Querrieu, and now had reached the place of its destruction.

PART II

Fighting

Mont St Quentin, 1 September 1918

By the time that Nine Platoon reached Querrieu, war had swept several times over the slopes of Mont St Quentin, a hill a couple of kilometres north-west of Péronne. The Mont itself is a character in the platoon's story, and its part in the war began earlier than any of theirs. As Garry later learned (and pasted references into his scrapbooks), invaders had passed this way for centuries — Henry V's bowmen marched past the Mont on the way to Agincourt. Péronne had withstood half-a-dozen sieges, and succumbed to several more, in 1815, when Wellington marched from Waterloo to Paris, and in 1870, when the Germans had taken it for the first time. (A memorial in Péronne commemorated Marin Delpas, the hero of the most recent siege.) The River Somme protected the southern approaches to the town, but the great French military engineer Vauban had built massive bastions around the old town, some of which survived on its north-western side.

Péronne's sufferings in the Great War began early. Late in August 1914, the Germans arrived again. Streams of refugees, including the mayor, fled westwards. A Colonel von Votberg, backed by a regiment of lance-carrying Uhlans, arrived at

Péronne's handsome town hall and demanded an indemnity equal to £12,000, to be paid within 24 hours. The cabinet-maker who stepped in to the mayor's shoes told von Votberg that, as the refugees had taken with them the municipal treasury, it would be impossible to comply. The German commander accepted £160 in gold and goods worth £16,000, but then allowed his troops to loot the town anyway. After breaking into wine shops, drunken troopers terrified and perhaps assaulted the people—one woman was said to have drowned herself in a well—before von Votberg restrained his men. Within three weeks, the town was back in French hands. The relieved citizens told returning French dragoons of their ordeal. Von Votberg left, warning, 'We shall soon be back', as indeed the Germans soon were.[1]

In 1916, the agonising and costly advance that was the battle of the Somme left the Allies just short of Mont St Quentin, which had been fortified by the Germans as a stronghold. The British and French sectors met hereabouts (the large French cemetery west of Cléry, beside the new motorway, remains a powerful reminder of their part). But British trenches on Bouchavesnes Spur looked out on the western slopes of Mont St Quentin. That winter—the coldest in twenty years—men of Captain Robert Graves's battalion of Royal Welch Fusiliers made their way to the front past a wrecked steamroller with the name 'Clery' chalked upon it. The village itself had no wall left standing higher than three feet, and otherwise comprised overlapping shell craters.[2]

When the Germans abandoned the Mont in their great withdrawal eastwards to the Hindenburg Line in the spring of 1917, British journalists found Péronne protected by 'acres of barbed wire' on the slopes of the Mont.[3] The town was already in ruins. The correspondents reported that the Germans had blown up all the houses (but that their own artillery had not shelled the town, and that there was not a shell-hole in the main square—obvious propaganda). The civilians had all fled. The only living things that the advancing British found were a German deserter vehemently claiming to be Danish, a tortoiseshell cat, and an abandoned cavalry pony.[4] Péronne became a rear area—Australian troops trained for defensive warfare around the town over the winter of 1917–18.

In March 1918, realising that America's entry into the war would eventually bring into battle millions of fresh troops, backed by a strong economy, Eric Ludendorff staked Germany's future on a gamble. Drawing upon troops released from the eastern front after Russia's collapse, the Germans launched their great spring offensive. In a terrifying, exhilarating month, the Germans burst between the British Fourth and Fifth Armies, and pushed the British Expeditionary Force far to the west. Further offensives directed against the French sent their armies reeling. For a time, it seemed that the Germans had achieved the long-expected decisive result that had eluded both sides.

Péronne and Mont St Quentin fell to the advancing Germans within a few days of the opening of the March offensive. Within a month, it lay sixty kilometres behind the battlefront. But the gamble failed. The British line bent, but did not break; the French gave up ground, but not the will to resist. The Germans failed to take the Channel ports, and failed even to reach the vital rail junction of Amiens. After a month of further German assaults on other portions of the Allied line, the German offensives ended and the Allies, their recuperative powers massively evident, launched the first of a series of offensives over the summer of 1918 that became known as the 'Hundred Days' (an echo of the hundred days that saw Napoleon defeated a century before) and which—as we will see—brought the German army to collapse and the Allies to victory, at last. The country over which the final offensives were launched had become a green wasteland. The Germans, determined to leave nothing useful when they retreated in 1917, had cut down trees, and blown up or burned buildings. Villagers had long before been driven out as refugees, their livestock commandeered, and their possessions looted. The rolling beet fields ran to weeds; the sites of villages marked by piles of rubble the colour of the dark, liver-coloured bricks of the region. The slopes of the Mont lay bare, seamed by trenches and wire.

If Henry Rawlinson's Fourth Army was to get across the obstacle of the River Somme, Mont St Quentin had to be taken. Mont St Quentin was not, as you might suppose, much of a mountain. Garry's friend, the sculptor Charles Gilbert, said that Australians would call it 'a bit of a hill'.[5] Charles Bean first saw the Mont on the sunny afternoon of 29 August 1918, when he and his little party of correspondents and artists walked over the brow of a ridge and looked down on the Somme below Péronne. They gazed across the broad valley, noticing 'a rather shell shattered wood' crowning a hill. He later realised it was Mont St Quentin, but shells bursting 70 and 50 yards distant persuaded him not to linger.[6]

On its summit, the village of Mont St Quentin lay in ruins, occupied by German machine-gunners and riflemen (the riflemen, often called 'snipers' in several accounts, were probably not especially trained or equipped as snipers). Many witnesses noticed a brick wall that ran along the western side of the village, with large gaps knocked into it by shells fired at the Mont throughout the war. Three times, Australian troops of Major-General Charles Rosenthal's 2nd Division advanced up the slopes of the Mont. The first attack began before dawn on Saturday 31 August, when battalions of the 5th Brigade went forward.

'IT WAS A SOLDIERS' BATTLE': THE 31 AUGUST ATTACK

Battles are confusing affairs, both to take part in and to write about. At first reading, the various soldiers' accounts of Mont St Quentin are simply baffling. Even when their authors had clear recollections of where they were and what they did—and they often did not—the task of describing what was an inescapably chaotic experience defeated all but the most determined. Even with Charles Bean's detailed interview notes, and the great stacks of war diaries and original orders that he and John Treloar badgered units into keeping, we have a scrappy and confused impression of what happened. Soldiers' accounts of the attacks on the Mont by the 5th Brigade on 31 August seem to bear out the Duke of Wellington's quip that 'one may as well write the history of a ball as of a battle'. Just as the hundreds of pairs of dancers forming and re-forming defy record and analysis, so the movements and reactions of thousands of men in action prohibit a complete or full account. Even John Monash, with all of the reports of his Corps headquarters, admitted that it was 'difficult to write a connected and consecutive account of the details of the fighting'.[7] Fortunately, concerned as we are with one platoon, we do not need a detailed account, but we do need to know where Nine Platoon fits into the bigger picture. For the first day of the battle, Nine Platoon waited to join it.

At 5.00 a.m. on 31 August, three battalions of Brigadier-General Edward Martin's 5th Brigade attacked the Mont. Though supported by the fire of no fewer than six brigades of field or heavy artillery (over 100 guns), and a machine-gun company of sixteen heavy machine-guns, the infantry committed numbered fewer than 1250 men. Contrary to the popular impression of 1918, no tanks supported the attack (indeed, most attacks, even in 1918, did not include tanks). In any case, they were too few, and the ground—slopes seamed by deep trenches—was too broken.

The 5th Brigade met fierce resistance from German defenders, many of them either men who had volunteered to hold the Mont, or members of the 'first class' 2nd Guard Division. Their swift and repeated counter-attacks stopped the Australian attack, broke its momentum, and forced the attackers to withdraw back down the hill, with many others hanging on in trenches and hollows, or in the rubble on the top of the Mont. The reports submitted to Rosenthal's divisional staff made out that the company commanders had 'decided to withdraw' to the trenches around Elsa Trench, just short of the walled wood on the Mont's western flank, but it is clear that repeated German counter-attacks and heavy fire drove them back.[8] Against that adversary in that place, it was no disgrace.

This much has been told before, in battalion histories and in Charles Bean's volume of the official history. But the story of the 5th Brigade's attack can also be told from a source that has never before been quoted. In the weeks and months after the battle, men of the 20th Battalion gave statements of what they recalled to Frank Brewer, a Brisbane journalist serving in the 20th. Though only a private and (it must be admitted) an unenthusiastic soldier, Frank Brewer was able to document his battalion's part in the attack on the Mont as did few other soldiers. The accounts that Brewer gathered have been in the Mitchell Library since the early 1920s, but only Bill Gammage has ever looked at them (in researching *The Broken Years*, in the early 1970s, and he was not interested in the detail of the battle). They give an impression of the 5th Brigade's attack. Exactly how Frank Brewer came to collect them will be told later. For now, these statements give a series of impressions of the attack of the 5th Brigade.

Weedy, bare fields lay on the Mont's slopes, uncultivated since 1914, seamed by trenches and littered with clumps of barbed wire. When he saw them a few days after the battle, the masses of barbed wire chilled the journalist-turned-soldier of the 20th Battalion. To Brewer, they looked like 'huge burrs' of metal, in such fantastic shapes that it suggested 'some gigantic spiders had crawled up from the slime of the Somme and spun these meshes of wire to trap men'.[9]

Frank Brewer asked his reader (not that there have been more than two since about 1920) to 'narrow the limits of his mental vision and concentrate his attention upon that battle within a greater battle'—the 5th Brigade's attack. He confirms what sounds like Bean's hyperbole, that they 'commenced the battle with a great shout'. Men called out catch-phrases and war-cries as they advanced—'Wild rabbito!' 'Bottlo!' and 'Cooee!'—hoping to sound more numerous. One of Brewer's informants said they were in 'a state of frenzy'. As they reached the first German dugouts in the village, 'Doc' Morris described a comrade standing at the entrance roaring, 'Anyone down there?' Rather than throw bombs in, he pushed into the gloom and found five Germans, whom he 'ratted'—Frank was not the only 'souvenir king'. Morris found time to talk with a badly wounded German sergeant-major. 'He asked me what I was fighting for', and told Morris that it was 'only a capitalistic war'. The sergeant-major (still coherent in English) told Morris he thought that Germany would soon collapse. As they reached the main road, they met German machine-gun fire. A sergeant said, 'I'll settle those bastards' and 'deliberately walked across the road', throwing bombs and killing the guns' crews. 'He came back to the mob with a good lot of souvenirs'.

'Doc' Morris, Lieutenant Daniel Anthon's runner, described how Anthon fired his revolver over the heads of a group of 'howling' prisoners. This quietened them enough for Morris, a man from the South Coast of NSW, to 'rat' them of revolvers, watches, 'photographs of Frauleins and other things that may not be seen at Helensburg'. The attackers sent the prisoners back, and sat drinking from their canteens and eating 'Anzac wafers and dodger' [bread], sitting and smoking 'as if nothing had happened'. Morris found a German doctor, from whom he took a tin dixie of coffee before sending him and his wounded as prisoners back down the Mont.

It seemed that the assault had succeeded through dash and sheer impetuosity: 'It was the initiative of the men that fixed the result', Private Daniel Peterson told Brewer. While some defenders had surrendered readily, the Germans reacted swiftly and strongly—their habitual reaction was to hold their most advanced positions lightly and to counter-attack the disorganised attackers. The 20th had begun on the left, the 17th in the centre, and the 19th on the right. The attacking battalions became badly confused, with sections and platoons from the three battalions mixed up. 'It was hurly burly', said a corporal.

The German company and battalion commanders—who were probably no more senior than captains or majors—reacted exactly as they had been trained to do. They launched a series of strong counter-attacks, using machine-guns, anti-tank guns, and *Minenwefer* (mobile mortars), all supported by heavy five-point-nine artillery fire. Survivors described how Lewis gun teams, at both the forefront of the attack and when called upon to meet the counter-attacks, lost heavily, and how the 'intensity of fire' from German defenders drove them back. The counter-attacks had often driven out disorganised attackers, and on the slopes of the Mont on the last day of August they succeeded again.

Another of Brewer's comrades summed up the attack: 'I do not think the Heads expected us to do as much as we did. It was a soldiers' battle'. But all the 'daring, bluff and determination' they showed could not prevail against the many local counter-attacks that the Germans made, and by day's end the 5th Brigade was spent. While odd Australian parties hung on in isolated trenches, by the late afternoon the attackers had mainly retreated back down the hill, forming a rough line along Elsa Trench, a couple of hundred yards short of the brick wall bounding the village.

At this point in the story—about breakfast time on 31 August—Australian accounts of the battle traditionally describe how General Rawlinson (in his headquarters at Querrieu) received a message while he was shaving: '5 Bde report having captured Mt St Quentin from which the Australian flag now flies', Les Carlyon quotes.[10] The message—from Edward Martin's 5th Brigade headquarters—appears in the 2nd Division war diary, and Monash seemingly passed it on, without seeking confirmation, but ignoring the cautionary addendum 'exact situation ... not yet definitely established'.[11] It was not literally true, not even in spirit. Both Les Carlyon and Richard Travers, the latest myth-makers of Australia on the Western Front, quote the 'flag' story as if it were true. Travers has the attackers 'falling back' to 'successfully drive off five German counter-attacks'.[12] Their implication is that Australian dash and determination had won through, against British pessimism. In fact, the first bold attempt on the Mont had failed: messages in the Corps war diary later that day reflect the more prosaic truth. No Australian flag flew on the Mont (or anywhere else within sight of a German artillery observer's binoculars), and the under-strength attackers held on by the narrowest of margins, a few hundred yards short of the summit.

Rawlinson, though at first rightly 'totally incredulous', accepted Monash's claim—he was astonished, but had no reason to disbelieve the message. His staff prepared and sent a 'message of appreciation' to Monash later that day. Without knowing the details, much less the truth, Rawlinson described the capture of the Mont as 'a feat of arms worthy of the highest praise'. Rawlinson said that he was aware of 'the natural strength of the position' and its value in overlooking Péronne, and was 'filled with admiration at the gallantry and surpassing daring of the 2nd Division'. Rawlinson congratulated the division's men 'with all my heart'.[13] In fact, as the primary sources show (and as the official history showed more than 60 years ago), the story was based on a mistaken report—not that accuracy bothers boosters. The Mont would not fall to the Australians for another thirty hours and until after two further attacks.

'FOUGHT TO THE DEATH': THE SECOND ATTACK ON THE MONT

By the evening of 31 August, it was clear that the signal sent to Rawlinson as he shaved had been impossibly optimistic: indeed, it was wrong. The only Australians on the summit were dead and wounded, or hiding from the Germans who had filtered back into machine-gun posts as men from Thuringia relieved exhausted Prussian Guardsmen. Was Monash genuinely mistaken? Had he jumped the gun, or was he misleading his army commander and hoping that his troops would make good on his promise? It seems that Monash accepted the 5th Brigade's report. Peter Pedersen, his principal military biographer, describes him as 'complacent' that afternoon, which he spent not following the battle, but 15 kilometres from his headquarters. Indeed, the flexibility and initiative so apparent across his Corps seems to have evaporated. While the survivors of the disorganised 5th Brigade beat off counter-attacks, no one took responsibility for supporting it or for renewing the attack. Not until mid-evening did Charles Rosenthal, the divisional commander, resume control of the battle. This is why Mont St Quentin was not Monash's triumph. He moved brigades in the general direction of the battle, but did not intervene to direct them to the decisive point when needed. His subordinates, expecting close supervision, did not at first take the initiative; but Monash accepted the credit when they finally did take charge.

If the Mont was to be taken, a new attack by fresh troops was needed, and Rosenthal ordered that James Robertson's 6th Brigade make a second attempt. Robertson's hard-pressed brigade-major, Captain Fred Sale, wrote new orders that he issued to weary battalion staffs in the early hours of 1 September. Rosenthal and Robertson's plan was for three of the brigade's four battalions to renew the attack on the Mont at 6.00 a.m., under the fire of three brigades of Australian field artillery and many British medium and heavy guns. (Though large numbers of guns were available, the confusion on the slopes of the Mont prevented them firing a barrage—they fired on fixed points on and behind the summit.) The 21st was to remain 'in support', ready to add its weight to the attack or reinforce the foremost units if (when) the defenders counter-attacked. The 22nd, 23rd, and 24th went forward as ordered but, as a 21st Battalion observer observed neutrally, 'were not successful'.

Fred Sale later collated reports from the attacking battalions and wrote a report that gave a vivid account of the attack that morning:

> The smothering [machine-gun] fire that opened as soon as the men went over the top broke up our formations and the advance had to be made in rushes—casualties were heavy in two companies [of the 23rd Battalion], all the officers were lost, and in one of these companies all sergeants except one. The leading men with magnificent grit ... eventually capturing [sic] Elsa Trench just west of the village'.[14]

There they found isolated parties of Australians hanging on, many wounded. Through the morning, Australians and Germans fought in the warren of trenches on the slopes of the Mont and in the ruins on the summit. Fred Sale gathered enough accounts from the survivors to write of 'intense fighting'. The defenders 'fought to the death, very few prisoners being taken … the enemy dead were strewn over the whole area'. But the defenders, the men of the 2nd Guard Division who had been unable to get out (or who may not have known they were being relieved), and the Thuringians who joined them, at least prevented the second attack from taking the summit. 'Very strong opposition was met with', the 21st Battalion war diary recorded (in the passive language that armies use to describe failure). Likewise, Fred Sale wrote, 'it was considered inadvisable to continue the advance'. Robertson found 'the whole line was held up', and later in the morning summoned his battalion commanders to a dugout in Lost Ravine. Bernard Duggan argued that the brigade could take the Mont, provided that the supporting artillery 'straffed' it heavily and that his fresh battalion joined the attack. Robertson agreed, and called by telephone to get Rosenthal's permission.[15]

'HOCHS': THE GERMAN DEFENDERS

Battles have two sides, but this book—like almost all Australian books of military history—tells the story almost exclusively from the Australian perspective. While Nine Platoon's is obviously an Australian story, we cannot understand the outcome of the battle of Mont St Quentin unless we look at the German side of the Mont. Who were the defenders; and why did they lose?

Even readers of the newspapers could see that the Germans were retreating. A series of offensives by British empire and French armies had driven them back again and again. Ludendorff knew that his armies could not hope to win, but equally he would not give up. On the night of 24–25 August, he ordered a retreat to what he optimistically (or misleadingly) called a Winter Line, a series of connected fortified lines reaching from the Somme at Péronne to the existing Drocourt-Queant line in the north—part of the outer defences of the formidable Hindenburg Line (known as the *Siegfried Stellung* to the Germans). But he knew that his units were disobeying orders, refusing to hold positions to the death, and talking Bolshevism.

Monash's intelligence officers also noted how their adversaries scrambled to hold their front with units called up from dwindling reserves—often, as Monash described it, 'single reserve Regiments of Divisions already deeply involved and sometimes even single Battalions torn from other Regiments', a 'heterogeneous jumble of units'.[16] Some Germans remained defiant. Bean and Dyson stumbled on a deserted German headquarters when they stopped to eat their bread and cheese while poking around Belloy, a few miles short of the Somme on 29 August. Dyson found a message chalked on an oilcloth:

> Tomy, you are the meaning to win? As you believe! I think else! You will loose it, and that is the troo! Good by![17]

The grammar and spelling were wonky, but the meaning was clear. Some German soldiers, especially the machine-gunners who became the mainstay of the German defence, remained defiant, many firing until overrun and killed.

But many others had become disillusioned and disheartened. The sequence of maps created daily by Rawlinson's intelligence staff shows as well as any document the Germans' desperation. Each evening, intelligence officers would collate the reports flowing to Rawlinson's headquarters in the chateau at Querrieu, a few hundred yards from the billet at Brewery Farm. They studied the reports of raids, the examination of corpses and, overwhelmingly, the interrogation of prisoners. These reports disclosed a perplexing picture. Almost daily, the identification of the German formations opposing the Australian Corps would change.

On 30 August, the tired West Prussian 41st Division held Péronne—it had already seen serious action twice since 8 August. It seemed that the 21st Division, from Hesse, was reinforcing it, holding the Mont itself, along with the seemingly fresh 232nd Division, from East Prussia, and the 2nd Guard—which had held Mont St Quentin facing Robert Graves's Welshmen eighteen months before. The following evening, the map showed that a battalion of the Thuringian 38th Division (like the Guard division, 'moderately fresh') marched in from ten miles south. Twenty-four hours later, advancing units identified Rhinelanders from the 185th Division and Bavarians of the 14th Division. The next day, *jägers* of the Bavarian Alpine Corps—actually a weak division—arrived. The defenders of Mont St Quentin not only reflected the regional diversity of the German army, but they also showed that General Georg von der Marwitz's Second Army was hustling units willy nilly to hold what it, too, regarded as a vital point. Of the divisions involved in defending Mont St Quentin and Péronne, only the Guards division was rated as 'first class'—the rest were ranked '2nd' to '4th', with the 232nd 'mediocre'. All were weak: most regiments had only two battalions of three companies.[18] The intelligence officers and the Fourth Army's general staff knew that this desperate rushing of tired troops from one threatened spot to another showed that the German army was, if not quite yet on the ropes, under severe pressure.[19]

The German army of 1918 was no longer the force it

had been. Every phase of the war had drained its strength and skill. The young, idealistic volunteers who had died in the *Kindermord* (the massacre of the children) of 1914, the battles of attrition at Verdun and the Somme in 1916, and the French and British offensives in 1917 had all taken their toll. By 1918, boys fresh from school outnumbered experienced men, and most experienced men had been wounded and knew the worst that the war could do. Sergeants led companies; captains commanded battalions. Already in May, Charles Bean was noticing, as he passed the big POW 'cages' behind the front, that three-quarters of the prisoners were 'boys'.[20] The German army had always relied on non-commissioned officers carrying far more responsibility, especially in battle, than their British counterparts. By 1918, their deaths in action had left German units dangerously short of the battlefield leaders that they needed to withstand the demands made on them. The Australians' nicknames for their enemies now included 'the Hochs'—as in *'hande hoch'* ('hands up').

Does this mean that the German defenders of the Mont were a pushover? They were certainly less formidable than Australian legend has assumed. The 21st Battalion men who spoke to some of the Germans they escorted as prisoners reported to Bernard Duggan that they 'stated that they had volunteered to stop the Australians'.[21] But James Edmonds, the British official historian, quoted from German records which suggest that the Mont's defenders changed between the 5th Brigade's unsuccessful attack on 31 August and the 6th Brigade's success on 1 September. Troops of the 2nd Guard Division met the first attack, and it was their resistance that pushed the attackers back down the Mont. But, overnight, Thuringians of the 38th Division replaced the Guards. These men came from villages and small towns in the forested hills in the heart of Germany. They had been the mainstay of the German army's long agony, but now they were losing the heart to go on. Though relatively fresh, the Thuringians had neither the strength nor the will to withstand the renewed Australian attack—the attack that the 21st Battalion was now to join.[22]

'KEEP YOUR BLOODY HEAD DOWN': THE 21ST BATTALION IN RESERVE

In Australia, 1 September had been celebrated as Wattle Day. Did any of the men as they woke in the dawn chill think of their young nation's floral emblem as they yawned and stretched on that Sunday morning? The 21st waited in reserve in trenches around Lost Ravine. No one bothered to tell the Diggers what was happening, and Tom Wignall recalled hearing 'a fair amount' of what he called 'furpheys'—the word had made the change from the name of a manufacturer of water-carts to an Australianism for a rumour. German shells fell among them, one killing Lieutenant Selwyn Dickson and a lance-corporal, Will Glasgow, struck in the chest by a shell fragment and dying instantly.[23] Godfrey Dobson was encouraged by the sight of batches of German prisoners being brought in. As each reached the 21st, a 'crowd of "Diggers" would rush forward ... ratting them for souvenirs'. Jack Castle described these men as including Frank Roberts and Ted Heath, 'both great souvenir hunters'.[24] In a more painful spectacle, they also saw mixed groups of wounded, Australians and Germans, helping each other toward the dressing stations in Lost Ravine. The 5th Brigade's wounded called out to the waiting 21st Battalion men, 'Don't spare any machine-gunners'. The 21st's men would heed that urging.

Australian soldiers did not conceal their willingness to kill prisoners rather than send them to the rear. Dale Blair has provided—in letters, diaries, battalion histories, ex-service journals, and in Bean's official history—abundant examples of Australians giving, as Blair called his book, *No Quarter*. Charles Bean 'so constantly heard our men and officers talk as if these things did happen, and laugh about them', that he became 'half inclined to think they must have happened more often than we would like to believe'.[25] Article 23 of the 1907 Hague Convention forbade combatants 'to kill or wound an enemy who … has surrendered', and the British *Manual of Military Law* paraphrased the convention and made the prohibition 'clear and distinct'. An explanatory circular summarising 'The Soldiers' Don'ts of International Law' told them 'Don't kill a man who has thrown down his arms' (though also, if they did, 'Don't be heartbroken').[26] It is an awkward fact that at Mont St Quentin, and at many other places, Australians killed men trying to surrender. This cannot be concealed: as Voltaire said, we owe the dead only the truth.

About 8.30 a.m., Bernard Duggan ordered the 21st to leave Lost Ravine, to march south-eastwards toward Péronne and then move north over the open ground toward the Mont, about 1500 yards distant and still in German hands. The companies moved off in 'artillery formation', walking briskly in loose groups with wide intervals between sections, platoons, and companies, so that exploding shrapnel shells would hit as few men as possible. They skirted or crawled under the barbed-wire entanglements left by successive occupants of the Mont. Wire, Noble Norwood remembered, was 'everywhere', the battalion intelligence officer describing it as 'a serious obstacle to attacking troops'. They soon came under fire. The lower slope of the Mont, Godfrey Dobson explained, seemed pretty much 'dead level', and they could be seen by German observers on the Mont. As they crossed this open ground, German machine-gunners on the Mont opened fire. Dobson thought the fire 'deadly', remembering 'men falling on every side', but the war diary does not record heavy losses. (The guns were firing at such long range that they hit few men.)

As C Company crossed the light-railway line running around the Mont (the bed of which can still faintly be traced) at about 10.20 a.m., German officers exploded a mine, throwing a great plume of soil and smoke into the air. The German who fired the mine electrically, probably from further up the slope, miscalculated, and the blast wounded no one. But German machine-gun fire increased as they continued. Some men broke into a run, while others lay down in the shelter of the railway line. As they lay there, Tom Wignall recalled, the machine-gunners 'pushed dirt all around us'. Here, Wignall recalled, 'a man heard a flow of language at men showing themselves'. As a platoon sergeant, he felt responsible for the men under him, and he showed his concern by abusing them. 'I think I called a few ... silly bastards', he told Garry Roberts, 'and to keep their bloody heads down'.

As the fire shifted and slackened, groups dashed toward a nearby German communication trench. They reached the trenches leading towards the Mont and jumped into them, safe below ground level from the bullets cracking overhead. 'Some never touched the ground', wrote Tom Wignall, but he and Jack Castle noticed that at least one man was killed while they ran.

They caught their breaths and made sure that no one was missing, now in one of the several communication trenches running more or less parallel up the slope of the Mont. It happened that this was Galatz Alley, though none of Nine Platoon seems to have known it. Peeping over the parapet, they looked out at the dead and wounded of the attacks launched the previous day by the 5th Brigade and their own brigade that morning. Passing wounded men who had not yet been collected by the hard-pressed stretcher-bearers, they met an Australian crawling back down the trench with his right leg blown off. 'His one complaint', Dobson wrote, was that 'his "fags" had run out'. Tom Wignall said that asking for a cigarette then 'was like asking a man for a tenner'—men in battle needed nicotine—but 'the boys managed to scrape one from somewhere'. They asked if they could carry him out, but the wounded man replied, 'You go and do for the bastards that got me', and said that he was sure he could get out.

Lieutenant Alfred Sennitt, who did know where they were, moved along the trench, telling the men of C Company that they would be attacking at 1.30 p.m. Later in the morning, they moved further up Galatz Alley, closer to the foot of the Mont. Machine-gun fire passed overhead. As they moved up the trench, they passed the body of Lieutenant Norman Holt, sniped through the head, they thought. It was a case, Tom Wignall wrote, 'of K.Y.B.H.D.': 'keep your bloody head down'. By midday, they crouched in communication trenches up the slope and leading towards Elsa Trench—a broad, deep trench (Godfrey Dobson called it a 'sunken road') that snaked in a rough curve following the hill's contours.

Tom Wignall's Nine Platoon was still together, organised into two Lewis gun teams. One team comprised Roy Smerdon (No. 1), Jack Castle (No. 2), Frank Roberts (No. 3), and Charlie Tognella (No. 4). The other team was Ted Heath (No. 1), Bill Rabling (No. 2), Albert Kelly (No. 3), and probably Noble Norwood (No. 4)—the records do not reveal much detail. Its other members comprised Sergeant Vic Edwards and Tom's 'runner', Godfrey Dobson, with Alf Crawford as a 'spare number'.

On a broader level, we know quite a lot about the detail of the 21st Battalion's part in the fight for Mont St Quentin. Much of the paper that the AIF created survived, largely thanks to men such as Charles Bean and John Treloar. We have three main sources. Each headquarters kept a 'war diary' in which the intelligence officer or adjutant recorded events as they occurred and later filed maps, messages, and reports. These documents, the war diaries and the related 'operations records', occupy kilometres of shelving in the Australian War Memorial. They provide the framework of the narrative that Charles Bean created in his massive official history. Both are daunting to tackle. The war diaries seemingly record everything that the battalion did. If picking the important from the insignificant is one of the historian's essential skills, the war diaries offer incomparable practice in navigating through the vast mass of faded field messages and flimsy typewritten reports. As ever, the useful stuff is in the crabbed, pencilled scribble on a little piece of squared paper, as well as the neat typescript of a report written days later.

Then there are Bean's notebooks. Bean made his way around the battalions — not just those in the 2nd Division, but as many as possible — interviewing officers and men about as many operations as he could cover. These notebooks, which were often stream-of-consciousness narratives taken down verbatim (and often without much indication of who he was talking to), provide a record from the survivors. Because Bean was able to question those involved in particular operations, and he generally knew the ground and had often watched the action, he was able to focus on incidents that he knew needed to be explained.

And then there are the 'private records', held in several archives and libraries, but also mainly in the War Memorial's collection. These include letters and diaries written within hours or days of the action, and memoirs and interviews recorded decades later. Rarely coherent and often lacking 'context', as the historian's trade jargon puts it, they shed all sorts of incidental light on the events in question, a reminder of the individual experience of battle, and how men shared its horror regardless of unit or rank. Their fragmentary nature, however—a letter from a man in one company; a memoir by men from two others, or whatever—means that these sorts of sources can usually only support or complement an account, and rarely form the guts of it. These sources are continually emerging as papers are donated to libraries and as researchers find them (often years later), and they demand stamina to use them effectively. These records give us a progressively more detailed account of the events of 1 September.

Pre-eminent among the private records are Nine Platoon's accounts gathered and edited by Garry Roberts. They are unique because no comparable group in Australian military history recorded their experiences in such detail. The platoon's own accounts allow the story of the fight for Mont St Quentin to be told, not just from the perspective of the battalion commander's dugout, but also from the very foremost trench. We will focus on the platoon's accounts after we see how Bernard Duggan and Charles Bean saw and recorded the fight.

'DISAPPEARED OVER THE SKYLINE': BERNARD DUGGAN'S VIEW

Lieutenant James Watt, the 21st Battalion's adjutant, distributed Bernard Duggan's orders around 9.00 a.m. 'The idea is to help the 23rd and 24th Bns to the Objective', it read simply. Three companies would follow to reinforce the first wave, and C Company's particular job was to 'mop up' the village on the summit of the Mont.[27]

From his headquarters near Lost Ravine, Bernard Duggan and his little battalion staff could watch the 21st's four companies moving up the communication trenches leading toward the Mont. Around mid-morning, they were waiting: D

Company in Oder Trench, C Company in Galatz Alley, and B Company in Agram Alley, with James Sullivan's A Company in reserve in Save Trench. There was little to see but occasional steel helmets bobbing above the parapet. This was the 'empty battlefield' created by machine-guns and shrapnel shells. The 21st's men threaded their way up winding trenches, passing dazed prisoners and wounded men of both sides making their way painfully to the rear. Through the late morning, the 21st's companies waited, hearing the sound of intermittent fire ahead of them and watching shells explode on the summit of the Mont. Towards lunchtime (though the documents do not mention food), men must have pulled out biscuits from their haversacks and swigged on their water bottles as the noise rose to a deafening roar. Duggan had asked for the 'intense fire' from the supporting artillery (and the British heavy batteries attached to Rosenthal's division), and the Mont erupted in smoke and dust for half an hour. Tom Wignall, watching the bombardment from Galatz Alley and with the eye of a veteran infantryman, thought it had 'little effect'.[28]

At 1.30 p.m., the bombardment ended and the company officers called their men forward and, once again, as they said, 'hopped the bags'. Duggan and his staff watched as the little khaki figures piled out of Elsa Trench and made their way forward. James Watt noted 'little opposition' as 'the men disappeared over the skyline at 2 p.m. going well'. From then, Duggan had to rely on runners arriving with notes: hastily scrawled notes in indelible pencil on squared pads or printed message forms. As an experienced commander, Duggan knew that for a time he would hear little, and even that would be late. Many messages brought by the runners sent back by company officers would describe the situation up to an hour before.

The battalion war diary and the operations files contain the messages that Duggan received. At about 3.30 p.m., he had his first reports, brought by lightly wounded men arriving at the aid post next to his headquarters dugout. They told him that C and D companies had pushed through the village, but had met 'strong opposition' east of the village. Lieutenant Norman Holt was dead. Fifteen minutes later, Duggan read a message that George Dearden had written fifty minutes before, reporting that the Germans seemed to be preparing a counter-attack. At 4.00 p.m., a message arrived from a B Company officer estimating '50% casualties' and asking for reinforcements: 'Enemy reported strong in front'. This message, too, reported the situation forty minutes earlier, and was wildly incorrect. Duggan's anxiety would not have eased when he received a message a few minutes later, but timed an hour before, reporting, 'Village and objectives cleared … All going well … casualties light'.

Bernard Duggan was asking exactly the same question as anyone who reads his battalion's war diary today. What was happening on the Mont? At five—an hour later—Duggan read another positive message from the left company, 'Going well … Much booty and machine-guns', but also asking for reinforcements. Experienced officers expected counter-attacks, though in fact none were made. A 45-minute late report from Sullivan reflected the confusion on the Mont. He had reached the further edge of the wood on the summit, and found ten men of the 23rd and six of C Company. Sullivan had met Hardwick, but he had 'only a few men' with him: C Company's commander had no idea of what Wignall's men were doing at the other end of the Mont. A belated message from a chastened Hardwick late that afternoon confirmed that his company was 'distributed'—that is, mixed up, and scattered—along the entire length of the 500-yard long battalion front. As the sun set behind them, the surviving company officers sorted out the confusion.

Meanwhile, Duggan and the other battalion headquarters

had reported to Robertson's brigade headquarters that 'All reports from the front pointed to very heavy enemy casualties'. The attackers had encountered more machine-guns than usual—clearly the Germans were also using weapons to substitute for men. 'Everyone was very tired but in splendid spirits', Duggan told Robertson. Although he had not visited the Mont, Duggan reported that it was 'one of the strongest defended positions held by the enemy': the legend of Mont St Quentin began on the day it fell. He also reported the battalion's casualties: four lieutenants (Norman Holt, Arthur Cope, Selwyn Dickson, and Alfred Sennitt) and eighteen men killed, and 60 wounded—about a seventh of the strength of those who had left the jumping-off trench that afternoon.

'A WONDERFUL VIEW': CHARLES BEAN'S ACCOUNT

Charles Bean started out from his billet at Mericourt later than he would have liked—the correspondents were setting up a new camp. He, the war correspondent Gordon Gilmour, and Will Dyson drove first to Gellibrand's headquarters in a chateau at Suzanne. He had already heard that Rawlinson had sent Monash his congratulations, though Monash did not really know whether his men were on Mont St Quentin or not. The news that Bean picked up was all about the attacks on the Mont. He heard that the 5th Brigade had reached the summit on the morning of the 31st, but had been driven off. But the reports were confused. Someone said that the attackers held their line along the main road running over the Mont; others, that they had been pushed back halfway down the slope. Rosenthal's staff did not know, and they disagreed with Martin's staff, closer to the action.

Bean had his driver, Herbert Boddy, drive on the north bank of the Somme towards Cléry. On the way, they were glad to see that the Somme's picturesque steep banks at Vaux remained unscathed (so rapidly had the Australian advance passed) and that this stretch of the meandering river remained 'still beautiful', as indeed it is today. Cautiously, they pushed on into the ruins of Cléry, leaving Boddy with the car, and setting out on foot to the north-west. Bean led his companions up Bouchavesnes Spur and past some Australian field guns. A hundred yards further on, they reached an artillery observation post, prudently moved fifty yards to its left, and got out their telescopes and binoculars.

'It was a wonderful view'. Bean saw Mont St Quentin directly opposite and a mile-and-a-half distant, with the Bapaume-Péronne road running down it 'like a scar'. By the time Bean arrived—later in the afternoon—the fighting had ended. 'I saw no movement on it the whole time that we watched', he noted. But he talked to some 3rd Division officers who had followed the afternoon attack through their binoculars, and they gave him a detailed account. A major in the 43rd Battalion told him that they had 'never seen a better sight' than the 6th Brigade's afternoon attack. The major said that as the barrage ended he had at first seen nothing, but then had noticed Germans running back through the wood on the summit, followed by Australians moving onto the 'nose' of the hill—exactly where Nine Platoon went.

The 3rd Division officers, including some gunners who had watched through their binoculars, had seen parties of attackers crossing the road—some driven back by machine-gun fire, others working their way across. They could follow the progress of the advance by the bursts of bombs and sudden rushes by little groups of tiny figures, and they saw Germans running back from the wood into what they recognised as a quarry. The Australians they had seen included Tom Wignall's Nine Platoon. If they had been watching between 2.00 and

3.00 p.m., they could have seen its fight for the strong-post in the quarry, clearly visible from Bouchavesnes Spur. Today, standing in the bean and beet fields that crown the spur, the Mont's northern slopes, and the site of Nine Platoon's fight for the summit, are clearly visible.

The major and his companions knew what the attackers were doing — they had done it themselves a dozen times. They described the 'bomb fight' around the quarry. They saw how 'one Australian would crawl up, throw his bomb and then get back as quick as he could', followed by another, each 'crawling up and delivering his bomb'. Germans replied with bombs — 'I fancy they said for 20 minutes', Bean thought. Then, the witnesses said that 'the Germans started to run from the quarry'. The Germans started back along the spur that ends in the 'nose' of the Mont, but the Australians did not pursue them far. The watching officers noticed that, for a reason they could not make out (but which, as veterans, they surmised was 'doubtless good enough'), the attackers did not follow the Germans very far, and halted just beyond the wood.

Bean, knowing that he would need to know more than he could put in his despatches, was concerned to record as much as he could, and stayed with the watching officers. Gilmour, unconcerned with detail, had seen enough for the colourful and broadbrush account that the censors and his proprietors would expect, and mooched off in search of souvenirs. Bean walked off to call him back so they could start for home. Perhaps this movement caught the eye of a German artillery observer, or perhaps he had seen the knot of half-a-dozen men with telescopes and binoculars. Either way, a German shell crashed onto the hillside a hundred yards away, followed by one much nearer, just fifteen yards away. Clods of chalky soil thrown into the air by the explosion rained down on the group crouching in a trench. Bean got several 'thumps on the top of the head'—he was wearing his customary officer's peaked cap, not a helmet—'as heavy as I have ever had from a shell'. They made off down the trench, seemingly followed by more explosions, 'quite nasty enough to make one keep pretty close to shellholes' for cover, and their rushes between shell holes between shells reminded him of musical chairs. Finding shelter in the gully at Cléry again, they made their way back to Boddy and the car, and headed back to Corps headquarters at Blangy Chateau to find out what had happened elsewhere that day.

Within a couple of months, Bean called on the 21st Battalion again. He had last seen it at Querrieu in May, when he had dined with its officers. Few had survived to fill him in on what they had done over the hundred days that had led to victory. Bean spent some time with officers and some of its NCOs, quizzing them especially about Mont St Quentin. His notes formed the basis of what he would write in the official history twenty years later. It's not clear who he talked to, especially in C Company—his notes simply run on—and several key witnesses to the attack on the Mont, as we will see, died or were wounded in the 21st's last action.

Bean's notes provide a more detailed account than Bernard Duggan's of C Company's part in the taking of the Mont. At 1.30 p.m., as the barrage ended, its men left Elsa Trench 50 yards behind the 23rd Battalion, moving toward the 'big brick wall' that everyone remembered. Extraordinarily, the defenders failed to fight from the cover of the wall; this was one of several perplexing aspects of the German defence of the Mont. The Germans did not try to hold the ruined village—the defenders had probably been killed, wounded, or deterred by the previous two attacks—but, among the houses, C Company captured two 'snipers'. One ran and they shot him; the other may have stumbled off to the Australian lines, perhaps with a wounded man.

As C Company passed through the wall, it began to split into two groups. The rightward-tending group emerged from the village to come under heavy machine-gun fire. Lieutenant Alfred Sennitt, who had joined the battalion only three days earlier, was hit by machine-gun fire while leading his platoon across the main road; as his widowed mother was assured, he died instantly. At the officer cadet battalion he had just left, his instructors had described him as 'rather colourless and lacking in personality': perhaps he now felt impelled to lead impetuously rather than cautiously.[29] (In both his notebooks and his history, Bean is often careful to note where and how officers died. To have done so with 'other ranks' was obviously unfeasible, but it reflects who he mixed with, and the essential perspective from which he wrote. For all that he hobnobbed at headquarters and eavesdropped on the men, Bean understood and recorded the war from the perspective of captains and lieutenants — as he would have been, had he carried a revolver rather than a notebook.)

Splitting up as they passed through the village, some of C Company under Lieutenant George Deardon moved to the left, or north, moving into a shattered wood. Today it is a dense green forest, its floor still bearing the marks of the years of bombardment that the Mont suffered. The ground resembles a frozen sea, with swells of craters and trenches still apparent beneath the accumulation of dead leaves, sharp bushes, and moss-covered fallen branches. Still, German resistance seemed almost non-existent. As they emerged from the wood, however, they found a clearing leading to what several men called a 'crater', but was actually a quarry, now heavily fortified. (In his official history, Bean has a bob each way: it's a crater in the text, but a quarry in the accompanying map.) Either way, this was one of the strong-posts around which the defenders planned the defence of the Mont, where they could meet attackers who had been split up and perhaps disorganised after passing through the obstacles of the village and the wood.

And at this point in Bean's notes, Alby Lowerson enters the story. A 22-year-old labourer from Myrtleford in the mountains of north-east Victoria, Lowerson had spent three years with the 21st Battalion since enlisting in 1915. He had crossed paths time and again with men in other platoons of his company. He had travelled to Britain with Tom Wignall aboard the transport *Osterley*, and he had been in the barnyard at Querrieu when Charles Bean had eavesdropped on the 21st's billets. Having lost contact with Lieutenant George Dearden, Lowerson led Ten Platoon into the fight for the quarry in which Tom's platoon found itself—a decision with profound consequences for him.

Sizing up the situation, Alby led his platoon and worked up what Bean called 'the straight north-eastern part of Varna trench', hurling bombs as he went. He captured two or three machine-guns—killing their crews—before reaching the lip of the quarry's defences. He led six or seven men across thirty yards of open ground and up a high bank immediately east of the crater. They threw about thirty bombs while the Germans fired machine-guns and threw bombs in reply. This was the classic 'bomb-fight' that the 3rd Division officers had watched from Bouchavesnes Spur. Men took trenches not with rifles and bayonets, but by chucking grenades at each other. Grenades caused shocking, often fatal wounds, driving jagged shards of metal into faces and bodies. Rather than face such wounds, men would often bolt: the bomb fight was in essence a contest of nerve—the trench went to those whose nerve lasted.

Meanwhile, another platoon (actually, Tom Wignall's Nine Platoon, though no one who talked to Bean mentioned it), attacked the quarry from the north. Tom had led those who survived around the curve of the hill to the left, throwing bombs as they went. This did the trick. 'The Germans started to clear out', an officer told Bean later. Lowerson himself did not describe the action to Bean; he had been wounded in the thigh just as he reached the edge of the quarry. There they captured twenty-five or thirty Germans and found the bodies of another twenty, along with fifteen machine-guns. But the fight was not over. It took them three-quarters of an hour to clear the quarry, with its warren of dugouts and communication trenches.

C Company, by now much weakened and mixed up with its flanking companies, ended up in an unfinished series of rifle pits just to the east of Mont St Quentin. Over the next couple of hours, they dug between the pits and made a trench, and there they stopped.

Bean's account makes perfect sense when compared to the messages and reports in both the battalion war diary and the operation records. It seems to be as detailed an account of the attack as you could wish for. But it doesn't tell us anything much about Tom Wignall's platoon. As we will see, Bean certainly did not interview Tom Wignall, nor Vic Edwards. The most senior rank available to describe Nine Platoon's part in the fight was a private, and Bean rarely spoke to privates. But Nine Platoon's contribution to the battle can be recovered, because we know more about its men's part than any other AIF platoon. It is to Nine Platoon's experience we must now turn.

'OVER WITH THE BEST OF LUCK!': NINE PLATOON ATTACKS

And then there are the accounts written by six men of Nine Platoon—Alf Crawford, Norrie Norwood, Vic Edwards, Godfrey Dobson, Jack Castle, and Tom Wignall (Phil Starr, Frank's friend, fought in a neighbouring company, and he wrote an account, too). These stories, ranging from sixteen lines to three typewritten pages, constitute the single most detailed accounts of an action by the members of any comparable group in Australian military history. They enable us to reconstruct the experience of Nine Platoon in unprecedented detail for the two days of its part in the battle of Mont St Quentin. They especially describe what happened from the time they rose from Elsa Trench at 1.30 on the afternoon of 1 September: exactly the moment and the place depicted in Charles Gilbert's diorama in the War Memorial.

In the communication trench leading towards Elsa Trench, they sat waiting for the bombardment to end, dispersed in case a shell fell among them — as likely to be a 'drop short' from a British or Australian gun as a German whizz bang. Noble Norwood recalled how Frank Roberts sat 'cheerily eating something'. Ted Heath sat a little way off, while Norwood and Alf Kelly sat together. A fragment of shrapnel came down through the brim of Kelly's steel helmet, missing him — for now.

About five minutes before the bombardment was to end, Tom Wignall looked at his watch and had them get up and move forward along the communication trench and into Elsa Trench — the 'jumping off trench', as they called it. They came upon a grim sight. The 23rd Battalion's leading officers had reported it to be 'packed with the dead of the 5th Brigade', as well as with dead Germans.[30] Norrie described many of them as having been shot in the head. By the middle of the day, many of the 6th Brigade's dead lay about, while wounded men of two armies slowly made their way back or lay waiting for stretcher-bearers. And all the while the sun beat down.

As the artillery bombardment ended, men of the 6th Brigade's Stokes mortar battery began to fire at likely machine-gun posts in the ruins of the village. Its men had carried their clumsy barrels and base plates, and heavy panniers of bombs, up the communication trenches, and had set them up in nooks and corners of the Elsa Trench—you can see them in the War Memorial diorama, too. As the Stokes bombs fell on the village, the Germans began firing green and white flares into the air, a signal presumably calling down retaliatory fire from their own guns and mortars. This seems to have been what Godfrey Dobson called 'a light barrage of shrapnel': a sign of how experienced Nine Platoon's men were. This was not just 'German fire': they were able to judge its nature (shrapnel) and its strength (light). 'Luckily no one was hit', Godfrey recalled—at least among his platoon.

Then, Godfrey recalled, 'the order came "Over with the best of luck"'. Who gave it he did not say, but it was probably the company commander, William Hardwick. This, Tom Wignall recalled, 'was the time I had to have my wits about me, for I was in charge of No. 9 Platoon'. Hardwick's company scrambled up out of Elsa Trench, their khaki uniforms smeared with whitish chalk soil, and moved forward—yelling and shouting, Godfrey Dobson remembered, though they kept in line, at least for the advance to the wall bordering the wood. Jack Castle remembered them being 'in good humour, talking to one another'. Jack must have asked Frank how he was, because Frank said to him, 'all right Jack'. They moved off in single file, walking rather than running, with Tom Wignall's platoon in the second wave, following B Company men.

Godfrey Dobson remembered what felt like 'the sweeping fire of hundreds of machine-guns'—a pardonable exaggeration. Several men (Norwood, Castle, and Starr) remembered approaching the 'broken brick wall' on their right—it angled away to the road and they were making for the left, so they walked more or less parallel to it for a hundred yards or so, warily looking towards it because it made such 'an admirable position for enemy machine-gunners'.[31] Their orderly formation soon broke down, and Norwood found he was following the men of Alby Lowerson's neighbouring Ten Platoon. Both platoons moved toward the left of the attack, moving in single file: the 'worm' of the tactical manuals later in the war. They could tell that a 'nest' of machine-guns in a 'ruined tower'—the village church—was firing at them as they moved into the houses. 'Nearly every man was quite composed', Norrie remembered, but all the same they 'looked furtively at every broken building'. 'We were going A1', Tom Wignall wrote.

In the village, just one or two houses wide on each side of the road, they met some scattered fire from the defenders who had survived the artillery barrage and the Stokes mortar fire. They saw and fired at Germans running back; though some were volunteers, the Germans did not resist. Godfrey Dobson saw Roy Smerdon using his Lewis gun from the hip, like a hose. Jack Castle wrote that 'Roy did good work with his gun'. He described him firing at a machine-gun, 'bringing it with a sweep as he fired'. This, he said, put the German gun out of action. Lewis gun instructors would not have approved. They taught that firing from the hip (which required some strength, even with the supporting webbing strap that some gunners used) was wasteful and inaccurate. (And dangerous: 'when the best of Lewis gunners fires his first burst from the hip', the instructors warned, 'it is highly dangerous for any of our men … in front of him'.[32]) Roy Smerdon turned his gun on another post further up the hill, perhaps in the upper storey of a ruined house. He could not lift his gun high enough, so Jack Castle had him hoist the Lewis gun's barrel onto his shoulder. 'That worked well', Castle recalled.

As they reached the main road, they met heavy machine-gun fire and 'a good deal of bombing' by both sides. Germans in the trenches and dugouts beside the road were hurling bombs at the Australians in the ruined houses and the overgrown, blasted gardens on the other side. The Australians were throwing

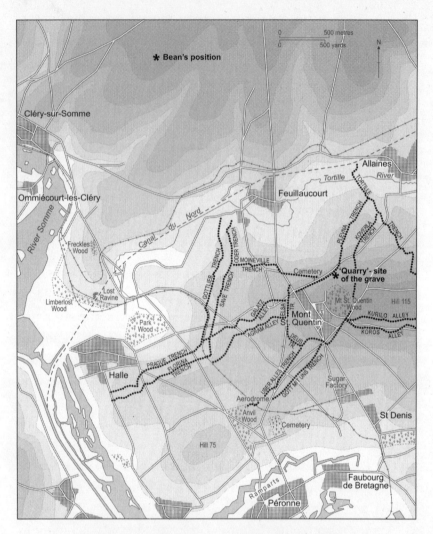

Mont St Quentin, 1 September 1918

their own grenades. This went on for some minutes. The numbers on each side were not great, especially on the German side, weakened by assaults and bombardment. As Australian corporals and sergeants saw resistance slacken, they would lead small groups to run across the road, scrambling across the ruined buildings into the trenches and dugouts beyond.

Once through the village, what Norrie called 'my platoon'—meaning the men of Ten Platoon whom he was with—moved into and through a wood. On a September afternoon today, the wood is cool and green, but in 1918 it had been shelled for a couple of years. While shellfire had stripped trees of branches, the undergrowth had sprung up in the spring and summer. Godfrey Dobson described cutting his way through bushes. Bare and splintered trunks lay among shell holes, trenches, and dugouts cut into the soil. The two platoons on the left of the attack were moving roughly northward: Nine on the left and Ten on the right. The rough ground—littered with fallen trees, pits, and trenches, rubbish and shell holes—broke up the attack even more, and the two became mixed up. Tom Wignall explained that they followed Germans along trenches toward the north, which explains their drift to the left of the attack. Wignall remembered: 'I turned to my platoon to say, "Come on boys, up and at the bastards."'

Pushing through the thick, debris-littered undergrowth of the wood, the attackers again acted on their training. They had been taught not to linger in woods (even though they seemed to offer cover). 'It is wise to get out of it as quickly as possible', instructors had stressed. Sooner or later, German artillery fire would fall on a clear target marked on the observers' maps, and the place would be full of deadly splinters and shrapnel. Instead, they had been told to press on to occupy a line just to the east of the wood. But between the wood and the objective lay a warren of German strong-posts, protecting one or more machine-guns and connected by communication trenches.

They soon emerged near the fortified quarry, the centre of a network of trenches, dugouts, and machine-gun posts. As the attackers moved through them, they saw a sight, as Godfrey Dobson wrote, that 'I shall never forget'.

The Mont had been shelled heavily for the past day, had been attacked twice, and had seen several German counter-attacks. The 21st Battalion now encountered the horrific results of that fighting. Germans—both dead and wounded, and men paralysed by fear and exhaustion—lay all over the trenches in the wood. They lay 'huddled together in heaps', the wounded crying out for aid. Men still fighting mingled with those trying to flee the attack. The Australians, grimly fulfilling their orders to take the hill, made no attempt to succour the German wounded, and treated all live Germans as enemies to be killed. Godfrey Dobson saw Vic Edwards shooting every German he came across, saying as he fired, 'There's another bastard—got him!', and 'another'.

The attackers also came across more Australians killed and wounded in the two days of fighting on the Mont. In the wood, Jack Castle found an Australian of the 5th Brigade lying on a stretcher. He called for Jack to get bearers for him. He had lain out for at least a day and a night, lucky to have not been wounded again by the bombardment directed onto the summit.

The machine-guns firing from the quarry stopped Tom Wignall's men's advance, and they took cover in trenches and shell holes. Wignall, in one of the communication trenches leading toward it, fired at the Germans running back. He killed the Germans trying to surrender: 'I ... accounted for a few more, who put up their hands', he wrote; 'none of us had any mercy that day'.[33] Roy Smerdon's Lewis gun came in useful again. A German machine-gun crew was firing on Wignall's men from the left. Wignall had Smerdon climb onto the parapet to fire at the gun. 'To get a good pot at them', Tom wrote, he had to stand up, exposing him to German fire, but 'he soon put Fritz and his gun to sleep'.

As they neared the quarry, Norwood saw the heads and arms of some of its defenders, saw them throwing grenades towards Nine Platoon, and then saw what he remembered as 'dozens' of Germans 'making off' away from him. Norwood called to a Lewis-gunner of Ten Platoon (Alex Gilmore, whose personnel file discloses that he had arguably the most uneventful war that a front-line infantryman could have) and directed him to fire into them. Whether Gilmore accidentally shot Norwood—something that you might call eventful—or whether the Germans fired back, Norwood felt a dull pain in his left shoulder. Looking down, he saw his tunic dripping with blood. Jack Castle came over to him and they shook hands: they both recognised a Blighty wound, a cause for congratulation. Norwood turned and slowly made his way back, through the wood and the village, across the road and back to Elsa Trench, where stretcher-bearers dressed his wound and sent him to the rear.[34]

Tom Wignall noticed that another group of his platoon was being held up by bombing and fire from a strong-post on the right side of the crater. He ran over—presumably along trenches—and saw what he called 'tons of Fritzes' looking as if they were preparing to make a counter-attack. His men—'the boys'—were firing and throwing bombs at them. (This suggests that they were as close as twenty or thirty yards away, able to see the faces of the men they fought.) Tom had Jack Castle fire his Lewis gun at them. Castle 'didn't need to be told twice', and he also climbed onto the parapet and fired off one magazine after another at the machine-gun.[35] Frank Roberts and Charlie Tognella handed him magazines. If the Germans that Jack Castle fired at were forming up for a counter-attack, it was the only one made against the left of the 21st's line. Despite the alarming messages that Bernard Duggan received, no counter-attacks materialised.

While his platoon attacked the strong-post, Tom Wignall stood, 'doing a little sniping myself' with his rifle at Germans who appeared over the parapet a few yards distant. As he crouched back down into the trench to replenish his magazine, a German lobbed a bomb into the trench. It wounded him in the stomach and the hand. Though in great pain, Tom continued to call directions to his platoon.

'IT LOOKED A HOPELESS TASK': THE FIGHT FOR THE QUARRY

As they emerged from the shattered wood, the attackers looked out across bare ground towards sand-bagged parapets. The defenders had left the area bare of cover to make a 'killing ground' for their machine-guns. This quarry, the 'strong-post' or 'the crater', became the focus of the survivors' accounts. It held up the attack, and the fight for it became the climax of the final assault upon the Mont. It involved a small group of men from Nine and Ten platoon, mostly Tom Wignall's men. There were another fifteen platoons of the 21st Battalion present, not to mention another thirty-two from the other two battalions involved, and many men from the 5th Brigade units still on the Mont. Beyond the Mont, battalions of the 3rd Division were fighting to the north, and battalions of the 5th Division to the south. Thousands of men went through experiences as intense: hundreds more men died or were wounded. The fight for the quarry was only one tiny fragment of what happened, occurring in just a small part of the battlefield. We know about this moment because several people troubled to collect or keep written records.

Jack Castle's Lewis gun detachment found cover—probably a trench or shell hole just short of the crater—and began hurling grenades toward the strong-post. Roy Smerdon threw grenades, perhaps because the others knew he could throw them furthest or most accurately: the hours of practice out of the line had given them skills that they used in action. But because he also carried a Lewis gun, Smerdon could not get the pins out of the Mills bombs quickly enough. Jack Castle, as Roy's Number 2 at his right elbow, straightened the pins for him. The Germans lobbed grenades back at the attackers. Jack Castle saw Frank Roberts fall. He knelt over Frank, saying, 'Well, Rob, has he got you?'

Vic Edwards, who had seen Tom Wignall wounded, did not pause as Wignall's Lewis gunners stooped to help him. Edwards headed towards the crater, joined by Hugh Smith and several other men of Ten Platoon, kneeling and firing as they went. He thought it was held by about fifty Germans and 'fully ten machine-guns'. 'It looked a hopeless task', and he thought that the only way to tackle it was 'to rush it'—in action, experienced and well-trained men acted more-or-less on a trained instinct.[36] 'Our platoon did not have an officer in charge of it', explained Jack Castle, but that did not stop Wignall's men from acting as they'd been trained to do. As usual, no one explained the things that were obvious to them. Did they call to each other, or use improvised signals? How did the sergeants like Vic convey to their men and to the men of neighbouring platoons their intention to rush the quarry? They don't say. The reason they didn't bother to record what they did was that they were following the drills that instructors had dinned into them in training. The instructors' lecture notes explain what Edwards and his men were doing. 'If an assaulting platoon is held up by a machine-gun', the instructors had said, 'that machine-gun must at once be engaged by the Lewis gun'. The Lewis gunner's task was to keep the machine-gun crew 'occupied'—make them keep their heads down 'while the bombers work round its flanks'. That was exactly what Edwards and his teams began doing.[37]

Godfrey Dobson thought that the distance from the edge of the shattered wood to the sand-bagged edge of the crater was about sixty yards, 'dead level ground'; Jack Castle thought it closer to eighty yards. A group of several men 'rushed' toward the strong-post, from which machine-guns fired at them and, when they reached within about twenty yards, the defenders threw bombs at them. Frank Roberts died in the rush. Godfrey Dobson wrote how 'several of our wounded mates' lay in this open ground. He described how, 'true to their name, the Huns opened fire on these poor helpless men' with machine-guns and revolvers. (The fact that the Germans were doing to Australians exactly what Australians were doing to Germans escaped him.) We don't know who these men were, but Ted Heath was wounded in the stomach at about this time. Alf Kelly, Ted's number 3, picked up his gun and continued to fire.

Several survivors of this rush piled into a trench facing the crater. They included Jack Castle, Bill Rabling, and Godfrey Dobson, no longer acting as the platoon sergeant's 'runner' now that Tom Wignall had been wounded. This partly explains why Bernard Duggan, watching in suspense from the bank of Lost Ravine, received almost no messages from his battalion's left flank: whole platoons were fighting, but separated from the reporting system based on officers. And, as Jack Castle mentioned, Nine Platoon did not see an officer after it left Elsa Trench. 'Things were looking real bad for us', Dobson thought, fearing that the attack (at least in this little portion of the battlefield) might fail.

Alby Lowerson had by this time reached their trench with two other members of Ten Platoon: Bert Bulluss, a young Ballarat labourer, and George Winnett, a Preston butcher.

Lowerson called on them all to make another effort on the northern side of the crater. At his word, they leapt up and charged forward again. The Germans threw bombs at them and fired machine-guns and revolvers. Running up to the edge of the crater, Lowerson threw Mills bombs into it, as did the others who had bombs left. By the time Vic Edwards and his party reached the quarry on the other side, they could see that Lowerson had started to bomb his way into it.

A fragment of a German bomb hit Roy Smerdon in the chest. 'He seemed to be in great pain', Jack remembered. Roy said 'give me a drink of water, Jack', but Jack would not. Medical officers had warned them that it was dangerous to give a man water if he were wounded in the chest or stomach. 'It was hard to refuse him', Jack explained, 'but I did it for the best'. Vic Edwards also saw Roy Smerdon hit, and told some stretcher-bearers he met to go and tend to him. But there was no time. Godfrey Dobson also saw Roy Smerdon fall, wounded. He saw Jack Castle stoop to assist him, and heard Roy say 'Don't, Jack, it hurts', before he died. Jack was enraged, and fired wildly at the Germans sheltering in the sand-bagged emplacements in the quarry.

With the loss of the platoon's two 'number ones'—Roy Smerdon killed and Ted Heath wounded—other men took over the Lewis guns. Jack Castle took Roy's; Alf Kelly, Ted's. Jack fired half a magazine into the Germans crowding out of the crater along the communication trenches leading towards their lines, until the gun jammed. As the last unwounded Germans withdrew from the crater, Alf Kelly fell, shot in the leg, and rolled into a shell hole. Jack Castle did not think that Alf had been badly wounded and was prepared to wait for help, but Godfrey Dobson went in search of stretcher-bearers. He found two of the 24th Battalion bearers, and told them about his platoon's wounded.

Just before the attackers had killed, wounded, captured, or driven off the Germans in the crater, Lowerson fell with a wound to his thigh. The citation that explained what he did—the basis of the award of a Victoria Cross—described it as 'a severe wound', but his AIF file records it as 'slight'. Either way, 'he refused to leave the front until the prisoners had been disposed of'—an ominous phrase. Godfrey Dobson remembered it somewhat differently, and his account suggests that the wound was hardly 'severe'. He recalled that Lowerson turned to him 'casually', indicating his wound, and saying 'I've got my issue'. Telling Dobson to 'carry on', Lowerson made his own way back to the dressing station at Lost Ravine, though he did remain with the battalion for another two days before accepting that the wound needed treatment. Bert Bulluss, however, also wounded in the leg, refused to leave the crater. 'I want some souvenirs off these bastards before I go', he declared.

Arch Green and Godfrey Dobson had carried Tom Wignall in a German blanket back some distance away from the fighting. They had found a German medical orderly and had him dress Tom's wounds, in his stomach and his right hand. Then, realising that their job was not yet done, they turned and made their way back towards the trenches on the summit of the Mont. Tom lay alone in a trench for a while. As Alby Lowerson limped past him, he said, 'Come on Wig, they have got me in the leg as well'. He helped Tom to his feet, and they limped off together. Lowerson found another German orderly, who helped to carry Tom back to the dressing station, though Tom lost consciousness on the way.

Vic Edwards saw Lowerson wounded and turn back down the Mont. 'Not far from him', Edwards wrote, 'Frank Roberts fell'.

'MOPPERS UP': NINE PLATOON ON THE MONT

According to Alf Crawford, the most taciturn of the platoon, they reached their objective—'an old sap [a trench] about 100 yards beyond the village'—at about 3.00 p.m.[38] The fight for the summit of Mont St Quentin had taken about an hour-and-a-half.

Though they had captured the strong-post, the attackers still had to hold the ground they had won: they knew that, time and again in the war, successful attacks had been driven out by German counter-attacks. What they called 'mopping up' was just as dangerous as the attack. Men had to find Germans who might be hiding or lurking in the maze of saps and trenches leading up the slope east of the ruins of the village. The attackers worked their way into the surrounding communication trenches, returning to the crater so as to keep in touch with their comrades and not become lost in the unfamiliar warren. They would hurl grenades into dugout entrances or around the corners of trenches; it was in one of them that Private Alex Walker, an émigré Scot from Ten Platoon, was killed. Alf Crawford remembered that Walker had been killed, but did not say how—only that it happened after the Australians had taken their objectives.

Vic Edwards and Hugh Smith, sergeants of neighbouring platoons, lost touch with their men, but somehow paired up and worked together. They bombed their way into the surrounding trenches, cautiously making their way along the communication trenches, hurling grenades around traverses, one covering the other as they turned each corner, rifle and bayonet at the ready. They found only dead or wounded Germans, with some frightened defenders running for shelter into dugouts. (As 'moppers up' were as likely to throw a Mills bomb into dugouts, this seems foolish, but perhaps they feared that attempting to surrender would see them shot or bayoneted anyway, as many were.) Edwards must have taken some men prisoner, because he mentioned sending them back down the Mont, presumably wounded. Then, Edwards and Castle related, an Australian trench mortar-bomb exploded in the crater, wounding Smith. Vic Edwards sent Smith back. Soon after, Edwards met up with the rest of his platoon—as a Lewis gun team, Jack Castle, Godfrey Dobson, and Bill Rabling had stuck together.

The mopping up continued. Vic sent Castle, Dobson, and Rabling to clear the trenches immediately in front of (that is, to the east of) the quarry. This was the most dangerous phase of the attack—with platoons weakened by casualties, and the orderly chain of command broken by death and wounds. Men were tired, the adrenalin of combat drained from their bodies at just the point that the Germans, if true to form, were due to launch counter-attacks with relatively fresh troops brought forward with the task of driving the attackers out of their gains. It had happened repeatedly: most recently, the day before, when the 5th Brigade had been pushed off the Mont.

The unfinished trench they occupied was wide and shallow, offering little protection from German shelling, so Edwards put men to work deepening it. He posted Lewis gunners on the flanks of his part of the line, able to direct fire against the expected counter-attacks. Men who had become mixed up with other companies made their way back to their parent platoons, and men asked about those who did not turn up. The surviving platoon sergeants (or the corporals who took over from the wounded and dead) made lists of those present, and pencilled in the likely fate of the dead and wounded men they had seen. News of the fight circulated between the companies. On the right of the battalion, down near Koros Alley, Phil Starr realised that, 'although we on the right were having no easy task', on the left 'the opposition was strongest'. German shells continued to fall on the summit and along the new front line.[39]

With the front line held, with sentries posted, and with Jack Castle and Bill Rabling manning Lewis guns, alert to a possible counter-attack, the platoon's survivors were able to find out who was left and to work out what had happened to the rest. Vic Edwards's platoon had lost three dead and four wounded, with only five men left unscathed. Jack and Bill were the only survivors of their gun teams: two out of eight men. Vic Edwards, who had seen Frank Roberts killed between the wood and the quarry, went back to collect his things — to empty his pockets and take his watch, before anyone looted his body. Vic only realised that Alf Kelly had been killed when he and a Ten Platoon man set out to find Kelly's Lewis gun. Jack Castle was surprised, because he had seen Alf take shelter in a shell hole: perhaps he bled to death before the bearers could find him; perhaps a stray bomb hit him; perhaps a German shot him before making away. We will never know.

Between Vic Edwards's taking charge of his stretch of the Western Front and the attacking battalions' colonels' orders to re-organise their mixed-up platoons and sections, Nine Platoon was saved from being wiped out. At this point, officers again enter Nine Platoon's story. It is notable that the only officers that the men's accounts mention are dead ones. C Company had at least three officers, but none of them led Nine Platoon onto the Mont, and they did not see an officer until George Dearden arrived at about 7.00 p.m. He had Edwards and the survivors of the platoon shift along to the right, or south, to allow a party of the 24th Battalion to take over the trench. Edwards described how the 24th men had not been there long when a German shell, a 5.9, landed right on top of them, killing five and wounding six.

That night, the rations came up — with ample seconds for those able to eat. The surviving officers sent patrols out to establish what lay before them in what had become the new no-man's-land—the password issued was 'Wowser'. Some men slept heavily, drained by the exertions of the day. Others remained awake, on edge. Some struggled against exhaustion, watching for another German attempt to re-take the summit. None came. Mont St Quentin at last belonged to the living and the dead of the 6th Brigade.

'TRACED BY THE SUN': HUBERT WILKINS'S PHOTOGRAPHS

There was another witness present with the 21st Battalion that afternoon. Describing the 'hop-over', Jack Castle recalled that 'the first thing I noticed was a man taking photographs of us as we went over'.[40] This was the official photographer, Hubert Wilkins. He followed the advance, from close behind the foremost troops.

Wilkins's photographs, taken on Mont St Quentin on the afternoon of 1 September, allow us to imagine the attack. As the infantry crossed the open ground between Elsa Trench and the big brick wall, Wilkins rested his camera on the parapet and took a photograph, though characteristically he omitted to make a note of exactly who it depicted. It shows that the attack was not, as some might have imagined it, a wild charge. Experience told the attackers to walk cautiously toward the wall and the machine-guns that might have lurked behind it.

Wilkins followed Captain James Sullivan's A Company into the fight for the Mont, taking several photographs of the right flank of the attack. Wilkins's image of Sullivan leading men up the Péronne-Bapaume road during the fight for the Mont became one of the 753 photographs that Bean selected for his *Photographic History* volume in 1923. It is one of the remarkably few photographs taken of Australian soldiers under fire in the war. It struck a reviewer, writing in a Melbourne newspaper, who noted Sullivan's 'eager figure ... stealing up the bullet-swept road at Mont St Quentin'. Sullivan's shadow, 'traced by the sun' lay on the page, the reviewer reflected—though by then, as we will see, Sullivan himself was dead.[41]

Frank's friend, Phil Starr, wrote a long statement describing A Company's part in the attack, and recorded that only after they reached the objective on the summit of the Mont did Wilkins leave them. 'He was a game man, and took some good snaps.'[42] Judging from Wilkins's biographies, it would have been an epitaph he would have treasured. Charles Bean heard him relate over dinner the next day what he had done. Wilkins 'let drop' how he (and the loyal Sergeant Jackson) had gone over the top with the 21st from Elsa Trench. He described their losses mainly to machine-guns firing on 'fixed lines' at shallow stretches of trench where attackers had to pass. Wilkins modestly claimed that he only went forward (into machine-gun fire) to avoid the shelling.[43] His photographs, identifiable by date and subject, became part of the War Records Section's 'E' series, but were not attributed to any particular photographer. Only now can they be identified as part of Wilkins's work, partly because of Nine Platoon's testimony.

'SOMME GOLGOTHA':
DEAD, WOUNDED, PRISONERS, AND SURVIVORS

The next day, 2 September, dawned bright and sunny. The day did not match the mood of the 21st Battalion's men occupying pozzies over the eastern crest of the Mont. Though Bernard Duggan had reported them as having been in 'good spirits' the previous evening, these were men who had entered the fight tired. Now the adrenalin of battle and the euphoria of victory had gone. On the morning after, many felt weary and flat, especially as they realised how few they were and whom they had lost. Visiting the day after the Mont's fall, Charles Bean described the summit as 'smoking and dust seething up from it against the hills behind'.[44] He, too, expected a counter-attack, though in fact the German artillery fire was covering the withdrawal of their battered and disorganised infantry. Observers looking out over the rolling hills could see German guns, wagons, and men snaking away in retreat, now pressed by units of the 7th Brigade steadily pushing eastwards.

On the Australian side of the Mont, among the first to get away from the fight were German prisoners, escorted by lightly wounded men to a collecting post manned by Light Horsemen near Cléry, close to where Les Baker had been wounded two days before. But survivors admitted that in the fighting for the Mont the attackers took few prisoners—perhaps 400, according to the brigade report. A 21st Battalion man told Bean that his platoon had taken twenty near the summit. 'These Germans put up no fight', Bean wrote in his notebook, 'but are not recorded as arriving back'.[45] They were probably shot. Phil Starr said that the men of A Company, attacking on the right of the battalion, 'were not in the mood to be stopped that day', and described how they had 'exacted a full penalty from the beaten Hun'. The savagery of the fighting for the Mont became legendary as a 'Somme Golgotha'. A reporter for the *Scotsman*, who explored the area after the armistice, heard that graves unit men had found 'more German dead ... on the slopes of the hill than in any equal surface area in the course of the war'.[46] Burial parties were still finding bones—mainly German, presumably—on the Mont months afterwards.

At first, no one knew who had been killed or wounded, or who might be alive and well but lost among some other company somewhere along the new front line. The platoon sergeants moved about, ticking off men they met and quizzing them about who had been hit. Vic Edwards knew that Wignall,

Norwood, Heath, and Tognella had been wounded. (Charlie had gone down with a bad, penetrating bullet-wound to the chest that had smashed into his upper left lung. He was carried out.) Casualties in the attacking units had been so heavy that they overwhelmed and exhausted the battalion stretcher-bearers. Men from the 7th Brigade battalions, waiting to pass through the next morning, came up the Mont to help to gather the wounded. 'They were lying around everywhere', Jack Castle wrote, but the volunteer bearers could not easily find them in the dark and in the maze of ruins and shell-blasted earthworks on the summit.

The 'walking wounded' had made their way down the Mont and along the communication trenches to Harris Mendelsohn's aid post in Lost Ravine. Tom Wignall walked back, leaning on Lowerson and a German prisoner. Australian stretcher-bearers and prisoners carried back more seriously wounded men. In his big, dirty, dangerous dugout, Mendelsohn treated and sent on about a hundred wounded over the two days of the action. The next day, Bean watched stretcher-bearers carrying white flags making their way from the Mont back towards the river crossings, running the gauntlet of shells bursting on the roads. After the near escape on the spur above Cléry the previous afternoon, Bean had a renewed respect for German gunnery. He insisted on his little group splitting up and moving 'two by two', rather than in a careless gaggle. But the shelling was directed blindly at the routes the Australians would use: the white flags were a sign to snipers, invisible to distant artillery officers.

The AIF's practised and efficient casualty-evacuation system carried the wounded, from the battalion aid-post in Lost Ravine through the 6th Field Ambulance at Halle, to the 53rd Casualty Clearing Station at Herbecourt and back by ambulance to Amiens and by rail to Rouen. They treated over a thousand wounded in the three-day fight for the Mont, and many wounded German prisoners besides. The medical units of three divisions shared a narrow corridor of roads, but distributed the load harmoniously in what the official medical historian called a 'happy confusion'—a further sign of the Allies' decisive material advantage in the war's final year.[47]

The medical units had gained a proficiency over three painful years of war—not that that comforted their patients. Noble Norwood's bullet wound to the left shoulder had him evacuated rapidly to Britain, and within a few days he was being treated in a military hospital in Weymouth. His was so clean and routine a wound that his file barely mentions it. Charlie Tognella's shoulder wound was more serious, and he too was swiftly carried back by hospital train and ship to London. Tom Wignall's 'medical case sheet' records how, at 12 General Hospital at Rouen, surgeons unwrapped his dressings to find a large open wound in his abdomen and three other wounds, as well as a bloody right thumb. They cleaned and dressed him, leaving him with a seven-inch scar that healed well but left him in pain while walking and on the toilet.[48] For all of them, the war was over, though they would carry scars and reminders of it every time the weather grew cold or whenever they bent over.

The most grievously hurt was Frank Roberts's souveniring mate, Ted Heath—the 'hard doer', the coach driver from Curdies River. Ted was at first reported as having been killed in action, before being re-classified as severely wounded. Admitted to the 53rd Casualty Clearing Station and then to the same hospital at Rouen as Tom Wignall, Ted also had a serious wound to the abdomen. A stomach wound was a grievous matter at a time when infection often claimed the lives of men who in later times would have survived. The best treatment was to debride the wound—that is, cut away the torn flesh—and leave it to heal. But Ted's stomach wound did not heal. Three weeks after the battle, Heath's family received a telegram telling them that he was 'dangerously ill', and six days later another, advising of his 'condition improving'.⁴⁹ Then, a fortnight later, he was dead, presumably of infection, probably from the 'gas gangrene' caused by microbes in the very soil they had defended. Another of William and Mary Heath's sons, Leslie, had been killed with the 23rd Battalion in the same attack. He had been wounded in 1916 and 1917, and was at last killed in 1918. At least another son, William, a prisoner of war, would return alive.⁵⁰

Garry recalled Ted from Frank's letters. He had described Ted as 'a tall, black scowling ... broth of a boy and a good pal of mine, one of the best'.⁵¹ Although himself bereaved only a few weeks, Garry wrote to William and Mary to offer sympathy and help, and they gave Garry's name in Ted's 'Roll of Honour circular' as the person from whom further details could be obtained. Sadly, he fell out of Garry's remembrance, which soon focussed on the men who shared Frank's grave.⁵² Ted Heath seems to have been largely overlooked by the platoon's survivors, but is reunited in memory now.

Because they were still under German observation and under artillery fire, no one thought it prudent to move about in daylight. The 6th Brigade stood-to all day in support of the 7th Brigade, pressing forward further to the east. The burial of the dead had to wait. In the meantime, they were probably covered with blankets found in the German dugouts. The 21st's dead were buried on the evening of Monday 2 September. (Even though 3 September was Jack Castle's 28th birthday, he was probably wrong in recalling that they were buried on the Tuesday.) Men of the battalion buried eleven bodies in a common grave in a chalk pit on the northern slope of the Mont, very close to where Frank, Alf, and Roy had died. Probably on the Tuesday (hence Jack's recollection), the battalion pioneers found time to erect a large cross from planks they found in the litter of war on the summit. Arch Green, a friend of Frank's, flattened a petrol tin and punched the men's names onto a sheet and nailed it to the arms. Someone added a black-and-red diamond colour patch made of leather and metal. The cross bears ten names, with one man (Scottish-born Alex Walker) marked as 'unknown'. Lieutenant Norman Holt was buried in an individual grave close by. 'There was no burial service', Jack Castle explained, 'as we were still under fire'.

As the front line shifted further east, the area in the lee of the Mont became safe for men to walk about. Men whose jobs took them there, and men best described as sightseers, walked about the slopes, still strewn with German dead, great bales of wire, and the litter of battle. Harris Mendelsohn and Donald Coutts, after their marathon stint in the dressing station in Lost Ravine, sent the last of their wounded off to the 6th Field Ambulance. Coutts walked up the trenches towards the Mont. He at least had a job—to look for a new aid-post site if the battalion moved forwards—but, all the same, he collected 'plenty of good souvenirs'.[53]

The AIF, from Monash to thousands of his privates, was obsessed with souvenirs—often grandly described as 'trophies'. Frank Roberts probably had watches and badges in his haversack at the moment of his death, taken from the Germans he and Ted had ratted that morning. Monash kept detailed lists of the number of guns, *Minenwerfer*, field artillery, and even field kitchens that his advancing battalions had picked up as they went. The number of German machine-guns captured on the summit varies in almost every source. Up to thirty were found in and around the crater. Godfrey Dobson helped to carry them to the road and load them in limbers that had brought up rations. Many ended up, as we will see, as 'war trophies' in small Australian towns.

At last, on the afternoon of 3 September, the 21st Battalion moved off down the Mont to make their way back to the reserve. The battalion cookers awaited them in cover near the river, and the cooks served out a hot meal. Then they set out on the long night march westwards across the battlefield of the past week toward Cappy.

'A STREET SWEPT BY BULLETS': TAKING THE TOWN

The capture of the Mont was only half the battle. A few hundred yards away down the road, the 14th Brigade fought to take the town of Péronne. Parties of the 54th Battalion forced their way into the town, racing along duckboards across the swampy Etang du Cam towards the remains of the old fortifications, and storming up the town's red-brick ramparts. German machine-gunners placed along the old walls fired, catching many groups in the exits from the belts of wire ringing the town. Fittingly, today this battlefield is the grounds of the Historial de la Grande Guerre, a museum interpreting the Great War.

Despite the fall of the Mont, the situation at Péronne remained confused. Fire from the 14th Brigade suppressed the German defenders' machine-guns to enable the 15th Brigade to storm the ramparts. By the evening of 1 September, the 54th Battalion held a series of posts halfway through the town, held up around the ruined main square by machine-guns, possibly firing in the wreckage of the Hôtel de Ville. Walter Downing, a member of the 57th Battalion, joined the street-fighting. He described how they 'climbed through a breach in the wall, stumbled among the heaps of bricks', and 'dashed across a street swept by bullets' as stones fell from the already wrecked buildings. He remembered seeing the moon through the broken windows of the ruined church of St-Jean-Baptiste.[54] Again, colonels and brigadiers ran the battle. When Bean tried to establish at Monash's headquarters on the morning of 2 September what had happened, he found that 'no one back at Corps seemed to know the position in Péronne at all'. Gradually, he pieced together the story of how the 54th and 57th had 'cleaned out' the town by the afternoon of 2 September.[55]

Impetuous as ever, Hubert Wilkins made his way into Péronne on 2 September. Both sides were shelling the town through the day in what Bean, a connoisseur of bombardments, called 'a very nasty fashion'. (Like many Great War veterans, even while knowing that artillery fire was utterly impersonal, he could not help describing it as if the searching shells had a malevolent will of their own.) The town remained dangerous for days. As Norman Nicolson led his battery of eighteen-pounders into Péronne in the days following its fall, he found the streets still littered with dead men and horses rotting in the muggy September heat. Norman noticed a placard tacked to a wall on what he assumed was the main street, 'a bit of old packing case' with 'Roo de Kanga' painted on it. They had no time to admire the soldiers' wit. A sentry advised Norman to shift his gun teams, and soon enough a German fighter swooped down, machine-gunning the streets.[56] As they passed through the town, making for the east, an official photographer, probably Wilkins, had his apparatus set up in the ruined streets. The image has not survived among Wilkins's glass plate negatives, which turned out to be much less robust than the photographer.

'LOWERSON AND SEVEN MEN': THE MONT ST QUENTIN VCS

Six Australians performed 'deeds' during the battle that gained them the Victoria Cross; three on the Mont itself. Private Robert Mactier of the 23rd Battalion died while charging three machine-gun posts during the second attack, and Lieutenant

Edgar Towner of the 2nd Machine-Gun Battalion kept his machine-guns firing at the Germans defending the quarry as the 21st Battalion's platoons attacked it. Brave though these men's actions were, they do not come into this story. (In any case, Australians do seem unduly preoccupied with the deeds of VCs, to the point that the blaze of glory that surrounds them blinds us to those who also served, such as the hitherto obscure men of Nine Platoon.) But one of the Mont St Quentin VCs became a part of Nine Platoon's story, because its members helped Alby to become 'Lowerson, VC'.

Sergeant Alby Lowerson gained a Victoria Cross for helping to capture the quarry. He had been an eighteen-year-old goldminer at Adelong in New South Wales when he volunteered for the AIF in July 1915. (Like many of the AIF, and several of Nine Platoon, Alby had been working away from home when he volunteered.) Alby had reached the front in July 1916, to be wounded soon after Mouquet Farm. In 1917, his officers noticed his knack for leadership. He became a temporary sergeant in April, before being wounded, seriously, at second Bullecourt in May. Rejoining the battalion in November—he probably survived the war by just missing out on the Ypres fighting—he led Ten Platoon into the attack on the Mont.

At Cappy, Bernard Duggan faced the unrelenting paperwork that oppressed a battalion commander, in or out of the line. His 'out-tray' held letters to the families of some of his men (probably only his officers) and the more rewarding recommendations for decorations. On 8 September, Duggan submitted a recommendation that Lowerson be decorated for his 'conspicuous bravery and tactical skill' in leading a small party against the 'Strong Point', the quarry on the Mont. He described how Lowerson had improvised seven men into a storming party, and how he had sent another party of three from the other flank, who were 'killed immediately'. They captured the strong-post, taking twelve machine-guns and thirty prisoners. Duggan recommended that Lowerson receive 'the highest possible decoration'. If accepted, it would be the first awarded to a member of his battalion.

Newspaper reports on Lowerson's deed mention that the position was taken by 'Lowerson and seven men'.[57] No one else's name was published in the citation published in the *London* and *Commonwealth* gazettes. Bean's official history describes the episode in just two sentences, though in a footnote he names five Nine Platoon men—Alfred Kelly, Frank Roberts, Roy Smerdon (killed), Jack Castle, and Vic Edwards, describing it as a 'spirited affair'.[58]

Among Duggan's thirty-two recommendations were two for the surviving men of Nine Platoon, both for the Military Medal—the most common gallantry award in the AIF, over 10,000 of which were awarded in the Great War. Vic Edwards (the senior soldier present, a crucial figure in the bureaucracy of bravery) witnessed Lowerson's actions, and recommended Godfrey Dobson for an award. Both Dobson and Edwards received a Military Medal. Dobson's recommendation described how, in the fight for the quarry, he had 'rushed forward' under fire and thrown two grenades that had killed and wounded German defenders. In the confusion that followed, other men had taken ten Germans prisoner and their three machine-guns. The other recommendation recognised Vic Edwards's work in organising and leading attacks on enemy strong-posts, instancing one in which Edwards was the first to reach a machine-gun post, where he killed four Germans, allowing his party to take the post without further resistance. Alby Lowerson would in time become a focus of the 21st Battalion's remembrance of its war.

'DRASTICALLY TREATED': MUTINY AND MONTBREHAIN

The 21st, including the four unscathed survivors of Nine Platoon, marched off from Mont St Quentin the way it had come a week before, only fewer in number. It reached the Somme-side village of Cappy on 6 September. Billeted in abandoned houses and barns for three weeks, the survivors enjoyed a more relaxed regime as part of the 'corps reserve'. Company Sergeant-Major Bill Trevascus recalled it as a time for 'resting and licking our wounds'. Their program included church parades, band recitals, kit inspections and issues (including welcome clean clothing), 'swimming parades' in the Somme, a brigade sports day (spoiled by rain), and inter-company cricket matches (ditto). Parties of men left for leave, and convalescents and reinforcement drafts arrived from the depots in Britain.

All seemed to go well until, on the morning of 20 September, James Robertson called Bernard Duggan to his nearby brigade headquarters, and dealt him and his battalion a 'sudden and unexpected blow'. Robertson told Duggan that he had been directed to disband one of his four battalions and to post its men to the remaining three units. Rosenthal had selected the 21st for extinction. What Robertson did not tell Duggan were the full reasons behind the decision. Despite its 'splendid fighting history', the 21st was numerically the weakest and least effective battalion in his brigade, with what Robertson thought was the poorest esprit de corps and the highest rates of 'crime'—25 per cent greater than the next unit.[59] Duggan told his officers the decision before lunch and his men that afternoon. The news, the war diarist recorded, caused 'great dismay'. Both officers and men met to elect deputations to 'wait on' Duggan and Robertson to protest against the decision.

For five days, Duggan shuttled between his officers and

his men, and Robertson and Rosenthal, trying to stave off disbandment and avoid scandal, all the while heartbroken at the loss of his battalion. Always up on brigade gossip, the transport drivers got wind of the coming change. Back from leave in Paris and the Riviera, Lawrence Polinelli had picked up the news while driving his limber about the brigade area, and recorded the 'worry and anxiety' that the men felt. 'The men are very sore about it', Polinelli wrote.[60]

Duggan ordered a parade in marching order for 10.30 a.m. on 25 September, but his officers reported that their men were refusing to comply. The battalion's senior NCOs had met and decided, as one remembered, to 'stand pat, refuse to transfer, and endeavour to run the battalion without officers'.[61] They had already elected Bill Trevascus, a Melbourne builder, as 'temporary Commanding Officer', and he picked Sergeant William Montgomery, a Melbourne artist, to be 'acting adjutant'. Montgomery was a sensible choice. No hothead, but a man with 'a perfectly balanced mind' and a winning manner, he ensured that the protest remained moderate.

At Duggan's order, the battalion paraded, immaculately turned out, with NCOs standing by with platoon rolls ready. Duggan and his senior major, Alfred Reed, arrived, and Duggan unfolded a brigade order that he began to read aloud, 'Instructions have been given for the withdrawal forthwith of the 21st Australian Battalion ...' Duggan, 'deeply affected', broke down and handed the order to Reed, who completed the job. Re-folding the order, Reed ordered that 'Officers will march their parties off'. The company officers repeated the order, but not a man moved. After some hesitation, the officers reluctantly marched off without their men. Trevascus and Montgomery marched the battalion off parade. The 21st Battalion was in a state of highly respectful mutiny.

Over two days, the officer-less but by no means leaderless

battalion followed its routine, even going for route marches, including the transport and the band, passing Robertson's headquarters, where the guard cheekily turned out to salute the passing column. Trevascus and Montgomery warned any who tried to take advantage of the crisis by going 'absent' would be 'drastically treated'. The companies paraded and marched off for football matches, and returned in 'an orderly manner', and that evening listened to a concert by the battalion band—all this, the war diary recorded, 'on the authority of the men themselves'. Throughout the crisis, the protesters maintained the guard roster, setting sentries as if officers were present.

The men had looked for 'a timely concession' from what they called 'the Higher Authorities'.[62] Astonishingly, they got it: their protest succeeded. Rosenthal told Robertson that 'the demands of the men were to be complied with temporarily'.[63] The 21st was to survive, merely reorganised into three companies, as the men's deputation had suggested—an expedient that Monash had dismissed 'for good tactical reasons'. Still under-strength, it was to serve on as a complete unit into its last battle.

The battalion had escaped being broken up, but C Company, the weakest, was not so fortunate. Survivors of its three platoons were sent to the other three companies, and it is impossible to tell where the five Nine Platoon survivors went. When it returned to the advance at the end of September, the brigade felt the pressure to press on. Robertson told the 22nd Battalion's officers that, 'I want you to report tomorrow morning that the line is a mile ahead'.[64] An advance of that distance had been feasible on the Somme a month before, but by then the Australian Corps was facing the Hindenburg Line, and such a rate was impossible.

Rosenthal's 2nd Division had returned to the advance on 1 October, pressing into the Hindenburg Line. It was due to be relieved on the night of 5–6 October. The 5th and 7th Brigades had attacked the Beaurevoir line on 3 October, so it was the 6th

Brigade's turn again. Vic Edwards, who had gone off to Britain on furlough immediately after Mont St Quentin, returned to find his battalion in turmoil over the disbandment, and then joined the advance to take part in what he described as 'the last stunt'.[65]

Montbrehain is one of the most tragic of Australia's battles on the Western Front. Not usually a bitter man, Bean called it 'the last, stupid, wicked fight' (though, decades later, he added, 'I don't believe this today').[66] Among the 21st's thirty-three dead were men who had survived Gallipoli and three years on the Western Front, only to die in a last, pointless fight. Bernard Duggan reported that half of the battalion's casualties had been caused by the 'erratic fire of our own artillery'.[67] The dead of Montbrehain included William Montgomery, the troops' delegate in the protest, who died of a gunshot wound at a casualty clearing-station. They included James Sullivan, whom Hubert Wilkins had photographed on the Mont, and Lieutenant William Hardwick, C Company's commander at Mont St Quentin. Hardwick died when he was struck by fragments of shrapnel as the battalion handed over its positions to the Americans. He became almost the last Australian infantryman to die in action on the Western Front, a fact that the 'i/c base records' had to break to his mother in Brecon the following year. Bill Trevascus's leadership was not confined to public meetings. He was awarded a Distinguished Conduct Medal for leading men at a German machine-gun post and capturing six of its defenders. Soon after, he was commissioned.

But, in the end, the 21st's temporary stay of execution could not be prolonged. The day after the battalion marched westwards from Montbrehain, Rosenthal ordered that the disbandment proceed. The 21st formed two '21st' companies in the 24th Battalion—although, as a returned man recalled, 'no 21st man ever thought of himself or his pals as anything else'.[68] In their Repatriation hospital records into the 1970s, the survivors of Nine Platoon always gave their unit as '21st Battalion'.

The survivors of Nine Platoon became part of a reconstituted Eleven Platoon, part of C Company, 24th Battalion, with Trevascus as Company Sergeant-Major. Vic Edwards and Hugh Smith became its senior NCOs, and it included Godfrey Dobson and Bill Rabling, as well as men who had fought alongside Wignall's platoon on the Mont, such as Alex Gilmore and Arch Green, who had helped to make the cross on the grave on the Mont. The survivors must have been conscious of the gaps in their ranks.

The amalgamation seems to have demoralised the old 21st men. While the 24th's men seemed to bear the newcomers no ill-will, it was clear that they regarded them as guests. 21st Battalion men were distinguished with the preface '21/' in the battalion's nominal rolls; and while they continued to wear their cherished red-and-black colour patches, the battalion magazine remained *The White and Red Diamond*, full of 24th Battalion gossip and in-jokes. On the day after the formal merger, 14 October, Donald Coutts, the medical officer of the new unit, inspected the cook houses of the 21st and 24th, which remained separate. He found the 21st's 'very dirty indeed'. Later that month, while inspecting the 21st's cells (also reported to be dirty, though wrongly), he found many men on minor disciplinary charges—another worrying sign that men had lost their edge.[69]

'SPECIAL PRAISE': COMMANDERS AND THE BATTLE

Even before the survivors of Tom Wignall's platoon made their way back from the Mont, its capture became the subject of laudatory press reports cabled to newspapers in Britain, Australia and, indeed, across the English-speaking world.

The battle soon became swathed in the cocoon of myth and exaggeration which so often envelops the high points of a nation's war history. Even as the battalions of the 3rd Division relieved the exhausted men of the 2nd on the forward slopes of the Mont, staff officers at various headquarters began drafting congratulatory messages.

Monash offered Rosenthal his 'warmest thanks' for his division's part in the capture of Péronne and the Mont. He singled out for 'special praise' Edward Martin's 5th Brigade, describing its achievement—'the Capture of Mont St Quentin'—as 'the finest single feat of the war'. 'No one will begrudge', he thought, him 'singling out' Martin's brigade like this. Or so he thought. Monash congratulated the 'subsequent defence' of the Mont by the 6th and 7th brigades, describing their work as 'not less able'.[70] This absolutely misconstrues what had happened: the 6th Brigade had attacked and taken the Mont, not defended it. Neither Monash nor his operations staff clearly understood even three days later what had happened on its slopes.

Monash had already begun to shape the understanding of what he regarded as his battle. He had a high opinion of both his corps and himself, and was disinclined to question the growing myth. In reality, he had pushed brigades over the Somme crossings, to be directed by his divisional and brigade commanders, and not by him. But the capture of the Mont, he claimed, resembled 'some of the surprise tactics of Stonewall Jackson'. Given the veneration of American Civil War commanders in British military thought at the time, this is high praise indeed, albeit self-directed. Monash enlarged upon the comparison between himself and the brilliant victor of the Shenandoah Valley campaign and Chancellorsville, claiming that it 'depended on accurate calculations of time and space and punctual execution of orders by all concerned'.[71]

Official and unofficial correspondents—who mostly relied on official communiqués approved by corps headquarters, and fed off gossip and hints from staff messes—remained equally misled. It is easy to understand why press reports, hastily typed, submitted to censors and published within hours or at best a day, should be so misleading. Neither Monash nor his staff, nor his subordinate commanders had much sense of the detail of what had happened across a broad, swiftly moving battlefield. Looking back, years later, with the official history making order out of chaos, with the official records neatly arranged unit-by-unit and month-by-month, it is easy enough to impose sense. But at the time, staff officers had no detailed picture of the shape of the operations they were living through. In any case, they were preoccupied with battles to come, with the Australian Corps approaching the Hindenburg Line.

Eager for favourable publicity, Monash kept a close eye on the London papers. He expected more from the journalists than he thought he got. Within a couple of days of the battle, he was complaining to the official artist John Longstaff that the London press had been 'strangely silent' about the capture of Péronne.[72] The 'English' press's denial of his due was one of Monash's preoccupations. Australian writers, echoing Monash without actually checking for themselves, have always claimed that British reports had attributed the successes of 1918 to 'English' forces, regardless of whether battles were won by Australians, Canadians, Scots, or British divisions.

Some British reports certainly appropriated dominion efforts (and Canadians and New Zealanders suffered as well). On the evening of 1 September, the official War Office communiqué described a success on the 'British front' where, after 'heavy fighting we have gained possession of Péronne with 500 prisoners and have made our hold on Mont St Quentin secure'.[73] It made no mention of Australian success specifically.

Bean railed against the easy attribution of Australian successes as 'British'. A British staff officer fatuously told him that 'The word "British" has always been used as covering the whole lot of us.'[74]

But the popular impression in Australia is largely wrong. Newspapers publishing news of the victory drew on the despatches of journalists who knew very well which corps was responsible. In fact, the reports of the 'Great British Week-End' published immediately after the seizure of the Mont gave the credit where it was due. Acknowledging the capture of the Mont as 'no smarter operation in this battle', *The Times* made clear that the attack was made by 'a comparatively small force of Australians', and 'Our Special Correspondent' claimed to have been present and to have seen German prisoners 'captured by the Australians at Mont St Quentin' straggling back. He reported, in a story written on the evening of 1 September, that the Germans had described the attackers in a captured order as both Australians and as 'storm troops'.[75] Again, accounts of 'Sir D. Haig's Story of Progress', published immediately after the battle, gave credit where it was due: 'Australian troops have seized the hill and village of Mont St Quentin', it read.[76] The popular impression is bogus — an example of Monash's characteristic egotism rather than a reflection of what occurred.

Monash made sure that his own contribution and that of the Australian Corps could not be overlooked. He circulated a 'Record of part of the Work Done in 1918' to influential figures, including prime minister Billy Hughes. His staff had tabulated the numbers of German divisions fought and defeated, prisoners and guns taken, towns and villages liberated, and the areas gained in square miles.[77] He made certain that journalists received these statistics, so much so that the impression that his corps made a disproportionate contribution to victory persists to this day. The effort was intentional. The grandly named H. Casimir Smart, fixer and factotum at Australia House, acted as Monash's London agent while he was busy winning battles in France. The day after the capture of Mont St Quentin, Smart reported to Monash that he had gone to the offices of *The Times* to ask the editor to 'do his best for Australia'. Smart's mission succeeded, at exactly the moment when Monash's corps was winning newsworthy victories. 'You will notice from today's *Times*', Smart wrote, 'that Jones has done us well'.[78]

'INVESTIGATING MANY DETAILS': FRANK BREWER'S QUEST

The taking of Mont St Quentin has fascinated many people, but few more than Frank Brewer of the 20th Battalion, who returned to his battalion after spending time in hospital with 'hysteria' (which had caused him to be absent for several days). Brewer, a 33-year-old Queensland journalist, had left his pregnant wife in Brisbane to enlist, transferring from the engineers to the infantry early in 1917. He reached France in May 1918, but soon after spent time in hospital, including three weeks in a VD ward. Though very different to the puritannical, prudish Charles Bean, and despite this unpromising career as a soldier, Frank Brewer did for Mont St Quentin what Bean did for the AIF as a whole; only, until now, no one has known.

As he reached his battalion the day after the Mont's fall, Frank noticed the evidence of recent battle: German helmets on the ground, stacks of German grenades, trees snapped and scarred by shrapnel, columns of German prisoners and clumps of battlefield graves, all overhung by the stench of dead men and horses. When he found them, the survivors of his battalion told him about the battle, and how only 96 men answered the roll afterwards. Two weeks after the battle, Brewer again looked over the battlefield, when he 'carefully examined the whole ground, and enemy defences'. In his diary, Frank recorded that he was 'so impressed by the pride the men took in this victory, that I devoted weeks to work of closely investigating many details'. He produced 'the most complete and exclusive' narrative, writing on YMCA notepaper and on odd sheets, tracing maps on greaseproof paper taken from cocoa tins. He interviewed surviving officers and men of his battalion, compiling notes that he combined with his diary. Sold to the Mitchell Library soon after the war, they were barely opened again for nearly ninety years.

The Mont's physical setting made a deep impression on Brewer. Standing on the ridge above Cléry—again, the same spur from which Charles Bean peered through his telescope at the summit on 1 September—he saw the ground as 'a vast amphitheatre or coliseum'. Admiring the sun sparkling on the river, he also saw the scars of the maze of trenches that lined the Mont's slopes. In the trenches he found signs of bomb-fights in gouts of flesh and teeth blown into the chalky trench walls.

Walking toward the Mont, he recognised it as a 'bastion' dominating the country for miles about, but also as a once-pretty village, 'nestling beneath the shade of a small wood'. He noticed how shells had smashed the wood, turning trees to matchwood and blackened stumps. The village was wrecked and, as a Catholic, Brewer was particularly struck by the shattered images of the Virgin in the church of Notre Dame du Bois. He became sententious at the thought of those who had died for France, hoping that 'beautiful France ... will watch over the relics of thy tombs'. Then he kicked over a board, and saw and smelt the rotting body of a Prussian guardsman killed a fortnight before.

Brewer walked over the ground with several men—'intelligent observers who took part in the battle'. Using 'the method I had been accustomed to follow as a Pressman', he took down their statements and had them point out where they had been and what they had done on rough sketch maps—Charles Bean's method exactly. Months later, on the transport *City of York* on the way home and after returning to Brisbane, Brewer wrote a report on what he had gathered. Brewer's report, written from 'the private's not the General's point of view', had a tendentious purpose—'to commemorate the glory of the 5th Brigade ... the most active and irresistible of the forces engaged'. Brewer, a member of a 5th Brigade battalion, naturally attributed the Mont's fall to his comrades' efforts. Who should have been credited with the achievement was to become, as we will see, a matter of contention.

'PUT A LITTLE MORE GLORY INTO IT': CORRESPONDENTS AND THE BATTLE

If there was any partiality in the newspaper reports, it came from the typewriter of the Australian official correspondent, Charles Bean. Writing from the 'War Correspondents' Headquarters' on the late afternoon of 1 September, Bean emphasised the attack of New South Wales troops—the 14th Brigade—pushing into Péronne from the west. He devoted less space to a vague account of a Victorian attack on Mont St Quentin, mentioning how, the previous day, Australians had been driven off the summit by 'an intense artillery bombardment'.[79] Bean's later accounts would give a more accurate version, but he never shook off his emphasis of troops from his own state of New South Wales.

Mindful of the need to keep his and his corps' successes in the public eye, Monash welcomed the arrival just after the capture of the Mont of a deputation of newspaper proprietors and editors from Australia. They were being squired around the battlefields as part of the propaganda campaign that the imperial government waged ceaselessly to persuade Britain and the empire of the need to continue to fight after four wearying years of war. They arrived only a couple of days after the battle, when the area still looked and smelled like a battlefield. The 'conducting officer', the urbane Richard Casey, a politically adept major on Monash's staff (later to become a cabinet minister and governor-general), made sure that they gained the most positive impression in the shortest possible time. Charles Bean was not the only one to decry Monash's desire for publicity: the editor of *Aussie: the Australian Soldiers' Magazine* reminded his readers that 'Aussies are not fighting for newspaper glorification'.[80] Monash did not agree.

Casey brought the pressmen to Rosenthal's headquarters at Cappy in time for afternoon tea. Though tired after a week of almost continuous action (divisional staffs worked around the clock, with no rest or relief while any of the division's three brigades remained in the line), Rosenthal's staff officers made them welcome and, naturally enough, talked about their most recent triumph, the capture of Mont St Quentin. But after a hasty cup of tea and some cake (perhaps homemade and sent, sealed, and wrapped from home, or sent from Harrod's in a hamper), Casey swept them off to pay calls on the other divisions. At each, commanders and staffs would make sure that their guests left with a good impression of their division in particular. On the afternoon of the fourth, Casey took them to see the front. Now that the corps had crossed the Somme and established a bridgehead on the far bank, they were able to see the Mont itself.

After lunching with Monash and Rawlinson, they piled into cars and puttered off to see the war. Gordon Gilmour, reporting for the Australian Press Association, kept his notebook handy. They drove to the summit of Mont St Quentin, seeing Australian infantry on the rolling downland to the east, still following up on the retreating Germans. From the old German observation posts, they watched British and Australian artillery bursting around the village of Flamicourt, south-east of Péronne. The journalists watched through field glasses, entranced to see clouds of red-brick dust boiling into the air. 'Few visitors', Gilmour inaccurately told readers of the *Sydney Morning Herald*, had 'ever been able to have such a close view of an actual battlefield'.[81] Gilmour had arrived at a quiet moment. Most of the shells fired were British: much of the German artillery was being dragged back eastwards ready for the next push by Rawlinson's army and Monash's corps. The journalists were taken to a nearby casualty clearing-station. By this time, all of the seriously wounded from the severe fighting of the week before had been evacuated to hospitals well to the rear, and few new casualties replaced them. Gilmour was interested to meet lightly wounded men—so lightly wounded that they were able to give blood for their more seriously wounded comrades. The journalists themselves became the objects of curiosity: soldiers from their home states gathered around, plying them with questions about how things were at home.

The Mont became a popular stopping-point for the parties of visitors that trailed across the Australian Corps area during September. They included Sir Joseph Cook (a nuisance making 'cheap witty remarks', Bean remembered), British press barons, and even Sir Arthur Conan Doyle. (Many soldiers knew he had created Sherlock Holmes, Bean noted: 'some thought he was Sherlock Holmes'.)[82] Two weeks after the battle, Bean showed Billy Hughes over the Mont. The encounter intensified Hughes's admiration for the Digger (if that were possible). Shortly before age and Alzheimer's destroyed his mind, Bean described his impression of the impromptu speeches that Hughes made to random groups of soldiers he met along the way:

Your deeds [will be] ... the basis upon which the future nation of Australians will be brought up. On the day you landed at Anzac the Australian nation was born. Before that day we were New South Welshmen, Queenslanders, Victorians—but on that day we became Australians'.[83]

Within months, a spat erupted over exactly who deserved the credit for the seizure of the Mont—a split on state lines.

In November, 'Our Correspondent', writing in the Melbourne *Argus*, reminded his readers that Charles Bean had given the credit for the capture of the summit to 'the New South Welshmen of the 5th Australian Infantry Brigade'. But, he pointed out, 'that hill-top was lost under a heavy counter-attack and re-taken the next day by the Victorians of the 6th Brigade'.[84]

Australian journalists had no doubt that their force had made decisive contributions to victory. Garry's old friend Edward Peacock, describing 'How the World Crisis was Turned' in the *Herald* in 1919, identified the capture of Mont St Quentin and 'the breaching of the world-famous Hindenburg Line' as the AIF's 'two most conspicuous successes'. Peacock argued that Mont St Quentin and the Hindenburg Line had been 'effective in forcing the enemy back towards his own front line'. This had been 'quite decisive'.[85]

By late November, further articles identified the capture of the Mont and Péronne as one of the key events in the victorious campaign. By then, snippets of Monash's congratulatory message had leaked out—probably from Monash—with the *Argus* describing the battle as 'the finest single feat of the war'. The magnitude of the victory that Monash told journalists he had won exacerbated a spat between newspapers in New South Wales and Victoria, each claiming the greater credit for brigades raised in each state. The *Argus* was indignant that Bean (a New

South Welshman, writing originally for the *Sydney Morning Herald*) should have described the Mont as having been taken by the New South Wales 5th Brigade. This exchange sparked a long-running dispute over exactly who was to be credited with the triumph—an example of how deep-rooted were state loyalties in a supposedly national and imperial force.

The men whom he so admired thought Bean's despatches rather dry. Soon after Mont St Quentin, Will Dyson (a much more matey type) fell into conversation with some soldiers at a roadside YMCA tea stall. They had read Bean's published reports. One said that, 'I reckon he does the right thing in sending … the dinkum story' to Australian newspapers. Others thought that unvarnished narrative might be 'all very well for the historian', but felt that, in sending reports read by their families and communities, Bean might 'put a little more glory into it'.[86] The contest between restrained and honest analysis and puffing Australian achievements has been an inescapable part of the telling of Australian military history ever since. The tension was also to be apparent in the depiction of the Mont in art.

'THE GREAT SUBJECT': ARTISTS AND THE BATTLE

The newspaper correspondents' coverage and the suggestions put about by headquarters staffs explain why Mont St Quentin soon became a subject for artists. Indeed, one war artist apparently recorded the action of 1 September 1918, even as it happened. Louis McCubbin, a stretcher-bearer turned official war artist, was said to have been 'present at the battle' of Mont St Quentin.[87] He depicted *The battle of Mont St Quentin*, claiming to have recorded it *in progress as seen from a ridge near Clery and painted between 2 am and 4 am on the day of the battle*.[88] McCubbin's description is very curious, since pre-dawn darkness does not usually afford much illumination, and anyway, the second attack did not begin until about 6.00 a.m. McCubbin painted several more scenes around the Mont, including the brick wall and, in time, the backdrop for the Mont St Quentin diorama.

In the weeks after the capture of the Mont, a succession of war artists visited the area to sketch it. The site was striking, significant, close to a relatively comfortable base in Péronne, and safely behind the lines. Their sketches, drawings, and paintings show that most were guided to the spot on Bouchavesnes Spur, close to where Bean peered at the Mont through his telescope on the later afternoon of 1 September. The visiting artists included Will Longstaff, James Quinn (a portraitist whose landscape sketches are at best half-hearted) and, above all, Arthur Streeton.

Streeton, already the most celebrated Australian landscape artist, returned to France in late October after a stint with the AIF earlier in the year, when he had painted and sketched the war-ravaged country further east. He was attached to the 2nd Division, and Rosenthal himself took the celebrity artist over the battlefield later that month. Streeton made many pencil studies of what he called 'the great subject'.[89]

He painted the Mont, like other artists, more or less at the spot from where Bean had taken out his binoculars—presumably Bean met him at the headquarters mess, and pulled out a map to suggest the best place. He captured the colour of the ground that Frank Brewer particularly noticed—'a sickly mixture of green and yellow'. However, visiting the place nowadays, and comparing what he saw with what he produced, reveals that Streeton grossly exaggerated the Mont's bulk and the steepness of its slopes in his painting.[90] Though he described the Mont as 'a thrilling sight', Streeton's painting confirms his conviction that the scenes of even strenuous combat are not necessarily more than stretches of spoiled countryside. He explained that 'unless a barrage ... is in progress, the battlefield is usually a lifeless expanse of wrecked fields and villages, silent and deadened in expression'.[91] Still, Streeton's *Mont St Quentin* represents the site of the Australian triumph as a hill of some eminence, its summit intimidating, thereby magnifying the achievement of its captors.

A reporter for the London newspaper *The British Australasian* saw Streeton's painting exhibited in London in mid-1919. He thought that the canvas, showing 'the terrible hill rising from the valley of the Somme', should 'certainly go to some Australian gallery'.[92] Though an official war artist, Streeton did not deliver *Mont St Quentin* to the War Memorial — he fell out with John Treloar (by 1922, director of the war memorial museum) over the price he was willing to pay for pictures that Streeton produced in addition to the number stipulated in his contract. He produced a work described, by the *Age*'s art critic, as 'a very large and magnificent painting of a hill in sunlight reaching up to a superb sky': you can't help but feel that he missed the point.[93] But the art of Mont St Quentin would continue to be part of its story, as we will see.

As Streeton and the other artists sketched and painted, men's diaries listed towns liberated as the Allied armies pressed the Germans eastwards. But no one expected the fighting to end in the near future. Lawrence Polinelli wrote pessimistically on 22 October that 'the war will go on for some time yet'. By 6 November, though, even he was writing that 'the Germans are retiring right along the line', and at last felt able to record that they were 'well beaten'. The news finally came through on 11 November.

Many fighting troops took the news of the end of fighting quietly, unable to grasp that they had survived. Lawrence Polinelli, driving a limber towards the front, recorded that the

French civilians around him were 'mad with joy', and of the 21st Battalion, that 'we are very pleased also'.[94] While some soldiers celebrated noisily—firing off coloured flares left behind by the demoralised Germans—Polinelli's flat response to the war's end captured the reaction of many front-line troops. The fighting was over: they had survived. Others had not, and the survivors were to live the rest of their lives with the consequences of serving in that war.

PART III
Grieving

'The War Took Him'

As we have seen, Garry Roberts felt too distraught to write anything in the days after he learned of Frank's death, but he did clip a verse from Guy Innes's paper a couple of days after. It might have been written for Garry and Berta, except that literally thousands of bereaved parents would have read the *Herald*. It asked the bereaved, 'How can we fail in our duty to them/who ne'er failed in the field?' Garry took this question to heart and found the strength to 'carry on'.

The day after they learned of Frank's death, Garry and Berta walked over to Ruby's parents' place, Warwick Farm. Ruby was in bed, prostrate with grief. 'It isn't true, father, is it?' she asked. When Garry confirmed the sad truth for her, too, she wailed 'Oh! My Frank, my little Nancy will never see her father'.

That afternoon, Garry and Berta walked in the forest roads to clear their heads, and then back home again. They sat in the dining room at Sunnyside talking of Frank's five happy years there, and of how he had cleared the ground and planted fruit trees and bushes, making a home in the hills they all loved. This place, they agreed, 'was endeared to us by a thousand memories'. That evening, Garry at last turned to his diary to record how he continued to dwell on those memories.

Ruby's distress at Frank's death must have been all the greater because the letter she read on the day she received the news of his death had been so optimistic. Frank had written it soon after the Hamel battle. He had described imagining her and Nancy as he waited for zero hour, looking up at what they called 'our lucky star'. He had written about their life together after the war, telling her that all the battalions were collecting for the war museums they expected to open in Australia. 'Perhaps years hence you and I and the *kiddies* will take a walk through some war museum'.[1] That walk would now never happen, and there would be no 'kiddies'—only her poor, fatherless Nancy.

Driven by an iron sense of duty, Garry prepared an *in memoriam* notice for Frank, of the kind he had read and clipped for the previous four years. He quoted from Frank's last letter: 'Death has lost a lot of terror and mystery for me … It's those left behind I think about.' It appeared in the *Age* and the *Argus*. Prompted by this public notice—people must have read the death notices regularly and with great attention—letters of condolence began to arrive. Hundreds of letters and cards fill Record Book 8. Some are short (the ladies in the Tramways Board 'Entering Room' conveyed their 'heartfelt sympathy in the loss of your brave son'), while others wrote at greater length, even though acknowledging 'there is so little one can say, but just to send sympathy'.[2] Some, fatigued by the need to send condolences so often in the fourth year of war, resorted to printed forms. C.J. Dennis heard of the Robertses' loss a week later. He wrote to 'Dad', admitting that 'a man usually dislikes receiving letters of this sort'; even so, 'as long as he knows, at least, that his friends do not forget', he offered his sympathy to Garry, 'mother and the rest'.[3] Receiving, and having to acknowledge, so many such letters became for Garry 'Very distressing', as he noted in his diary.

Garry's colleagues received him in the office 'with great sympathy'—it was not the first time they had worked with someone who had just learned of the death of a brother or son.[4] Letters arrived from neighbours in Hawthorn and, after a time, from more distant friends and family overseas, from cousins Lucy and Emily in Wexford, and from Edith Alston in Paris. She passed on comforting snippets recalled from Frank and Norrie's Paris leave: that Frank had spoken fondly of Ruby and Nancy, and that he thought Garry 'the best Dad in the world'.

There was no place for Christian consolation in Garry's (or, it seems, Berta's) grief. While a clergyman (unnamed, but almost certainly Anglican) brought the first news of Frank's death to Eumana, the Robertses did not again seek his solace. Nor did any of their many expressions of grief contain any religious element. The Robertses were not church-goers. Churches were for weddings and christenings: they spent their Sundays in the bush. Garry's and Frank's beliefs at least seem to have been materialist or at most pantheist. Garry's scrapbooks are unvaryingly materialist—cathedrals, for example, were works of art to him, rather than of faith. But rationalist belief did not lessen his grief, nor that of his son's comrades.

'I MISS HIM KEENLY': FRANK'S COMRADES

It bears saying that 'the grieving' included the men who served with the dead, as well as those at home. Late in October, the first letters arrived from Frank's comrades. Phil Starr, who had gone away with Frank on the *Ascanius*, had sent a green-crossed 'active service' envelope (one not censored within the unit) as soon as the battalion reached Cappy. Mont St Quentin, he wrote, had been 'one of the hottest corners they had been in'. Frank had been 'got by machine-guns', but his body had been buried and the grave recorded. Starr had not been in Frank's company, but said that Frank had been 'my best friend over here ... I miss him keenly'. Phil explicitly wrote to say that he did not offer sympathy or condolence; but, having lost his own two brothers in 1917, he could 'understand how you must feel'. (Starr's brothers, Michael and Patrick, had been reported missing and killed on the same day, in the mud-bound attack on Broodseinde at Ypres.[5]) Ruby's brother Percy (who had fought at Péronne in Pompey Elliott's brigade) confirmed the news. He sought out Starr. Six weeks after the battle, Phil was 'so sorry he cried' telling Percy about the attack and Frank's death.[6]

A fortnight later, Noble Norwood wrote to Ruby. Wounded in the shoulder, he had been in a military hospital at Weymouth when he heard of Frank's death, and at first did not believe it. He told her how he had lain awake that night, thinking of Nancy and Ruby, 'and how Frank loved you—and I said "It's impossible"'. Norrie's sister lived at nearby Manningtree Road in Hawthorn, and he asked her to contact Ruby.[7] Many of the Robertses' circle knew each other independently of (or as a result of being introduced through) the family. Web Gilbert had cabled Garry to tell him of Frank's death because Norrie Norwood had written to Gilbert from hospital in Dorset, having been introduced to Gilbert by Frank.

Letters also arrived from Vic Edwards's brother in Launceston, enclosing a watch and ring that Vic had taken from Frank's body. Garry had given Frank the silver 'wisket' watch shortly before he embarked on the *Ascanius*, and his cousin Lucy had given Frank the ring when he visited them the year before. (It had belonged to her brother, a ship's captain.) Edwards had got to them before looters ratted Frank's body, and sent them to his brother for safekeeping.[8]

In December, to the family's distress, the first of the letters and parcels that Garry had sent to Frank began to arrive back, unopened. Garry pasted the label from each one into his Record

Book: the book documenting Frank's death deals with just the fortnight following Frank's death, but comprises hundreds of pages of clippings, copies, correspondence, and other items recording the events following his death in great detail.

Garry had printed a memorial card, eventually sending out some four hundred of them. The card, dozens of examples of which appear throughout Garry's diary and Record Books, bore the photograph that Frank had had taken when he and 'Norrie' went on leave to Paris, and the 21st Battalion's red and black diamond-shaped colour patch. Garry also arranged for mourning brooches for Ruby, Berta, and Gwen: a small enamelled red-and-black diamond with a miniature portrait of Frank in the middle. Garry especially dwelt on Frank's loss. He pasted in page after page of consolatory verse, 'To the Dead', 'They are not Dead!', 'Our Triumphant Dead', and 'Sons', and dozens of casualty lists and *in memoriam* notices. The Robertses knew that they were not the only family to lose a son — a fact that may have brought them some comfort.

So far, the Robertses had only known that Frank had been killed 'in France'. Early in October, though, Garry met William and Jane Dickson, the parents of Lieutenant Selwyn Dickson, who had been killed earlier on 1 September. William, an insurance broker from Armadale, told Garry that their sons had died in the attack on Mont St Quentin. Jane Dickson (she asked Berta to call her Bessie) explained that 'General Monash had ordered an attack but not in sufficient strength': a succinct and essentially accurate summary of the events of 31 August–1 September. It was the first time that the name 'Mont St Quentin' appeared in Garry's diary. He had already clipped cabled stories describing the attack ('Capture of Hill', 'Fine work of Australians') early in September, but without realising the significance it held.[9] It was to give him a focus for the increasingly detailed, not to say obsessive, compilation he was making in his Record Books. Garry already had press reports cabled from France describing the capture of Mont St Quentin and Péronne. He now went back to those reports to annotate them as the place where his son had died.

On 11 November, Australians, along with millions of people across the world, celebrated the war's end with public rejoicing. In Hawthorn, too, people hung out flags, rang school bells, and attended thanksgiving services—ten thousand people crammed Glenferrie Oval, standing in silence as the Last Post sounded. Garry's diary reveals none of this public celebration. The photographs of cheering crowds do not reveal those who had cause for bitterness and grief rather than jubilation and relief. Garry simply made the flat observation in his diary that 'the war is practically over'. For him, the significance of the date was that it had been 'a year and a half since dear old Frank sailed for the War'. 'The War', Garry wrote, 'took him'.

'THE EXACT SPOT': FRANK'S BURIAL PLACE

Garry's desire for 'particulars' centred especially on Frank's grave. His application to the Red Cross on the most awful day of his life began to produce results early in 1919. Red Cross officials had obtained statements from Jack Castle and Alf Fox (a testimony to the AIF's record-keeping, since both had been wounded—Alf in August and Jack in October), but the 21st (or rather, now, the 24th) Battalion orderly room was able to identify who had been in Frank's platoon and where they could be found.

Soon, accounts of Frank's death reached Garry or Ruby. Chaplain Sydney Buckley had written to Ruby on 12 September. Having spoken to a man present, he described Frank as having been wounded by a German grenade. Buckley said that Frank 'only had time to say "I'm done" when he expired'.[10] Over the

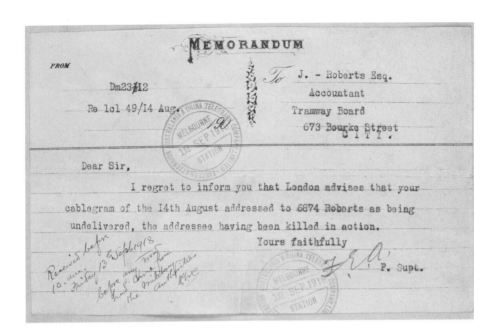

The telegram Garry Roberts opened when he got to his desk in the Tramways Building on the morning of 13 September 1918. (SLV Ms 8508, Record Book 7)

The Robertses (minus Gwen) and friends at Sunnyside, 1914 (from top) Johnny, Berta, Garry and (holding pipe) Frank, with Charles Web Gilbert (centre) and Robert Croll. (Courtesy of Jan Fraser)

Frank and Ruby after they were married. Ruby may well have been pregnant with Nancy by this time. (SLV Ms 8508, Record Book 7)

Alf Kelly, the forty-year-old Boer War veteran who died near the quarry on the Mont. (SLV Ms 8508, Record Book 25)

The label of a parcel Garry had posted to Frank in August 1918, returned to sender 'deceased' in March 1919. (SLV Ms 8508, Record Book 7)

Roy Smerdon, from Murrayville, one of two sons the Smerdons lost to the war. (SLV Ms 8508, Record Book 25)

Les Baker, 'a wasted man'.
(SLV Ms 8508, Record Book 8)

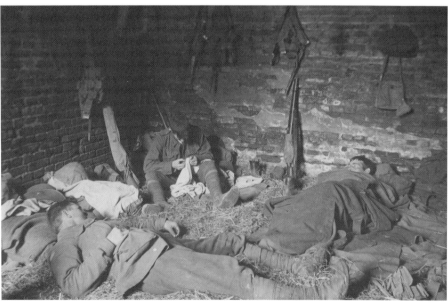

Hubert Wilkins's photograph of men of the 21st Battalion in the barn at Brewery Farm, Querrieu. (SLV Ms 8508, Record Book 25)

The forthright Vic Edwards: 'if you know of anybody with a better service I would like to here of his name'. (SLV Ms 8508, Record Book 8)

Hubert Wilkins's photograph of Mont St Quentin at 1.30 on the afternoon of 1 September 1918, the minute at which Nine Platoon attacked it. (SLV Ms 8508 Record 25)

Jack Castle: 'I went to war so you'll never have to'. (SLV Ms 8508, Record Book 8)

Hubert Wilkins's photograph of a platoon of the 24th Battalion awaiting zero hour in Elsa Trench on 1 September 1918. Though of a neighbouring battalion, this group is exactly the same size as Tom Wignall's Nine Platoon, and is also equipped with two Lewis guns. (SLV Ms 8508, Record Book 25)

Noble 'Norrie' Norwood, a portrait hinting at his artistic sensibilities. (SLV Ms 8508, Record Book 8)

Len Woolcock's photograph of John and Bertha Monash at Frank's grave in the war cemetery in Péronne in May 1919. (SLV Ms 8508, Record Book 7)

Godfrey Dobson, MM, who was to spend his life coping with the war's effects on his health and happiness. (SLV Ms 8508, Record Book 8)

Godfrey and Janet Dobson had one child, Kenneth. This snap, sent to Garry around the sixth anniversary of the battle, does not disclose the war's life-long effects on Godfrey. (SLV Ms 8508, Record Book 17)

Bill Rabling, the last of Nine Platoon to die. (Eveline and Ken McLeod)

Alby Lowerson, VC, whose 'deed' Nine Platoon supported at the quarry on the Mont. (SLV Ms 8508, Record Book 8)

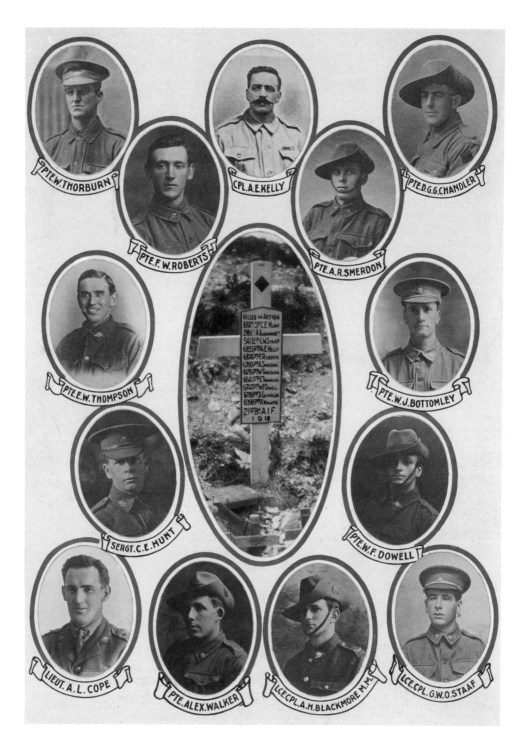

Garry Roberts's montage of most the 21st Battalion's dead of 1 September 1918 (Ted Heath continued to be overlooked), and a photograph of the second cross erected over the men who shared Frank's grave. (SLV Ms 8508, Record Book 7)

Charles Web Gilbert sculpting figures for the Mont St Quentin diorama in the Australian War Memorial's workshops in Melbourne in 1921. (SLV Ms 8508, Record Book 7)

Charles Web Gilbert's initial model for the Mont St Quentin diorama, photographed on the battlefield in 1919. It shows the second wave – including Nine Platoon – going over the top towards the brick wall. (SLV Ms 8508, Record Book 25)

A rare newspaper photograph of May Butler-George working on one of the panels mounted on the plinth of the 2nd Division memorial on Mont St Quentin. (SLV Ms 8508, Record Book 7)

Berta and Garry Roberts with Ruby, Nancy and Barbara at Sunnyside, 1929. (SLV Ms 8508, Record Book 19)

The *Argus* reported the unveiling of Gilbert's memorial in October 1925. Garry clipped this photograph, and probably stared hard at it, trying to discern Frank's likeness. (National Library of Australia)

Charles Bean's view of the final fight for Mont St Quentin, photographed from Bouchavesnes Spur. The quarry where Nine Platoon's men died was located in the wedge-shaped clearing to the left of the photograph. (Peter Stanley)

'Eumana', Hastings Road, Hawthorn, today; recognisably the same house from which Frank called 'Goodbye, Sweetheart' when he left for the last time, and from which Garry Roberts set out on 'the most awful day' of his life. (Peter Stanley)

Descendants of some of Nine Platoon at the Shrine of Remembrance, Melbourne, November 2008. From left Ken and Eveline McLeod (Bill Rabling), Vivienne Lewis and Jilba Georgalis (Frank Roberts), Gordon and Greg Castle (Jack Castle). (Peter Stanley)

The Mont St Quentin cross at the Australian War Memorial. (Peter Stanley)

Ruby (sitting) and Nancy in the 1980s. (Jilba Giorgalis)

Relics of Frank Roberts's death – his medals, Berta and Ruby's Female Relatives Badges, and Nancy's bootees, the ultimate symbol of the sadness that permeates the Robertses' story. (Peter Stanley)

Peter Stanley besides the graves of the Nine Platoon men buried in the war cemetery at Péronne, 2008. (Jane Capel-Stanley)

following six months, the Robertses received several different accounts of Frank's death. Even men in Frank's platoon disagreed over the exact details. Vic Edwards—who had also been present—told his brother Edward that Frank's death had been 'instantaneous', and later told the Red Cross that Frank had died 'in a few moments'.[11] But Jack Castle, who had been in the same Lewis gun team, told the Red Cross that, 'I saw him hit in the chest by a bullet and he died in about 2 minutes'.[12] And Godfrey Dobson, who had been 'in the same party' in the crater, told a Red Cross official that he had been hit by a bomb in the abdomen and that he died ten minutes later.[13]

Garry's desire for 'particulars' of the circumstances of Frank's death became for a time his only interest. Eventually, the Record Books would go on to document the travails of the Tramways Trust and its political, managerial, and industrial troubles, and the local history of the Dandenongs, and the doings of the Scarsdale school's old boys and girls. For the moment, though, Garry spent his evenings mulling over the letters and clippings he was collecting, and writing to try to gather more details and to share his burden with others. Ruby's brother, a sapper, Ted, took the first photograph of the common grave and its 'very nice cross' within three weeks of the burial. He had come over from the 5th Field Company's billets, at Cappy, where he must have heard about the 21st's mutiny. Ruby contributed her portion to the 'particulars' that Garry was compiling. Her other brother Percy, also an engineer, had made his own enquiries in France. He reported that Frank and fourteen others had 'attacked a machine-gun emplacement … and made it easier for the battalion to follow'.[14] This story of sacrifice provided some comfort.

AIF 'Base Records' had written to Ruby in October. Referring to 'the regrettable loss of your husband', it advised that Frank had been buried 'in an isolated group of graves, in a shell hole, in a valley, near a Lane, just East of Mont St Quentin'.¹⁵ This sounded quite exact, but it did not satisfy Garry. The Red Cross's Information Bureau affirmed that it had obtained a statement from Private Harold Smedley of the 21st Battalion. Smedley had testified that, on the evening of 2 September, he 'buried three men, with six others in a crater at Mont St Quentin', and that Frank, Roy Smerdon, and Albert Kelly were among them. (This was a day earlier than Jack Castle's later account, and the number differs from the names that Arch Green punched onto the sheet of tin he nailed onto the cross.) 'The ground was held', Smedley wrote—removing any suggestion that the bodies may have been disturbed by further fighting. Even more comforting, Smedley added that 'before I left I saw the cross for their graves'.¹⁶ The cross would have a story of its own.

Several letters arriving towards the end of January 1919 gave Garry what he needed. He wanted to know 'the exact spot' at which Frank had been buried. A letter from the new officer commanding C Company of what was now the 24th Battalion gave a map reference—I.9.d.9.4—that established its location as precisely as possible. By about the end of January, Garry had a map reference, a photograph of the grave, and a list of those it contained.

'OUR SACRIFICE': THE SHARED GRAVE

Frank did not lie alone in the grave near the quarry on Mont St Quentin. The photograph from Ruby's brother, Edward, gave Garry a list of eleven other names on the cross, which enabled him to trace the dead men's families.¹⁷ He confirmed this from the Red Cross. By late November, Garry knew enough about those who had died and been buried with Frank to begin to contact the families of other 21st Battalion men killed on the

Mont. He wrote to their families, sending 'particulars with the hope that you will be comforted to know ... where the body lies of the one dear to you'. These letters went to elsewhere in Melbourne, to Malvern and Windsor, to Echuca and Murrayville in rural Victoria, and as far as Alberta in Canada and Aberdeenshire in Scotland. By the end of the first week, six families had replied.

Like the Robertses, all the families that Garry contacted were struggling to come to terms with their loss, the more so because it came so close to the war's end. Mr John Blackmore, father of Albert, spoke for many by acknowledging that 'victory comes for Liberty, Freedom & Righteousness', and they knew that 'our sacrifice has not been in vain'. Had it not been so, Mr Blackmore wrote, 'it would have been bitter indeed'.[18] Like Garry, the Blackmores wanted 'particulars', too: they all wanted to know what had happened. Garry also contacted the Chandlers, who had a terrible war. Three sons were killed; the third, Dave, at Mont St Quentin. The surviving son, Robert, died in October 1921 of a seizure at work. Robert had 'not enjoyed very good health since returning from the war', his father Dave explained to Garry.[19]

Garry conducted an intense correspondence with the Walkers of Rosehearty in Aberdeenshire, whose son Alex had been killed in 'mopping up' the quarry, but who was at first recorded as 'unknown' on the cross. Garry had already enquired of AIF Base Records about Alex Walker's effects—his parents received none and his kit bag in the AIF's stores had none. Alex's parents (George, a shoemaker, and Janet, a nurse) corresponded through their daughter Bella. They appreciated Garry's letters, no copies of which are preserved in his Record Books—only replies like the Walkers', which suggest that he must have been a warm correspondent, able to transmit feeling across great distances. 'We so often talk and think about you',

Bella wrote, 'to think we have found such a friend', though 'one we have so little chance of ever meeting'. Later, Garry sent the Walkers Jack Castle's account of the fight for the Mont, the published history of Alex's battalion, and C.J. Dennis's *The Sentimental Bloke*. Bella lent Dennis's book to 'ever so many' of her friends, and her Presbyterian minister pronounced it 'the right good real stuff'.[20]

From Coronation, Alberta, a hamlet on the vast Canadian prairie 200 kilometres north-east of Calgary, came a letter from Mrs Isabel Kelly. She and her two young children, Albert and Grace, had been given a passage back to Canada by the Australian government. Mrs Kelly's Australian brother-in-law, Jack, had sent on Garry's letter. She was 'so glad to have' the photograph of Albert's grave. Mrs Kelly speculated that 'maybe I will be in a position to go and see those graves sometime'. She also offered reciprocal sympathy, saying how sorry she was that Frank 'was not spared to come back to you'. 'I know something of how hard it must be for you', she wrote.

Garry exchanged several letters with Isabel Kelly, who had just returned to Canada with her two children. He later sent her a copy of Jack Castle's statement, in which Jack described how he had seen Albert hit in the leg by a machine-gun bullet, speculating that he must have been hit again—'I could not believe it when I heard Kelly was killed, but I saw him later lying near the crater'. Garry confessed his bitter feelings toward those who had neither volunteered to serve nor had supported conscription. Remembering how divisive conscription had been, Mrs Kelly replied warily. 'Well I think conscription is the fairest way,' she replied—Canada had conscripted from 1918—but she could not understand how 'when they got the returns of the soldiers' votes most votes were against conscription'. This was not all that puzzled Mrs Kelly. Having left Australia, she was now denied the full pension, but was ineligible for a Canadian pension. Canadian veterans had promised to take up her case. Writing from the depths of her second winter on the prairie, she confessed to being 'just a little bit afraid that the cold winters here might be hard on the children', but she was relieved that 'so far they are standing it very well'. With that, Mrs Kelly fades from the story: attempts to trace Grace and Albert in Canada ninety years on came to nothing.[21]

Months after he first wrote, Garry received a letter from the Smerdons of Murrayville. Ann and John Smerdon had also had a letter from the 21st's chaplain, Sydney Buckley, soon after the battle, but nothing since then. They had received Roy's diary in the 'effects' returned to them, but 'Mr Smerdon ... has never felt inclined to open it'. Garry sent the Smerdons Jack Castle's account, which explained Roy's death as well. The Smerdons replied, through their daughter Ann, as Mrs Smerdon had hurt her hand after being thrown out of a cart, and Mr Smerdon seemed not to relish writing. In April 1920 the Smerdons wrote again, apologising for being tardy correspondents, but explaining that they were preoccupied with the drought. 'We are still looking Heavenwards for the approach of some stray rain drops', Miss Smerdon explained. 'We are milking nine cows and we can only manage to make butter for ourselves ... but all considered we get off light, when you think of [what] the masses in the city have to pay for all kinds of produce'.

While the remains of Albert Kelly, Roy Smerdon, Frank Roberts, and the other eight men had been exhumed and moved in March 1919, it was not until early 1920 that the Imperial War Graves Commission was ready to install headstones. Its Australian office contacted all the families, asking them to specify an inscription for the grave of their loved ones. Of the twelve dead in the quarry, ten families chose to add an inscription. The commission's requirements were exact: 'There

is space for 66 letters less spaces between words', it advised.²²
Garry specified that Frank's stone bear a star. He explained that,
in his letters home, Frank had 'used frequently to refer to his
"lucky star"'. The commission explained that the star it meant
had been a Star of David, and that its use was restricted to Jews.
Garry asked if he could have a seven-pointed Australian federal
star, but that was forbidden also. In the end, the family settled
for an inscription: 'Not lonely with the boys—I'm one of the
"Aussie" family here (letter)'.²³

Garry's Record Books include photographs of Frank's
comrades, particularly on the memorial card that Garry had
printed, and his books constitute a memorial to them. But
Frank's face predominates.

'THE LITTLE TASK YOU GAVE ME': THE SURVIVORS' ACCOUNTS

Meanwhile, the survivors began to return home. Despite two
plebiscites on conscription, the AIF remained a volunteer
force. Its dead had, in a sense, chosen their fate—more so than
the conscript soldiers of both enemy and Allied armies, whom
Australians had looked down upon. That fact of volunteering
coloured the thoughts of at least one 21st Battalion man as he
thought of the comrades he left behind in France:

> Shed thou no tears
> This road they chose, this way of pain
> Was theirs
> Who drank the cup of bitterness
> And lie in alien soil, hungering
> For home.²⁴

Hungering for home, the 21st's survivors were at last able

to return. They came back in the same way that most of them had left: not as a battalion, but in drafts, sorted by length of service and by other obligations (for example, to families and educational opportunities), and despatched on 170-odd ships through 1919 and into 1920.

In December 1918, Garry's clippings show that he had begun to take an interest in the advice published in the daily press of the names of those men returning from active service. The first to arrive was Charlie Tognella, who embarked from the Royal Albert Dock in London aboard the ambulance transport *Somerset* on 30 November 1918. He travelled with a draft of 1914 men lucky enough to go home on furlough, a detachment of twenty underage boys combed out by more diligent checking in the depots and, among several hundred other convalescents, thirteen other wounded members of his old battalion, suffering from gunshot wounds in various places: his was 'GSW chest'. Garry seems to have missed Charlie, who went straight back to northern Victoria, but he found everyone else.

By the end of January, several men had arrived home. In March, Norrie Norwood, Vic Edwards, and Tom Wignall arrived, as well as Alf Fox, who had been gassed in August. In May, Alby Lowerson and Godfrey Dobson visited the Robertses, followed by Tom Wignall (who brought maps, and who presumably sketched for Garry the exact details of where on the Mont Frank had been killed and buried). Soon after, 'Norrie' introduced Phil Starr, and Jack Castle brought Bill Rabling along later in 1919.

Garry took to shouting groups of Frank's comrades to lunch at Carlyon's Hotel, at the corner of Bourke and Spencer Streets, where he had entertained Frank and his friends when they were at Broadmeadows. Speaking to him directly, they were able to say more than they had felt able in letters. Vic Edwards told Garry that Frank had been shot in the chest, and that he knew this because he saw blood on his chest.[25] Norrie Norwood said he thought that Frank had been killed at about 1.50 p.m.[26] Dobson was able to tell Garry more of the moment of Frank's death, and he gave a slightly different version in person. He said that Frank had said, 'They got me, Dobbie', and had asked him to 'turn me over'. Dobson did so, so Frank was lying on his back. Then he asked Dobson to 'straighten my legs'—a request that Vic Edwards mentioned, too. Dobson did so, as Frank's face turned yellow, and he died 'in a few minutes'.[27]

But not all of the veterans who turned up were either welcome or trustworthy. In March, a Sergeant Henry Bevern arrived—the only man in the AIF to bear that surname. Bevern, a timber clerk from South Australia, had enlisted in 1914, but had been discharged as medically unfit twice before re-enlisting when the recruiting officers became less choosy. Like Frank, he had arrived in France late in 1917; unlike Frank, Bevern had kept his stripes. Though less qualified than Frank, he had ended up as Nine Platoon's sergeant for most of the next five months. He and Frank fell out immediately—it was Bevern whom Frank meant when he told his parents that 'I've fallen out with my sergeant'. Bevern gave Frank more fatigues than he should, and managed the platoon's rations so poorly that they were often short. Now he arrived at Garry's office as Frank's old mate. In fact, Bevern had been gassed late in July and so could tell Garry nothing about what he wanted to know most. He wangled a couple of lunches at Carlyon's before some of Frank's friends told Garry the truth. Vic Edwards—a straight talker, as we will see—said they 'all had a good opinion of Frank, but a very poor one of Sgt Bevern'. Norrie Norwood told Garry that hearing of Bevern having his legs under the Robertses' table 'makes my blood boil', describing his regime in the platoon as 'the tyranny of a bully'.[28] Garry must have recalled Frank's references in his letters to the 'bastards' who had made his life miserable, and Henry Bevern thereupon disappeared from Eumana and from the record. But the record includes, as we have seen, the survivors' incomparable testimonies.

Garry Roberts had a clear and understandable motive for inviting his son's comrades to lunch and dinner. He wanted to collect 'particulars' of Frank's life in the AIF, and his death at Mont St Quentin, as a way of retaining a precious bond. The snippets and stories that Frank's comrades recalled over the meat and veg at Carlyon's Hotel or in the dining room at Eumana helped him to grieve. When Alf Fox thanked Garry for an evening, he suggested that 'you may find reward in the fact that we all regard & respect you as the father of one of our dearest & best comrades'.[29] Garry could absorb the ebbing warmth that his friends shared. One of the ways he coped with his grief was not to push it away and deny it, but to wrap himself in it.

Part of the gathering involved Garry pressing his son's friends to record their memories of the day on which Frank died. Amazingly, Garry persuaded seven of the eight survivors of Frank's platoon, and Phil Starr, to write memoirs of Mont St Quentin: only two men promised accounts and did not deliver. Les Baker proved to be, as he said, 'a bit slack', for reasons we will soon understand—not that his account of Mont St Quentin would be very informative, since he was wounded on the evening of 31 August.[30] Alby Lowerson faced again the VC's dilemma, to talk about his 'deed' without seeming unduly modest or a big-noter. He found Garry's request 'no easy matter', and solved the problem by simply not writing or saying anything.[31]

Phil Starr, for example, came to dinner on 19 May (1919), and two weeks later sent Garry his first account. 'It is a "plain unvarnished tale"', he wrote, 'without any elaboration'. Phil claimed that it told 'exactly what happened on that memorable morning'. He had 'no doubt ... it will pass into history as something worth while': meaning the taking of the Mont, not his version of it.[32] But Starr continued to work on a longer version, and eight months later announced to Garry that he had 'at last ... finished the little task you gave me'.[33]

Jack Castle completed his account by December 1919. Garry continued to question Jack about Frank, too—not because he did not accept his account, but because he thought so highly of Jack's memory and ability to express it. He sent it to Guy Innes, the *Herald*'s editor, whom he had met on the fateful tram journey to Bourke Street on the most awful day of his life. Innes replied enthusiastically. Castle, he thought, had written 'quietly and methodically'. He thought it 'beyond the expression of one merely trained in the artificial use of words', but an authentic and sincere account.[34] Another writer, Jeannie Gunn, agreed. 'I felt I was living through that awful day with him', she wrote.[35] Mrs Gunn was much preoccupied by the war and its effects. Not only had she devoted herself to patriotic endeavours during it, but now that it was over she was caring for Joe Jones, a one-handed, one-legged man suffering from a mutilated jaw and tuberculosis. Jack's account showed his ability not with the pen, but with his voice. The manuscript is not in his hand, but in the handwriting of Ethel, whom he had married in 1917 while convalescing in Britain and who had joined him as a 'war bride' soon after the war.

Alf Crawford's is the shortest account. He had returned to Gippsland and, besides sending his statement from Orbost, in east Gippsland in September 1919, had nothing more to do with Garry, the platoon, or the battalion association. His medical file was later lost by the 'Repat' Department, so we know almost nothing of Alf Crawford's life besides what is recorded in his AIF file and in his one-page account of this battle. My attempts to find relatives were unproductive until weeks before this book was completed.

The last survivor's account came from Perth, when Noble 'Norrie' Norwood posted his early in September 1920, 'heartily ashamed' at the time it had taken him. Norwood relied not only on his own memory, but on 'several books' giving 'the account of that memorable affair'. 'It's not a comprehensive account', he warned, 'but it's the best I can do'.[36] Recalling the events of 1 September 1918 obviously upset some of the survivors.

Garry carefully annotated and amended each man's handwritten pages before sending them to be typed by the Tramway Trust's typistes and stuck into the Record Books. The various versions show how Garry edited the accounts to make them clearer, and how he asked their authors to seek further details. He also circulated accounts between members of the platoon—Godfrey Dobson, for example, replied that he agreed with Castle's account, except for two mistakes, though Vic Edwards wrote to say that 'it's just how things were', correcting only the name of the lieutenant shot in the head as they worked their way up Galatz Trench: it was Cope, not Holt, he thought (wrongly).[37]

'How I persuaded men, who swore they could not write', Garry later told Charles Bean, 'is quite a story'—not that he ever told it. His appeal rested not only on his own obvious need to know about Frank's final days, but on his broader desire to record what had happened 'for the benefit of relatives of those who had fallen in the fight'.[38] Of the platoon, the only man he could not prevail against was Charlie Tognella; going on Charlie's AIF and Repat files, it would seem that he was more or less illiterate, and covered his embarrassment by simply not replying.

Frank's former comrades wrote, as Garry said, 'simply, accurately and in detail'. Their accounts range from the page submitted by Alf Crawford to the long narratives of

Godfrey Dobson and Jack Castle. They amount to over ten thousand words of detailed, vivid, and often moving first-hand testimony. Garry encouraged Frank's friends to write further memoirs, but without success. In 1922, Phil Starr replied to Garry's suggestion that he write an account of 'the strike of the 21st'—the disbandment protest—but he seems not to have.[39] Even so, the narratives of Nine Platoon constitute the most extraordinarily detailed account of one platoon's experience of battle, a source unrivalled in Australian military history. Without them, this book would not have been possible.

'A WORTHY AND STRIKING MEMORIAL': THE MONT ST QUENTIN MONUMENT

The idea of erecting a memorial on the summit of Mont St Quentin arose within days of the battle. With his division resting at Cappy, Rosenthal had visited the Mont twice in the week after the battle. On 6 September, he walked over the ground, clambering in and out of trenches only just cleared of German dead, and looking at the mounds of rusty barbed wire littering the slopes. He came to appreciate 'the difficult nature of the task and the gallant work done by our infantry'.[40] He must have mused on this overnight, because the next day he took his divisional engineer and his French liaison officer with him to pick a site for a memorial he wanted to build on the Mont. Just on two months after the battle, Rosenthal, lecturing in Britain at the Staff College on the capture of the Mont, had secured permission for the monument's erection (presumably through Australia House). He had already contacted two Australian sculptors working in Britain: Miss May Butler-George, and Frank and Garry's friend Charles Web Gilbert. An expatriate Gippslander, known in London for painting miniatures, Miss Butler-George had taken up bas-relief sculpting in plasticine while ill in bed. By the year's end, both had been engaged to create a memorial, and soon both had visited the Mont. Miss Butler-George claimed to be 'the first woman to see the devastated battle areas' (presumably she meant the first woman who was not French and not a nurse), but she certainly saw some of the first residents of Péronne return to what remained of their town, and described the poignant scenes in the *Argus*.[41]

The Robertses first learned of the idea of a memorial being placed on Mont St Quentin from a clipping of a story reprinted in the *Age* from the *Scotsman* at the end of 1918. Soon, a letter arrived from Gilbert, telling Berta and Garry that he had been asked to create a memorial to Mont St Quentin, and that 'if possible he wanted to use Frank's head for the figure'.[42] This, he told Garry, he saw as 'a compliment to your good self'.[43] Frank had visited Gilbert in London, meeting Mabel, the new Mrs Gilbert. Presumably Gilbert had sketched Frank then, so he had the raw material at hand, as it were. Garry naturally took a close interest in reports about the proposed memorial. In February 1919, he read of Gilbert's intended design: an Australian with a rifle driving a bayonet into a symbolic Prussian eagle. 'As Frank appears to have lost his life while attacking with the bayonet', Garry thought that 'the design suits his ending as well'.[44]

Rosenthal invited the men of his division to contribute to a fund to build their monument. By March 1919 he had collected over £1230, including the contribution of a few bob short of £100 by the 24th. Its magazine encouraged men to imagine the effect on 'the friends and relatives of the brave men who died on this hotly contested field' when, on visiting the scene, they found 'a worthy and striking memorial'.[45] They were told that the monument would be placed 'near Elsa Trench', which many of the 5th and 6th Brigades would remember from the attacks they made from it.

Despite getting off to a rapid start in 1919, work on the

monument slowed. In 1925 Miss Butler-George was still working on the reliefs in a studio behind the Chapel Street drill hall in Richmond. Soon they were to be sent to be cast in Paris. Still, it promised much. Gilbert's massive figure was impressive, and, according to a reporter for *Table Talk*, Miss Butler-George's panels were 'life-like in the extreme' and were expected to 'appeal strongly to living members of this famous division'.[46] She seems to have rendered the division's 1916 battle, Mouquet Farm, as 'Moquet Farm', suggesting that no one kept much of an eye on her work.

In the course of its completion, a small mystery emerged. Jack Castle's account of 1 September described how Roy Smerdon rested his Lewis gun on Jack's shoulder. In the margin of Jack's account, Garry Roberts noted that 'Gilbert shows this in his memorial', though it did not. Perhaps he meant May Butler-George's bas reliefs on the plinth, though she did not depict Roy and Jack's exploit. The monument's two bas reliefs show gunners hauling artillery pieces, and infantry advancing. Neither depicts a man resting a Lewis gun on a comrade's shoulders. Did Garry refer to a vignette in an early version of Web Gilbert's diorama, only to be removed later in one of the several refubishments it has undergone?

'FRANK'S BOOK': GARRY'S MEMORIAL VOLUMES

By March 1919, Garry was working on what he called 'Frank's Record Book' into the night—until 1.00 a.m. for several nights running—pasting, reading, and re-reading, annotating and, I suppose, just sitting and thinking, in a pool of light in the quiet of the night. This effort continued for years. He seems to have begun two series of scrapbooks. Four are labelled 'F [i.e. Frank] I' to 'FIV', but many of the other twenty-odd scrapbooks held in the State Library of Victoria contain documents, photographs, and related material pasted in. The books are so many and massive that they form a small mountain on the desks in the Library's Australiana room.

Garry was equipped to produce a book: he mixed with writers and was known as a minor author, and he published a detailed history of the reunions of his old school, Scarsdale, and small local histories of goldmining sites around Ballarat. The Robertses' circle and Frank's comrades naturally came to know about Garry's project—and to realise that it became his perpetual obsession. They took to asking, as Norrie Norwood did, 'when Frank's book is being published ...?' Norrie made the mistake of writing a hastily crossed out 'if'.[47] In 1921, Garry told John Treloar that he hoped to publish it 'next year'. The following year, a week after the fourth anniversary of Frank's death, Garry told John Treloar that he had been compiling a 'memorial volume' for nearly three years, a book to be distributed to his comrades and not sold. He asked Treloar for permission to use official photographs, and the War Museum Committee gave its permission 'with pleasure', hoping to receive a copy 'in due course'.

'In due course' became 'never'. As the 1920s advanced, it became apparent that Garry could not corral the massive lode of clippings, correspondence, papers, and photographs he had gathered.[48] There are biographical snippets preserved in the 'F' books, notes taken from Fred Cutlack's *The Australians: their final campaign*, John Monash's *Australian Victories*, pages cut from Sir Walter Scott's mediaeval romance *Quentin Durward* (because it mentioned Péronne), and many other references. But the business of writing an account that did justice to Frank and to the battle in which he died clearly defeated poor Garry. Overwhelmed by the amount of material he collected, unable to cut anything that reminded him of dear, departed Frank, the heartbroken father never published Frank's Book.

That the Record Books were more about grieving than about writing a coherent publishable account is obvious from the photographs they contain. About twenty of Garry's Record Books begin with photographs of Frank, the *in memoriam* cards that Garry had printed, and photographs of Frank's grave or of the family, including Ruby. From September 1918 they became not just a commonplace book record of domestic happenings and general news, but an explicit memorial to Frank. Garry pasted into the books every letter he received with any connection to Frank or his comrades. Other documents in Garry's memorial scrap book are a mystery. For example, it includes a list of men in C Company and a detailed plan of where Nine Platoon went on the Mont, and where Frank had been killed and where he was buried, but the sheets give no indication of who wrote them. They probably came from one of the sergeants—probably Tom Wignall, who kept his notebook recording men's names.

Garry had asked his old friend Robert Croll to write a foreword. It became one of the few parts of Frank's book that reached the typescript stage. A decade after Frank's death, Garry abandoned any hope of its publication, and Croll's foreword appeared ten years later as an Anzac Day feature in the *Sun News-Pictorial* in 1929. If it was not the emotion of writing about Frank's death or controlling the vast range of materials he assembled that defeated him, Garry found himself unable to decide on whether the battle in which Frank died had truly been a triumph.

'CLOSE SCRUTINY AND HONEST TALKING': JUDGEMENT ON THE BATTLE

Mont St Quentin was becoming known as one of the AIF's great achievements on the Western Front. However, within the paeans of praise, two controversies rumbled in the background. One was primarily of interest to members of the two brigades that had attacked the Mont; the other is of relevance even today. The first essentially concerned the question, 'Which brigade had really taken Mont St Quentin?' The second revolves around the question, 'Was this battle fought well?'

Those involved in the battle of Mont St Quentin soon began to produce different versions explaining what had happened. From a distance of over ninety years, the arguments, the emphases, and the claims seem unimportant. After all, the victors were all Australians: all dressed in that faded, dusty pea-green khaki, and all commanded by Monash. What did it matter exactly which unit or brigade did what? It mattered a great deal to those involved, the more so as the tag 'greatest single achievement' became attached to the battle, and particularly the capture of the Mont itself.

Fred Cutlack, another of the official war correspondents who had been working with Bean in France, published *The Australians: their final campaign, 1918*, within months of the war's end. Cutlack, who had written the book while recuperating from a motorcycle accident in July, did not witness the battle, nor even see the ground on which it had been fought. He also relied on the slapdash accounts filed by staff officers and pressmen in the days after the battle. He gave the credit to the 5th Brigade, though conceding that 'the 6th Brigade played a great part too'.[49] Cutlack underplayed his description of the climax of the attack, in which 'the 6th Brigade line … rushed the position', though admitting that there were 'very few prisoners taken'.[50] He paid more attention to the brigade that had not in fact succeeded in taking the Mont, while giving short shrift to the troops that had.

Men of the 6th Brigade never resiled from their contention that they had taken the Mont. Jack Castle complained to Garry about an article in the *Herald* on 31 August 1922 'claiming that date as the anniversary'. But he pointed out that 'it was then that our Battalion ... was brought up' and 'we took and held it'.[51] A disinterested evaluation of all the available records ninety years on leads to the conclusion that while the 5th Brigade did not fly the Australian flag on the Mont on 31 August, it wore down the defenders by beating off repeated counter-attacks by the 2nd Guard Division. The Thuringians who relieved the Guards did not offer such a stout resistance (nor did they make any counter-attacks), but the 6th Brigade did gain possession of the Mont. The details mattered only to men who are long dead.

The broader significance of the battle is of more enduring importance. As we have seen, boosted by press reports, paintings, photographs, and sculpture, the taking of Mont St Quentin swiftly assumed epic proportions in the AIF's story. An article in the Melbourne *Herald* marking the battle's first anniversary described it as 'one of the greatest achievements of the war' (the qualifying 'Australian' had been lost), and talked of the two hundred machine-guns the attackers had captured at a cost of 'less than 50 casualties'. This, Australian journalist Edward Peacock remarked, was 'little short of a miracle'; but it was also inaccurate—errors soon gathered around the battle for the Mont.[52] (Peacock was another old friend of Garry Roberts's.)

The superlatives were made in Australia. The British author Sir Frederick Maurice, describing *The Last Four Months* in a book published in 1919, did not ascribe any special pre-eminence to Mont St Quentin. Working from Rawlinson's reports, which, as we have seen, were written on the basis of an anticipation of the Mont's capture, he dated the capture to 31 August and gave the credit to the 5th Brigade.[53] Mont St Quentin is the finest single feat of the war only in Australia—because the country was told so by none other than John Monash.

The Australian account that carried the most weight was Monash's—hardly a disinterested observer. While still in Britain as director of repatriation in mid-1919, Monash obtained a publishing contract for £1100 and delivered a manuscript of about 115,000 words after a couple of months of intensive writing. The result, *The Australian Victories in France in 1918*, was a complex mix of boosting, boasting, evasion, and exculpation. It sold in large numbers, and essentially determined the standard Australian interpretation of the war's final year. It appeared twenty-two years before the detailed (but almost indigestible) chapters of Charles Bean's official history. Its racy, confident narrative portrayed the battle for the Somme bend as a calculated bit of bluff, dash, and biff, and pretty much set the dominant tone for the succeeding ninety years. Bean was not fooled—his notes for Volume VI include the telling line 'I attach no value to JM's account of fighting in Péronne'.[54] Many later chroniclers have been less sceptical, mistakenly regarding *The Australian Victories* as reliable history rather than as the propaganda it clearly was. Indeed, a willingness to accept Monash's book as history separates the sheep from the goats.

Monash represented the manoeuvres that preceded the attack as 'all part of a comprehensive plan' (as a sub-heading read when his *Australian Victories in France* ran as a serial in the *Sydney Mail* early 1920).[55] Naturally, Garry clipped and annotated many instalments for his Record Books. Based on Monash's declared aim, though, you would have to question that his plans for the capture of the Mont and Péronne were as successful as he made out. He rightly identified that the Mont's importance was that it 'dominates the whole of the approaches to it', and correctly foresaw that it needed to be seized by a sudden attack. But he claimed that the effect of taking the Mont would be 'to open a wide gate through which the remainder of the Fourth and Third Armies could pour, *so as to roll up the enemy's line in both directions*'.[56]

Commanders throughout history have dreamed of 'rolling up the enemy's line'—it was a particular obsession in the American Civil War, which Monash had studied, and also of Douglas Haig. It proved to be equally illusory at Mont St Quentin. There was no gate; there was no rolling up; there was no break-through. There was just the relentless pressure that gradually forced Ludendorff to continue to give ground. Writing of the capture of Mont St Quentin and Péronne, the best that Monash could offer was that 'doubtless the loss of Mont St Quentin was a controlling factor in the decision which was forced on him to undertake a retreat'.[57] This qualified admission did not seem to deter those who portrayed the battle as the greatest feat of the war. Nor did Monash reveal that he had done nothing to press the faltering advance for most of 31 August.

Gradually, as Garry collected accounts of the battle for Mont St Quentin and sat night after night reading and musing over them, he began to form a suspicion, growing into a conviction, that much of what he had read was neither consistent nor justifiable. In September 1921, just over two years after the battle, Garry wrote beside a clipping that he had realised that after the 5th Brigade had attacked the Mont on 31 August, 'the Germans had recaptured it'. The attack made by Frank's brigade, the 6th, the next day, 'was not consolidation but an absolute recapture of what had been lost'. He believed this to be so and indeed, 'so say the men I have questioned'. Checking with the memoirs of John Monash, he found that 'Sir John Monash does not seem to have stated this fairly in his work'. Later, Garry returned to this point, writing in the margin, 'This deserves close scrutiny and honest talking'.[58] In his grief,

Garry was not equipped to contest the view of a man whom he revered. It is now clear, though, that Monash misrepresented the taking of the Mont, taking credit for a battle essentially run by his divisional and brigade commanders, and allowing readers to believe that it was taken by the 5th Brigade on the 31st, and not the 6th on 1 September.

Garry Roberts entered only once into this argument, to advocate the claims of Mont St Quentin against other major actions. Early in 1920, he wrote to the *Argus* as 'De Facto', taking issue with Senator George Pearce, the minister for defence. Pearce had said that Mont St Quentin had been 'won on the 31st of August and lost, but was recaptured and held by the 6th Brigade on September 1st'.[59] It was important to Garry that Frank had died at the moment of victory.

'SEARCH FOR PRIVATE ROBERT'S GRAVE': THE MONASHES ON THE MONT

Meanwhile, the communal grave on Mont St Quentin did not remain undisturbed for long. The Imperial War Graves Commission had written to Garry late in March 1919 to advise that the men's remains had been moved from the common grave on the Mont to graves in the Péronne communal cemetery extension, and they had been re-interred by the spring. The bodies were identified, and each was given a separate plot. Amazingly, among the first visitors to the new grave were Monash and his daughter Bertha.

Bertha and John Monash were enjoying a trip together, as they had not for the past five years. Early in 1919, with the submarine menace at last over, Bertha and her mother, Victoria, had travelled to Britain. Neither had any idea of John's affair with Lizette Bentwitch, and Victoria never would. When Bertha got wind of the extent of John's dalliance, relations between the two would cool, to Monash's lasting regret. In the meantime, Bertha and Victoria—as much as her chronic illness would allow—enjoyed the social round on the arm of the newly knighted senior Australian officer, meeting the royal family, politicians, generals, and Society generally in the first peacetime spring Europe had seen since 1914.

In May 1919, John Monash returned to France with Bertha, whose diary—'My Trip with Dad to France'—offers an insight not only into his relationship with his only daughter before they became estranged, but also opens a further chapter in the saga of Mont St Quentin and, remarkably, even the Nine Platoon story.[60]

The Monashes had crossed the Channel by the boat train, on a troopship packed with soldiers bound for the army of occupation in Germany. After spending a night in Boulogne, they motored across to the Somme Valley. Their driver was Len Woolcock, a Queensland mechanic with bad teeth who was waiting for demobilisation. (His ticket came through a month later: did he ask a favour of the director-general of repatriation?) Len knew his way around the Somme—he had driven ambulances and lorries in 1918. They travelled by Montreuil, the beautiful walled town that had housed Douglas Haig's general headquarters, and the chateau at Bertangles, 'where Dad was knighted'. On a Saturday afternoon, Len had parked the car on a steep hill overlooking the Somme valley, with Amiens in the distance, while 'Dad explained the importance of the high ground at Villers-Bretonneux'. It was not, it seems, the first holiday lecture that Bertha had heard from Dad.

After a night in Amiens, they motored out along the road to Querrieu, Monash pointing out to Bertha where a German shell had narrowly missed his car near Glisy during the desperate days a year before. Monash had Woolcock cadge some petrol from a War Graves detachment working on a cemetery and where Monash uncharacteristically lost his glasses. (He left them on the road, it seems. Before they returned to look for them, a party of German prisoners repairing the roads marched over them. The AIF were not the only troops who souvenired anything not nailed down.)

Then they turned eastwards and drove along the straight Roman road that had more or less formed a flank of the Australian advance in 1918. Though the weather was bright and sunny, with spring wildflowers blooming on ground still heavily pocked with shell craters, the scene was one of desolation. Bertha found Warfusée Lamotte 'completely demolished', Foucaucourt 'in ruins' and, when they reached the Somme in time for morning tea, they found the sign—still preserved in the Australian War Memorial—that announced 'This *was* Villers-Carbonnel'. Soon they were in Péronne. As they walked along the Rue Saint-Sauveur, past the sign 'Roo de Kanga' still hanging on the wall of the partly demolished Hôtel de Ville, they saw signs of life returning to the town: a few wooden huts, even a restaurant opening. Bertha and her father did not, however, eat at the restaurant. They motored north along the road to Bapaume, and a few minutes after noon reached the summit of Mont St Quentin.

There they stood, on the site already prepared for Rosenthal's monument to his division. Monash led Bertha out to the edge of the Mont, still bare of trees. Unlike today, they could see for miles over the rolling countryside. They looked down on Elsa Trench—not yet filled in—and Bertha noticed the bare slopes and the piles of wire entanglements still strewn about the fields. Woolcock fetched a hamper from the back of the car, and Monash and Bertha sat amid the ruins of the village and ate a frugal picnic, the new spring growth and buds contrasting with the devastation about them. And then something unusual happened. Rather than (as you might expect) delivering another fatherly lecture on 'Another of My Great Victories', John went looking for a grave, accompanied by Bertha.

They drove back down the road towards Péronne, turning right towards the old municipal cemetery on the town's northern outskirts, already known as the Péronne communal cemetery extension, finding it easily because it stood in bare fields, uncrowded by houses, ruined or otherwise. There, they searched for a particular grave and, Bertha wrote, 'soon found it'. (There would still have been a War Graves unit detachment stationed there, and their lists and cemetery plan would have been exact.)

Bertha 'went with Dad on a search for Private Robert's grave'. Only one Australian named Roberts had been buried at Péronne: Frank. Bertha took some photographs but, finding she was short of film, borrowed Woolcock's camera, and took some more 'snaps' of the grave, still marked by a wooden cross—the uniform headstones and the manicured grass and roses were years away. Monash had wandered off, perhaps uncomfortable at being surrounded by the graves of men he had commanded. He found a party of American and Australian soldiers (perhaps looking after one of the thousands of 'dumps' the army had left behind as it trailed across France), and found their lively company more congenial.

Early in the afternoon, they motored on northwards. At Fleurbaix, they stopped by the only other grave that Bertha mentions, that of Harry Cathie of the 8th Battalion, a family friend who had died in the AIF's earliest months in France. Seeing the country he had fought over, and perhaps especially the graves of his men, seem to have disoriented Monash. On the way back to Boulogne he lost his wallet, and then found it. First his glasses, then his wallet: not what you expect from the organised, disciplined Monash. But if the visit to the old front upset him, Monash concealed it well from Bertha, though she seems not to have been particularly emotionally attuned. After just three days in France, they were back in London with Victoria. It was the only time that Monash was to return to the scene of his victories, or to visit the graves of those who did not come home.

Why did John and Bertha Monash go in search of Frank's grave particularly—one of only two graves that they visited? Monash's meticulously indexed papers give no clue. There is no record of his receiving a letter from or writing a letter to Garry Roberts in the war's final months or in 1919. Likewise, while Bertha's correspondence is incomplete, she neither corresponded with the Robertses nor wrote about them in her long, chatty letters to Dad in the war's last months or while she fretted impatiently for the boat that would take her and Mum to see him again. The answer emerges in hints and surmises. When Monash returned to Australia on Boxing Day 1919, among the crowd assembled on St Kilda Pier was 'one whose son lost his life at Mont St Quentin'. That one was Garry, writing anonymously in *Our Empire*, the magazine of the Sailors and Soldiers' Fathers' Association. Garry described how he had sent his son a copy of *Our Empire* and the verse 'Carry On!' Shortly before he died, the son (Frank) encouraged the father to 'Carry On, Dad!', a motto that the grieving father took as his own. In fact, Garry carried a flag bearing the legend 'Carry On, Dad' when he lined up with hundreds of others to greet Monash. In his article, Garry disclosed that the key figure in taking the photographs was Bertha Monash. 'Shortly after her arrival in England', Garry wrote 'it was made known to her that the Father was anxious to have a photograph of the temporary grave of his son'.[61]

But who made it known? While his family believed that Garry knew Monash, they were not 'friends'. In fact, Garry's half-brother, Arthur, happened to be in London after the war.

He knew Bertha from a choir they had belonged to, and she remembered having met Garry a year before. Arthur asked the Monashes (who were about to go to France) to find and photograph his nephew's grave as a favour. Because it was communicated in person, no single document explains why among the 30,000-odd graves the AIF left in France and Belgium, Monash visited the grave of an orchardist from the Dandenongs. In the last few folios of Garry's massive scrapbooks, next to a newspaper clipping reporting Monash's death in 1931, there is a scribbled explanation.[62] Len Woolcock's snap is yet another of the extraordinary relationships that cluster around Nine Platoon's story.

'TOO PERSONAL AND SAD':
MONT ST QUENTIN AND THE WAR MUSEUM

The 21st Battalion had contributed its share to the collection of 'relics' that John Treloar gathered in the war's last two years. Indeed, Treloar, the young lieutenant-colonel who had run the War Records Section, told Bernard Duggan that his battalion had 'sent in probably more captured maps than any other unit in the AIF'—another 21st Battalion first. Treloar's file on Mont St Quentin includes a sheaf of receipts for German documents and maps taken from the dugouts on the summit of the Mont.[63] But the cross that the battalion pioneers and Arch Green had made remained on the ground next to the graves-site on the Mont, rejected as a reminder of the cost of war.

Garry Roberts soon developed a friendship with Treloar, who in 1920 became the director of the war memorial museum about to open in the Exhibition Building in Melbourne. Garry allowed the War Museum to advertise its 'Battle Pictures Week' in 1920 on his trams ('Digger! See Yourselves in Action!') and, as a result, Garry 'and Lady' were invited to the opening of the show at the Town Hall.⁶⁴ One of the lecturers in Battle Pictures Week was Charles Rosenthal, the 2nd Division's commander in the battle.

Rosenthal, again practising as an architect, retained his energetic attitude to life and broad interests in music and urban development (though we might be glad that his ambitious plans for a sweeping re-development of the Rocks and Woolloomooloo did not come off). But the war had forged steel in his soul in some way. D.H. Lawrence is said to have used Rosenthal as the model for the authoritarian demagogue Benjamin Cooley in his 1923 novel, *Kangaroo*. A sometime Nationalist member of the NSW Parliament, Rosenthal took an interest in the idea of a war memorial museum, and supported it by lecturing. Garry and Berta met Web Gilbert and Mabel at Rosenthal's lecture, 'hoping to see dear old Frank' in his slides. They were disappointed, but Garry must have seen the photographs already, including those taken by Hubert Wilkins, since he had already ordered dozens from the War Museum to be glued into the Record Books.

In February 1919, Garry heard through the Red Cross from a man who had not seen Frank killed, but had been among the party that buried him and helped Arch Green to erect a cross over it.⁶⁵ Jack Castle later told Garry that he remembered seeing Arch Green punching the names of the dead onto tin sheets.⁶⁶ Gilbert saw this cross when he visited 'dear old Frank's grave' in the first winter after the war. He later told Garry that the original cross ('with the names written by nail point through a sheet of tin') would have been collected for the War Memorial but—extraordinarily—'it was thought to be too personal and sad'.⁶⁷ Fortunately, this view did not prevail. The cross that Gilbert had photographed lying beside the grave but which he thought 'too personal' did, in fact, become part of the War Memorial's collection.

Indeed, by the time Garry had received Gilbert's letter, the Australian War Records Section had collected it from the graveside and carried it to a collecting depot to return to Australia. The details of the cross's journey from Péronne to Melbourne are obscure; but it is clear that, once it arrived, John Treloar immediately saw the cross as a symbol of the link between the relics he had collected and the idea of remembrance that was at the heart of his museum. Garry soon learned of its arrival. He suggested to Treloar that it would be a 'gracious act' if he could send copies of a photograph of it to the families of the men who had shared Frank's grave. Treloar accepted at once, and copies went out to suburban Melbourne, rural Victoria, Alberta and Aberdeenshire, to addresses that Garry provided.

The replies that Treloar received hint at the depth of the emotions that the photographs stirred up. Alex Walker's father wrote from far off Rosehearty to say that the photograph had arrived 'in excellent condition', and that he and Janet Walker 'appreciate your kindness very much'. The words surely do not convey the depth of emotion they felt. Those closer to Melbourne visited the museum to thank Treloar in person, and to see the cross. John Blackmore let slip that he and members of his family had visited the museum several times, describing how they 'seemed to get riveted to that spot' in front of the cross that bore his son's name.[68]

The Robertses kept in close contact with John Treloar. He invited Garry and Berta to the official opening of the Memorial in Melbourne in April 1922. Characteristically, Garry clipped articles about the new museum for his Record Book. Did Garry and Berta visit the War Memorial to look at the cross, standing perhaps in busy exhibition galleries or in crowded store rooms to look upon, or even touch, the wooden marker that represented their greatest loss? Garry's vast papers, so detailed on external matters, are strangely silent on this most intimate moment. In 1999, by serendipity, it became part of the permanent display in the memorial's 'exit corridor' as a reminder of the sacrifice of war. Those who selected it for display had no idea of the rich story of loss it represented.

Many of the 100,000 people who visited the museum in its first ten weeks were returned men, including some of the Melbourne members of Nine Platoon. Jack Castle visited a couple of months after it opened. 'They have a fine collection of things', he told Garry—so many that Jack and his wife Ethel did not have time to see all of it, but they were going again. But Jack did seek out the Mont St Quentin diorama, which he thought 'splendid!'

'INSET PICTURE MODEL NO. 5': THE MONT ST QUENTIN DIORAMA

In their billet at Querrieu, Charles Bean and Will Dyson had conjured up the idea of what they called 'picture models', the perspective models that are still among the most popular of the War Memorial's exhibits. Treloar credited the idea to Bean, who advised on the selection of subjects and the progress of the scheme, and believed it to be second only in importance to the collection of the AIF's unit war diaries as a record of the force's achievements. The first of them is connected to the story of Nine Platoon's part in the fight for the Mont. Besides sculpting the memorial that was to be erected on Mont St Quentin, Charles Web Gilbert was to create the first of what were initially called 'inset picture models'; later 'dioramas'. The subject of 'inset picture model no. 5' (in fact, the first to be created) was the attack on Mont St Quentin.

Treloar thought that models should befit inclusion in a memorial (hence the selection of fine artists to create them), but also—practically—that they should be able to be transported from where they were begun in Europe to where they would be completed and displayed in Australia. By early 1919, he proposed depicting six of the AIF's most important actions in large picture models, at first envisaged as six feet wide, later on a much grander scale. Of the six models first envisaged, only Mont St Quentin and two smaller models (Pozières and Ypres–Broodseinde) were completed. Why Mont St Quentin should have been selected above all is unknown: perhaps the battlefield struck Bean and Treloar as strongly as it did Frank Brewer.

Gilbert, now a lieutenant in the AIF, embraced this task eagerly. He travelled to France to inspect the site of this (and other battles), taking photographs and making sketches so he could translate the scene of the action into a sculpted perspective model that would suggest what it had been like. The modelling section camped on the battlefields, working in bitter cold, slogging along muddy roads to try to record the terrain, finding trouble in obtaining everything from modelling supplies to maps and aerial photographs. At last, the weather improved and they completed the first plaster 'draft' model of Mont St Quentin. After all this, the model was almost destroyed at Péronne when a passing train hit the case protecting it and spun it around on the platform. It was not the first time that the model would be physically endangered.

But what would the diorama depict? Treloar's initial scheme had specified that it was to show the 6th Brigade attacking at dawn—the second attack, the one the 21st Battalion watched 'in support'. At the same time, his instructions gave the modellers latitude to depict 'dawn or such time when 6th Brigade were attacking forward slope, before reaching summit', which fitted the afternoon attack just as well. Someone—Bean or Treloar—later amended 'dawn' to '1.30'.[69] Certainly Bean had to referee a spat between Wilkins and Gilbert, who had recorded and interpreted the 1 September attacks in photographs and in a diorama respectively. They disagreed about whether the diorama should show the 21st or the 23rd Battalions. Wilkins's photographs were a key source for the diorama's construction. He recalled taking photographs of the 23rd, while Gilbert carried a torch for the 21st, partly at least because of his connection with Frank and Garry Roberts. Bean (who knew that men of both battalions climbed out of Elsa Trench, and no doubt knew from the colour patches that Wilkins had photographed men of the 21st, such as James Sullivan) diplomatically decided that 'probably both Wilkins and Gilbert are right'. Bean decided that the photograph of the troops approaching the brick wall were probably of the 21st, and that the figures in Elsa Trench in the diorama should be '23rd … with some of the 21st working up near … the left of the wall'.[70] In the event, figures bore the colour patches of the two battalions, satisfying honour equally.

By this time, Gilbert was back in Melbourne (at last able to express his sympathy to the Robertses in person) on the War Memorial's staff and working on the full-scale diorama. Visitors to his Fitzroy studio found his twin boys, Hugo and Charles, playing with German machine-guns, used by Gilbert as prototypes for his model. It changed as he worked his way into the task. Photographs of Gilbert's first 'draft' diorama are quite different from the one eventually installed. He sought Treloar's permission to extend it, but also reduced the number of figures included. He kept up with Garry, sending him photographs of the model, which Garry then pasted into his scrapbooks, to go with the stories about it that he clipped from the illustrated papers.

Dioramas had previously been regarded more as fairground attractions than as means to communicate historical interpretation. The ones that Bean, Dyson, and Treloar envisaged were versions of a novel and risky form of conveying history—'it has never been done yet', Bean wrote to Treloar soon after their talk at Querrieu.[71] 'Much depends upon the first model', an *Age* reporter observed.[72] Gilbert worked closely with Treloar, experimenting with materials and techniques, even introducing shrubs loaned by the Botanic Gardens into the foreground of the diorama—it has to be said, unsuccessfully. (The diorama's background was more successful, rendered by Louis McCubbin, who had painted the battlefield in the pre-dawn darkness of 1 September.) Gilbert's intention was not to be 'scientifically accurate'. It was to offer 'a graphic reproduction of the battlefield ... easily identifiable by the soldiers who took part'.[73] This proved to be the case, and not just for an admiring Jack Castle. A *Herald* reporter watched other AIF men stand 'spellbound', one saying 'There's the very spot where I was knocked', and another, 'I hopped over that very bit of parapet'.[74] Gilbert confirmed that the diorama depicted the moment when 'the second wave is just leaving the trenches'.[75] This was the wave that Nine Platoon was a part of, and the one that Hubert Wilkins joined. It was the wave in which Gilbert's young friend Frank had been killed.

Gilbert did not go on to create the ambitious program of dioramas that Treloar and Bean had planned. Soon after the museum opened in Melbourne, cabinet disallowed the nine-year contract that the memorial proposed. Gilbert, 'overwhelmed with offers and opportunities for private work', decided that he did not need to be mucked about by bureaucracy, and resigned.[76] He completed several other major works: *The Wheel of Life* at the University of Melbourne; the Melbourne memorial to Matthew Flinders; and the monumental *Australian soldier*, Broken Hill's war memorial, unveiled within days of his death, in October 1925. Mabel, with three young children and nearly destitute, was allowed to sell back to the War Memorial the plasticine, tow, and copper wire in her late husband's studio and returned to Britain.[77]

The diorama remained on display in the memorial, in Melbourne, in Sydney, and in Canberra, for most of the succeeding ninety years. The memorial continued to encounter problems, particularly over the figures. Gilbert had cast them in plasticine, but they drooped and broke away from their wire stands (or 'armatures'). The sculptor Wallace Anderson and the artist George Lambert took an interest in the problem, disagreeing over whether they should be re-cast in plaster or bronze—the more robust and durable bronze (championed by Lambert) won out.

It was just as well. The diorama seemed jinxed. Having almost been scuppered by a French goods train in 1919, twenty years later (when the memorial's relics and dioramas were being installed in its new building in Canberra) a barrow-load of bricks fell through a skylight, and smashed figures and landscape. Ironically, the builders responsible were Simmie & Co.—Jock Simmie had served with the 21st and was a benefactor of the Association, but he paid up £28.16 for repairs very reluctantly. Leslie Bowles (the sculptor supervising the installation) complained that, 'if I had known he was such a bad payer I'd have charged him more'.[78]

With the opening of Gilbert's diorama in the War Memorial in Melbourne, Mont St Quentin's place in history seemed secure. Monash's *Australian Victories in France* had enshrined it as 'the finest single feat of the war'. Not for a further twenty years would anything more substantial be published about the battle. The battle of Mont St Quentin was in the past. What lay in the future was the rest of the lives of Nine Platoon.

PART IV
Remembering

Shadows of a Battle

As they returned from the Great War, the survivors of Nine Platoon faced the challenge of getting on with their lives. Some came back to families and jobs, to support and respect, but also to responsibilities and pressures that they had not known for several years. All must have been affected by their war service—not that its effects were apparent immediately or obviously. Manning Clark, who grew to be one of Australia's greatest historians, was a child in the years following the war. He remembered seeing returned men 'break down and cry' when they met, able only to console each other with 'I know, Charl., I know'. Children like him, coming suddenly upon men in distress, were told, 'He's ... crying. Can't stop ... don't be frightened'.[1] Seeing men in tears, or women in black, was a common, unremarked part of that time.

Edith Alston, who returned to Melbourne from Paris early in 1920, at last met the Robertses. 'Norrie' Norwood had described Miss Alston and her sister to the Robertses as 'congenial, broadminded & intelligent women', and they shared everyone's affection for Frank.[2] Garry and Berta were able to hear from Miss Alston her memories of her guest in

Paris in March 1918. Garry passed on the various accounts he had collected from the men of Frank's platoon and, like Guy Innes, she was struck by Jack Castle's account. Horrified by his matter-of-fact description of the fight for the Mont, she asked Garry 'how can these men settle down again?'[3]

But 'settle down' they did. 'Funny how most of our battalion chaps have married since they returned, isn't it?' wrote Norrie to the Robertses.[4] Despite whatever daytime visions or nightmares they grappled with, the returned men of Mont St Quentin did get on with life. Most married and had children, inevitably becoming preoccupied with the struggle to earn a living and to rear their family. All but Charlie Tognella and Noble Norwood married early in the 1920s; coincidentally, two to women they met in Britain (Ethel Castle in England and Anne Edwards in Scotland).

But it cannot have been easy to live with a returned man. An official photograph of King George V ('H.M. the King' to them) inspecting men of the 6th Brigade after Mont St Quentin suggested something of the standing of their feat. The photograph, available as an 'enlargement in Natural Colour', featured in the exhibition by the Colourgraph Art Company of Windsor, Victoria, entitled *The Hundred Best Photographs of the World War*, which toured Australia in the early 1920s. The entrepreneur behind this venture had an eye for photographs that depicted the war as noble and picturesque—a reassuring impression for both returned men and bereaved families. 'What could be a more suitable present for a returned soldier's bride', he asked, 'than a coloured enlargement of one of these pictures?'[5] What indeed? But it seems unlikely that the brides of the Nine Platoon survivors would have agreed. Even if they did not have a reminder of their husbands' war hanging on the wall, they had surely married it anyway.

Of Nine Platoon's nine survivors, we know least about

Alf Crawford, the Delegate labourer who wrote the shortest account for Garry Roberts. Alf's Repat file has been lost, though his story can be pieced together from family memories. Alf returned to Gippsland in 1919, married, and had three children. But his marriage broke down, and caring for his children seems to have been beyond a man who worked as a labourer for the Main Roads Department. Alf's sons went into care, his daughter fostered by a relative. He had been gassed in 1918, suffered from respiratory complaints and, in 1945, became the first member of Nine Platoon to die after the war. Thanks to the survival of the records, we can trace in greater detail how other Nine Platoon men reacted to the challenges of coming home. The most pressing need for all of them was a job—sadly, Roy Smerdon had anticipated that need in a postcard he sent to his family in Murrayville from near Querrieu in 1918: 'will you give an old soldier a job?'

'I MAY BE ABLE TO EARN A LIVELIHOOD': CHARLIE TOGNELLA

Helped ashore from the ambulance transport *Somerset*, Charlie Tognella was the first of the Mont St Quentin men to return to Victoria. He went back to the area around Graytown that he had left in 1916 as a wood-cutter earning ten shillings a day, and began looking for work. He told the Repat that he needed no help in finding it. A Repat clerk asked him 'Employment desired', and he told the clerk 'Labor'. Charlie's chest wound—the most serious wound of the survivors of the platoon that had fought on 1 September—left him 'permanently unfit', but gave him a pension of only a pound a week, so he needed to work. For a time he thought little more about it, but soon discovered that his wound had changed everything. In August 1919, he completed a statement for the Repat:

My prospects as regards future employment are not good, as on account of the wound received on active service I am unable to do any work of a laborious nature. On several occasions I have tried to do fairly heavy work, but have had to knock off after a couple of days as I was unable to continue working. If my health improves I can get very light work I may be able to earn a livelihood.[6]

Charlie Tognella was not shamming. A local official endorsed his statement, affirming that 'I do not think he has refused any offer of employment'—Charlie was 'a sober steady man'. But his doctor confirmed that the bullet that had smashed into Charlie's chest had damaged his lung and left him feeling pain in his shoulderblade—a handicap for a man who had always been a woodcutter and had very few options. (Charlie was virtually illiterate and did not, for example, know his birthdate.) As a returned man, life for Charlie was to get much harder.

'I WISH THAT I COULD FORGET': NOBLE NORWOOD

Noble Norwood returned briefly to Melbourne, where he offered his commiserations to Garry and Berta. The book department of Boan's department store in Perth gave him his old job back, and he obtained a railway warrant to return to the west by the new Trans-Continental railway. Back in Perth, he felt restless. The Repatriation Department agreed to fund courses in book and magazine illustrating (through the Perth branch of the 'International Correspondence School' of London), but Norrie confessed that he did not think he could settle down until he had seen more of the world: Sydney, New Zealand, even South America. 'Do you think I am selfish …?', he asked

Garry. His mentor evidently pressed Norrie to think of settling down, but he remained wary. He had had a 'misunderstanding' with a girl in Melbourne soon after returning. He defaulted on his obligations to both the Correspondence School and to the Repat, whose local commissioner, a Gallipoli veteran, remained patient in granting extensions and exceptions. When he submitted work, the college gave him high marks—94 or 96 per cent—but he finished few courses.[7]

Norrie decided to go into business on his own account, setting up a music and book shop in Baird's Arcade in Perth. Within months he had employed a 'young lady' pianist to promote his sheet music, and before Christmas sold a hundred copies of the music to Valentino's *The Sheik*, then playing in Perth.[8] He continued to correspond with Garry, possibly because he confessed that he felt lonely so far away, 'not knowing any of the men who I met in France'. He owned up to some of the symptoms of what today we would call post-traumatic stress. When Garry pressed him for further details of Frank and Mont St Quentin, Norrie wrote that 'there are some things I want to forget'. But he also described seeing visions of France and of dead comrades:

> Curiously enough, quite often during my daily work, there comes before my eyes a scene in France—as plainly as the real thing—and such things depress me. I wish that I could forget. I cannot exactly explain these visions—for visions they are—but they are most real, and several times Frank has figured in them.[9]

Norrie reassured Garry that 'there are many things that I do not want to forget', including Frank's comradeship.

'I NEVER HEARD FROM ANY OF THE BOYS': VIC EDWARDS

Like Norrie, Vic Edwards had returned to another state, travelling to his brother's house in Launceston. Before the war, Vic had been employed as a labourer at £3 a week. He registered with Repat's Tasmanian office, where an official minuted that he was 'endeavouring to get employment and seems anxious to get settled down again into civilian life'. Vic was healthy, proud that he was 'never in hospital [in] 4 years continuous service'. The best he could do, at first, was to get work as a carpenter's assistant at 10/- a day, which was rather less than he had made labouring before the war. He applied for an allotment of land under the *Returned Soldiers' Settlement Act*, but was unlucky to miss out—or perhaps not, given the sorry history of so many soldier settlers.[10] Soon, Vic also wrote to Garry, from the remote hamlet of Weldborough, that he had married. Anne McIntyre—known to her new family as Nan—was a Scottish woman who had followed him to Australia. Vic did not tell Garry his wife's name, but did say he 'like[d] the life tip top'.[11]

Having returned to Tasmania, Vic was cut off from the comradeship he had known in the battalion. 'I never heard from any of the boys since I came home', he wrote to Garry when he sent his account of Mont St Quentin in February 1920.[12] Peace brought sadness rather than solace. The Edwardses lost a baby the following year, but the stoicism Vic had learned in the war had uses in peace, though Nan may not have felt the same way. On or just before the first of September 1921, Garry posted out a fresh batch of memorial cards. They stimulated cards and letters in reply. Vic Edwards, writing from the Tasmanian bush, wrote to thank Garry: 'One can hardly realise that three years have passed since that day I lost so many of my Comrades.' And he told his wife—still unnamed in his letters to Garry—about them.[13]

Except for those able to secure steady positions, such as working on the Tramways, work remained uncertain for many men. Les Baker and Charlie Tognella depended on casual work, and were out of work for weeks at a time; and Vic, a casual timber-getter, worried about timber mills closing—in 1922, he told Garry that 'this year I think I will cut out all the Blackwood in this part'.[14] As an unwounded, healthy man, Vic did not apply for a war pension. In fact, in 1930 he asked the Repat to confirm that he had never sought one, to counter 'some malicious person with a view to injuring me in business' who had 'made the false statement that I am receiving a full war pension'. But his independence meant that he left few records besides his details on the electoral roll. His family recall that he and Nan did well, taking over the post office at Weldborough from 1923, and in the early 1930s buying a bakery at Railton.

'TROUBLE & WORRYS': TOM WIGNALL

Tom Wignall's grenade wound in the stomach left him 'permanently unfit', as the 'Medical Report on an Invalid' described him in 1919. He received a pension based on the calculation that he had lost three-quarters of his earning capacity. Formerly a gardener, he could no longer bend or stoop, sought 'private tuition' in clerical work, and by 1920 was working for the Red Cross at its MacLeod Sanatorium. Tom wrote to apologise for not visiting Garry from nearby Malvern, explaining that he had become a father, with all that entailed. 'You know what trouble & worrys a man has to go through when he receives that honour', he wrote.[15] Tom's worries grew when, first, his infant son and then his wife fell ill. After two 'serious operations' and several months off work, he had to sell his house in Malvern and shift in with his in-laws in Northcote. This was just for a few weeks, he thought optimistically, but it turned out to be for a longer time. Tom's worries were internal as well as external. Wearing an elastic belt to support his scarred stomach, and suffering from daily headaches, he ate carefully to avoid bloating, diarrhoea, and indigestion. 'Bomb specks' prevented him from gripping anything firmly, and he suffered from occasional tremors in the right hand. Even so, he lost no time from sickness. Not until 1960 did Tom apply for a Repat pension and, as we will see, he became the only one of Nine Platoon to seek out the company of his wartime comrades over the coming years.

'HONEST AND TRYING': LES BAKER

Les Baker returned to Agnes and his five children, and almost immediately fathered a sixth, Beryl. He began looking for work around Ringwood. AIF men were entitled to a 'War Gratuity' of 1/6d per day of service. Les's gratuity (according to a ready-reckoner in a pamphlet, *All About the War Gratuity*, written by none other than Frank Brewer, back home and working as a journalist) was about £109.[16] Most men took their gratuities in war bonds, but those in 'necessitous circumstances' were allowed to take cash. Les was among them. He used his gratuity to build his own weatherboard house, just by the railway line—Garry and Berta passed within fifty yards of it when they travelled between Hawthorn and Belgrave.

The shell that exploded in the 21st Battalion's bivouac on the banks of the Somme on the day before the battle left Les with shrapnel scars above and below his right knee. His fortnightly pension was the same as Jack Castle's, plus amounts of between 2/6 and 7/6 for the children. This was about a quarter of the maximum rate, but the total—£2/8/6—was far less than the minimum wage of about £4 a week. Les still had to seek work, to support his family and to re-establish their home. While he was away, Agnes had been forced to sell their furniture (pressed by debts, she could not store it), so, late in 1919 Les applied for a loan from the Repatriation Commission of £34/18/2 to buy furniture, repayable at 10/- a month.

By April 1921 he was 'considerably overdue', unresponsive to reminder letters from the local repatriation committee, whose voluntary members oversaw its work. Its secretary reported that Les was out of work but had promised to make a payment within a month. He recommended 'lenient treatment'. By December 1922, though, Les was 25 instalments in arrears. The committee organised a local whip round and repaid ten pounds, explaining to the deputy commissioner in Melbourne that 'he has a large family and is [still] trying to pay off the timber for the house which he has built'. They again asked for lenience. By this time, Les owed six pounds in interest on top of the original loan, and early in 1922 the commission warned that it might have to re-possess the furniture.

In the winter of 1922, a Repat 'Senior Business Inspector' visited Les and Agnes's house to assess their assets. He found they had a boiler and two saucepans, a table, eight blankets, and a quilt (but only three mattresses and one pillow), a dinner service but only six table knives, and 17 yards of lino. He asked around Ringwood, and learned that Les was regarded as 'a hardworking & honest man'. Six months later, and after Les defaulted again, the inspector recommended another reprieve—the Bakers' assets were, he reported 'worthless'. He called repeatedly, in July 1924 finding that the dinner service was even smaller than before.

Les was 'honest and trying': Agnes said he was 'straight and a good father'. But he was in and out of work, had six children under fourteen, and was 'not getting enough to pay for sufficient food for my family'. He confessed that he could not pay anything off the loan. The Repat inspectors took pity on Les, and simply wrote off the debt. There the report ends; but, as we will see, life never got much easier for Les and Agnes and their six children.

'MADE POSSIBLE OUR FUTURE': GODFREY DOBSON

For several men, their main problem was to find work, and Garry Roberts's patronage became invaluable—for Jack Castle, Les Baker, and Godfrey Dobson especially. Garry had already helped men in various small ways when he sought out the returning men early in 1919. Godfrey Dobson became a serial supplicant. In the winter of 1920 he wrote to Garry, apologising for again asking for help, but he explained that he had become disillusioned working at his old trade of lithographer. His employer, while benefiting from his skill, refused to pay him as a journeyman, even though he was '100% efficient'. Godfrey asked if Garry could find him work with the Tramways Trust—he would 'tackle anything at all', he said.[17] The risk paid off. In the winter of 1922, Godfrey wrote to pass on the news that he was 'doing well'. He had 'not been on the mat once since job started'. He, too, was to be married, to Janet. Godfrey and Janet 'often talk of you ... it was your kindness and interest in me that made possible our future'.[18]

By 1925 the Dobsons were living in a 'Type (5) State Savings Bank house' in the new outer-Melbourne suburb of Maidstone. Godfrey and Janet hoped, as he coyly put it, for 'provision for an additional seat at the table'. Godfrey was working on the trams at the Footscray Depot, where he was 'Third Delegate' on the shop committee. He was disillusioned with what life post-war had brought. He thought life 'sham & shoddy', especially his fellow tram employees. He had become 'sick & tired of hearing men use the word comrade'. A year later, writing again in September, he proudly told Garry that he and

Janet had had 'a bonza boy', Kenneth. But still thinking of the war, he 'very often' wondered 'whether it was all worthwhile'. He had felt like 'jumping up & starting a fight'.[19] But he did not: Godfrey stood for election on the local council. With the support of other returned men, he 'romped in'.

Godfrey Dobson had occasion to visit the employment section at Anzac House. There, in a badly lit underground passage, he found the place crowded with returned men seeking work. 'Many of them were poorly clad and looked half-starved'. Godfrey mused darkly on the cruel hand that fate had dealt some former comrades. 'The multitude has soon forgotten the lessons of those times', he thought, 'and does not like to be reminded'. Still, he was grateful to Garry. 'We have never looked back since that time you extended a helping hand', he told Garry, 'along with you and others who gave of their dearest … there are those who will never forget'.[20]

'A RUN OF BAD LUCK': JACK CASTLE

Jack Castle had returned from the war minus a finger—it had been amputated in 1917 after he had been wounded on the Somme in 1916—but with a British wife, Ethel. The missing finger was worth a pension of 30/- for himself and Ethel, which was a quarter of the maximum rate. He still needed to work, but for much of 1919 looked fruitlessly for employment. He sought Garry's help, and in November 1919 the Tramways Trust offered him a labouring job at £3 a week. A year later, Jack gratefully wrote 'just a few lines' to let Garry know that he and Ethel were settled in West Brunswick, with a garden, a lawn, vegie patch, and fowl pen.[21]

Hints in letters to Garry disclose what men were too proud or embarrassed to tell him. Late in 1921, Tom Wignall let slip that Jack was 'having a run of bad luck'.[22] Garry was prepared to help out Frank's comrades. Alf Fox, now also married and with a son, Bobbie, wrote to tell him he had 'got over that business trouble I told you of'—perhaps after Garry had lent advice, a word to a bank manager, or even money.[23] Jack Castle, too, had asked for help over an insurance claim, because he had unknowingly served under a pseudonym. His birth name, he learned, had been Gordon Stewart Castle. He decided to continue to use Jack and to save 'Gordon Stewart' for Sunday best.

Nine Platoon men continued to write to Garry and Berta occasionally—after a gap of three years, Jack Castle wrote to let him know that 'our trouble is over. We have got a Daughter'.[24] The Castles continued to visit the Robertses throughout the 1920s. Most did not: the war became a memory, as families, jobs, and houses claimed the returned men's immediate attention. By the late 1920s most of the Nine Platoon men no longer had regular contact with the Robertses. Norrie Norwood, for example, briefly returned to Melbourne in the winter of 1928, as a member of the Margaret Bannerman theatrical company, and the understudy to the leading man in a drama playing in a city theatre. The theatre did not appeal to Norrie. It was 'an unpleasant sort of life, and not always harmonious', and he gave it up to return to the west. He seems to have seen the Robertses once, and never again.[25] As Garry's list of visitors shows, Jack Castle visited occasionally with Ethel and their children ('Frank's mate in C Company ... with Frank when he was killed', Garry added to one of Jack's letters).[26] Ethel and Jack sent cards to Garry and Berta on New Year 1933, which was to be Garry's last. The bonds of wartime grief loosened as time passed.

'THE RED ZONE': MONT ST QUENTIN AFTER THE WAR

Engaged to create the first of the 'inset picture models' for the war museum, Gilbert had no sooner accepted Rosenthal's commission than he tried to defer doing anything about it for a year while he shivered and sketched on the battlefields. Australia House tried to persuade Rosenthal that having Gilbert on the battlefields might even turn the delay to advantage. Before shelving the sculpting of the memorial in favour of the diorama, Gilbert had at least decided what form the memorial should take. Word of the 2nd Division memorial aroused interest among editors and journalists. Many stories appeared, many of which Garry clipped. They showed a striking design—a hatless Australian soldier driving a bayonet into the breast of a crowned Prussian eagle, the most vigorous of the five divisional memorials that the AIF left in France. Not everyone admired Gilbert's bellicose design. Charles Bean, who believed that memorials should not perpetuate wartime enmity, told John Treloar it was 'a cheap conception' that 'bears no shadow of the spirit of the AIF'.[27]

By mid-1921, Gilbert, now back in Australia, was working on the clay figure that formed the first part of the process of creating the memorial figure. He used Corporal Roy Guest of the 11th Battalion as his model for the uniform and kit, though making the finished figure's torso more 'classically' proportioned than the stocky Corporal Guest's. 'I am not a photographer', Gilbert said; 'I might as well make a plaster cast of him'. Whether the idea of giving the figure Frank's face survived to the final memorial is unclear. Photographs of Gilbert's drawings, the maquette, the clay figure, and the final cast figure are not sufficiently clear. Meanwhile, May Butler-George had started work in Britain, visiting the artillery depot at Woolwich to sketch the field guns that she felt she had to get right. She, too, was soon to return to Australia, and by 1923 was at work in Melbourne.

When French civil servants came began to assess the extent of devastation in war-ravaged regions, they shaded the worst areas in red on their planning maps. Péronne and Mont St Quentin lay in the centre of what was to be called 'The Red Zone'. In the summer of 1919, a 'special correspondent' from *The Times* made a 500-mile tour of the old Western Front, investigating the continuing work of finding and re-burying the dead. Already, he reported, British empire war graves units had registered 375,000 graves—more bodies than had served overseas with the AIF in total. At first, graves lay in over 1200 plots, although war graves units gradually consolidated them into fewer, larger graveyards. Péronne became the headquarters of the southern area of the British zone, which included a thousand men of Australian war graves parties.[28] Péronne's mayor asked that the town's ruins be cleared of graves so that the task of re-building could continue unimpeded.

In the country, nature made the graves units' work more difficult. Tall grass and nettles grew over shell-pocked fields, making it hard to find traces of graves. The Australian journalist Boyd Cable, a former gunner, rode his motorcycle along the old front line in search of 'The Vanishing Front', and found farm buildings on hillsides that he remembered as having been bare, villages reappearing, and woods—low but dense—where he recalled only scatterings of naked stumps. Cable visited Péronne. He described the little suburbs of ex-army Nissen huts standing outside the town. Within the ruined ramparts, he found many houses being rebuilt. The new houses, hotels, and shops, he thought, seemed 'all very spick-and-span and new-looking, giving rather the effect of an imitation town erected all of a sudden for some sort of exhibition or fair'. On the main square, the Hôtel de Ville remained untouched, the church of

St Jean still lacking a fourth wall, his hotel 'brand new from cellar to roof'.[29] Indeed, much of Péronne is physically no older than the communities that Nine Platoon had left—Murrayville, Curdies River, or Hawthorn.

When, like John and Bertha Monash, Boyd Cable travelled to France on the boat train from Victoria, he noticed in the dining car other travellers poring over trench maps, pinpointing the cemeteries they sought. Here were the first bereaved families searching for the graves of their dead. By the middle of 1920 the *Times* could mention 'the battlefield tourist', observing that the French called them 'pilgrims'.[30]

The first member of a family of the 21st Battalion's Mont St Quentin dead to visit was probably Mr Andrew Staaf, father of Gustaf Staaf of Echuca. He had relatives in Sweden, and visited France en route, making a point of visiting Péronne in 1922. Mr Staaf wrote to Garry to tell him that he had visited their sons' graves, and enclosed a poppy picked from the slopes of Mont St Quentin. Handling the poppy and fixing it in the Record Book was as close as Garry was ever to get to Frank's grave.

Norrie Norwood, the most assiduous of the platoon's correspondents, asked Garry 'do you still contemplate going to France?'[31] Garry and Berta must have discussed making such a visit. Presumably, they made enquiries and discovered that the cost would be prohibitive—perhaps £400, about the Robertses' annual income after Garry's retirement.

But Garry never stopped thinking of Frank's grave, and continued to collect and annotate photographs of it. In 1928, the Church Army sent him a photograph of the grave in the communal cemetery, now showing neat rows of headstones and a garden. His brother William visited France in 1926, and placed flowers on Frank's grave. He was 'very proud' when he saw Gilbert's sculpture bearing Frank's likeness.[32]

Just as the countryside of the Somme became green again, with trees growing and trenches filled in, so time also softened the raw edges of grief. From 1919 to 1926, Garry and Berta always placed *in memoriam* notices in Frank's memory in both the *Age* and the *Argus*. Often 'his friends' placed them—members of the Sunnyside set, Robert Croll and the artist John Shirlow—and former comrades such as Tom Wignall and Jack Castle. Garry kept in touch with the families of the men who had shared Frank's grave. In September 1921, he received letters or cards from the Staafs, Bottomleys, Copes, and Ann Smerdon, who wrote to say that it had rained, and that the first aeroplane to visit Murrayville had caused great excitement, until it crashed. But that contact, too, came to an end by the mid-1920s. For all of the shared emotion of *in memoriam* notices, bereavement was a private feeling: it was hard to share on paper, even with those who had themselves experienced it.

Web Gilbert's statue, and May Butler-George's reliefs adorning its base, were unveiled by Marshal Ferdinand Foch on 31 August 1925, more or less the seventh anniversary of the battle. Ceremonies of remembrance continued to be held at the memorial on the Mont on 1 September, and were occasionally reported by the Melbourne newspapers. In 1932, for example, Major Frank Berryman (who had joined Rosenthal's headquarters at Cappy immediately after the battle) travelled from the Staff College at Camberley to represent Australia. But who was the memorial for? Hardly any Australians and almost no veterans were able to visit the Mont between the world wars. Not for about fifty years would any substantial group of veterans return to the Mont.

'THIS WILL INTEREST YOU, ROBERTS':
MONT ST QUENTIN AND THE OFFICIAL HISTORY

Charles Bean devoted his life to establishing the war memorial museum that became the Australian War Memorial, and to writing the official history. He worked chronologically, finishing his first Gallipoli volume in 1921, but not publishing the final volume, on the second half of 1918, until 1942. Garry had already sent Bean one of the hundreds of memorial cards for Frank. Bean replied politely that he was glad to have it—which was probably true—and that 'it may be of help later on', which was gilding the lily somewhat. Three years and one week after the battle, Garry and Berta Roberts were taking tea with Charles Gilbert and his wife, Mabel. Gilbert passed to Garry a letter from Charles Bean to John Treloar, saying, 'This will interest you, Roberts'. In it, Bean adjudicated in the dispute between Gilbert and Hubert Wilkins about which battalions should be depicted in the Mont St Quentin diorama. By coincidence, Garry had visited the War Memorial's temporary displays in the Exhibition Building earlier that day. Garry grasped that here was a chance to ensure that Frank's memory could be preserved fittingly. The following day, he gathered some of the papers he had been collecting for almost three years and sat down to write again to Charles Bean.

By the spring of 1921, Bean had been at work for just over two years. Knowing from almost the outset that he would write something more substantial than newspaper despatches, he had kept a detailed diary throughout the war. He now had over two hundred of them securely stored at Tuggeranong, the sheep property near Canberra where he was writing the second Gallipoli volume. Bean's notebooks provided him with the spine of a narrative and with the on-the-spot evidence that, for a time, the official records lacked. Until the amateur soldiers of the AIF learned what to write and file in their official unit war diaries, Bean only had what he had described in his diary as the basis of his history.

By the war's end that dearth was long over. With the appointment of John Treloar as head of the Australian War Records Section in May 1917, Australian units at last began to compile detailed and usable accounts of their actions in and out of battle. For 1918, all sixty Australian battalions were submitting folders several inches thick, including copies of orders, maps, reports, and returns, month-by-month. These records enable us to see the battle from Bernard Duggan's dugout. As the records were shipped back to Australia to the War Memorial's warehouses, Bean and Treloar must have looked on the piles of crates with mixed feelings. Bean's assistants worked their way through this massive stash of documents, noting, copying, and summarising. But even when filleted and gutted, the war diaries still made a mountain of paper. No wonder Bean tended to use only three main sources: his own notebooks, the few published memoirs of senior commanders, and the war diaries. He either had no time for anything else or he decided that he could not afford the time needed to check the veracity of the private records he was offered.

In giving Bean Nine Platoon's accounts, Garry assumed that they would be useful, and used. Garry explained what he had done and why. After Frank's death, Garry had been 'anxious to obtain as full a report as possible of how he died'. He sought out many of Frank's comrades as they returned and 'suggested to a number of them that they should write their experiences of the attack on Mont St Quentin, simply, accurately and in detail'. It was not only for him, but for all the relatives of men who had died in the fight. He obtained photographs from the families of the men killed in the fight, 'fine manly faces, not a weakling amongst them'.[33]

Garry sent to Bean copies of Nine Platoon's statements in July 1922. Bean thanked him for 'the data', and hazarded that it would be 'of considerable value' to him when he came to write the account of the battle in his history.[34] Bean passed at least some of the accounts on — those of Jack Castle and Noble Norwood were bound into the records assembled to help Bean write the official history. He probably looked at them when he drafted the chapters on Mont St Quentin, early in the Second World War, but he did not quote from them. The paragraph he wrote about the third attack shows that he read the accounts, but he gave no hint that he possessed soldiers' versions of what happened on 1 September. While several historians in the early twenty-first century found and discussed the Robertses' story in seeking to understand bereavement, they did not quote or mention the accounts that Frank's comrades left Garry. They are used in this book for the first time.

Bean's chapters on the battle for Mont St Quentin are detailed, but they are not among his best. The battle was complex, and happened across a wide, swiftly changing front. Bean's account, dealing as it does with the doings of battalions and companies, and even platoons, is often confusing. An ailing, ageing man, exhausted by the demands of two decades of intense labour, he was unable to do justice to the later actions of 1918; the final volume is more detailed but much less clear than those dealing with 1916 and 1917. His weariness can be seen in the line he wrote on its completion: 'Now it is there for anyone to do as likes with'. What just about everyone did with Bean's account was to ignore it, though with great respect. No one has investigated the battle in any detail; even this book examines just one small part of it. Mont St Quentin is still ripe for re-evaluation — particularly applying a more astringent eye to Monash's self-serving account and the massive lode of original records still almost untouched. The one conclusion that

Bean offered was concealed beneath what seems a deliberate obfuscation. 'The capture of Mont St Quentin and Péronne', he wrote, 'is held by many Australian soldiers to be the most brilliant achievement of the A.I.F.'. The qualification 'is held by many' is a clue to what he really thought, because he goes on to say that 'Monash himself realised that it was also largely a soldiers' battle'—and therefore not a generals' battle.[35]

'THE LEADER OF THE DISTRICT'S SOCIAL LIFE': GARRY'S LAST YEARS

The official history appeared in 1942, and by then Garry had been dead for a decade. The early 1920s brought further change for the Robertses. In March 1923, Garry retired from the Tramways Trust. It had proposed abolishing his position of 'Manager of the Cable System' and to make him 'Chief Controller of Stores'. Garry consulted Berta and decided that, 'under doctor's advice', he should decline. He disclosed that he had been close to nervous collapse twelve years before, and seems to have feared that at the age of sixty-two the strain of getting on top of a new position would undermine his health. He accepted a generous settlement of four months on full pay and six months of 'retiring allowance' on top of his pension.

By the mid-1920s, the Sunnyside set that the Robertses had known before the war had dispersed—Gilbert was dead, Dennis had moved away, and only Robert Croll remained a steadfast friend. With Garry and Berta ageing and burdened by Frank's death, the Robertses' carefree weekends in the Dandenongs ended. But Garry became friendly with other artists. The great impressionist Tom Roberts returned to Australia in 1923 and settled at 'Talisman', just up the road from Sunnyside, for his last eight years. Roberts painted Garry in gratitude for his help (though the whereabouts of the portrait is unknown), and his friendship with Garry and Berta contains a local connection with Mont St Quentin that seems to have eluded the Robertses. Tom Roberts had been great friends with Arthur Streeton, who also returned to Australia in 1923 and lived some of the time near Olinda, close to Ruby's old home and just a few miles up the track over Beagley's Bridge. As we have seen, Streeton had sketched Mont St Quentin, and then painted the face of the Mont that Tom Wignall's platoon had attacked, including the site of Frank's first grave. *Mont St Quentin* was among the 'war pictures by Mr Arthur Streeton' exhibited at the Victorian Artists' galleries in Melbourne in April 1920; however, Garry and Berta seem to have missed this viewing, though Garry clipped a notice of it.[36]

In 1926, Streeton gave away 117 paintings and drawings that he had produced in France, but none to the memorial. (Charles Bean lamented to Treloar that it had been a pity they had quarrelled with Streeton.) He gave Charles Rosenthal a painting of the Mont and several pencil sketches, and other works to various officers and the remainder to officers' clubs in Sydney and Melbourne. *Mont St Quentin*, a major work, the first listed in the catalogue he published to document his generosity, went to the National Gallery of Victoria, where it remains today. Seven years later, Streeton wrote a conciliatory letter to Bean, telling him that he regretted giving the painting to the National Gallery, 'when it is hardly seen', rather than to the memorial, where it certainly would have become a treasure, like his *Amiens, Key to the West* and *Bellicourt tunnel*, which Bean secured as a job lot for the knock-down price of £350.[37]

Surely Garry would have been interested to see a painting of Mont St Quentin in a Melbourne gallery, a work painted by one of his neighbours? Tom Roberts and Streeton knew each other well. Streeton was a notable figure in Australian art who had painted many works around the Dandenongs, and who had donated a painting of a place precious to the Robertses to the state gallery in Garry's city. But the connection seems to have eluded Garry entirely; it seems that Tom Roberts never mentioned Streeton's *Mont St Quentin* to him. While a reproduction of it appears among other works in one book, there is no mention of Streeton in any of Garry's Record Books. If he had met Streeton, Garry would surely have clipped any reference to him. It seems extraordinary that this connection could have been missed, and sad that Garry and Berta were denied an opportunity to see a painting of Frank's place of death.

Garry became what Tom Roberts's biographer recognised as 'the leader of the district's social life'.[38] He held the first wireless licence in the area, and became a central figure in local organisations, such as the Dramatic Society. In the mid-1920s, he led the push to change the name of South Sassafras to Kallista—South Sassafras was not only nowhere near Sassafras, it was almost unreachable from it. Melbourne businesses would cheerfully and carelessly consign goods to buyers in 'Sassafras', leaving off the 'South', so that items took days longer to arrive. Residents finally decided that they had had enough of this, and pressed for a change. Garry seconded the motion put to the shire to change it to Kallista. Edie Eastaugh, who had been with Gwen when she learned of her brother's death, was by this time classics mistress at Wesley College. Still an occasional weekend guest at Sunnyside, she suggested that 'Kallista' was fitting, being the name of an island in the Aegean meaning 'most beautiful'. The change was accepted, and Garry as ever made sure that the change-of-name ceremony proceeded smoothly.

Garry tried to rationalise his huge collection of Record Books. The Mitchell Library in Sydney declined to buy his hundred Federation Record Books. Further disappointment would follow: despite his friendship with John Treloar, the War Memorial declined to buy any of his Record Books, even those that documented the Gallipoli campaign and the four that traced Frank's war service in particular detail. The memorial was unwilling to pay the asking price—£125—entertaining a quite groundless scepticism that Garry could have assembled anything of value. Someone whom posterity has rendered anonymous minuted in 1932 that 'it would appear unlikely that he would be in possession of any important documents', but did not take the trouble to travel to Kallista to check.[39] Accordingly, twenty-seven of the Record Books, all the Federation volumes, and some of the diaries ended up in the State Library of Victoria, through John Roberts, in about 1940. With the exception of a few odd scrapbooks, Garry's entire 'hand-made encyclopaedia' has vanished.

Early in 1933, Garry Roberts died at his brother's house in Kew. Then Berta moved away, suffering a stroke and dying at her surviving son's house in 1936. Sunnyside was sold, and burnt down in yet another Dandenong bushfire, and within a couple of decades even the remains of the 'bus camp' could not be found on the slopes above Sassafras Creek, though today the property is remembered by the naming of Sunnyside Avenue.

The Roberts family, so close in the happier years 'Before the War', grew apart. Gwen eventually married her fiancé, Geoff Eastaugh (Edie's brother). They lived on a property in the upper Yarra Valley, not well off. A cultured woman, Gwen often lamented the life she found herself living. Johnny (who later threw off his boyhood nicknames and insisted on John) had a tragic life. Having overcome the handicap of his mutilated hand and become a commercial artist (he even published a children's book, *The Little Old Man*, in 1928), he married and had a daughter, but an addiction to gambling drove him and his wife apart. Like his father, he worked for the Metropolitan

Tramways Board, as an engineer, and died in 1967. Sadly, both Gwen and John lost touch with Ruby and Nancy.

'TONS OF LOVE AND HEAPS OF KISSES': RUBY, NANCY, AND THE ROBERTSES

Ruby naturally kept in close touch with Garry and Berta, Nancy's grandparents. Garry helped her apply for Frank's war gratuity, and helped her financially, though she lived with the Barratts at Olinda. But in the early 1920s Ruby unexpectedly disappears from Garry's Record Books. Berta and Garry's *in memoriam* notices for 1926 make no mention of Ruby or Nancy. What had happened?

In fact, Ruby had married again, to Percy Minter, who had served on Gallipoli and in France. Percy had already known the Robertses, and perhaps Frank and Ruby. She remained affectionate — she sent 'tons of love and heaps of kisses' in letters to Garry and Berta, though the Minters moved to Deepdene, closer to Melbourne.[40] Ruby and Percy had a daughter, Barbara, born in November 1923. Percy was an easygoing man, able to cope with the ebullient Robertses and willing to be a part of Ruby's first husband's family. As Garry's Record Books show, he often visited Sunnyside, and in 1929 even drove Berta, Ruby, and her daughters on a motoring holiday through the Western District of Victoria. But Percy was not Frank, and never could be. Ruby thought of Frank every day, her granddaughter recalled. Though a stoic, patient woman, cheerful and loving toward her grandchildren and great-grandchildren, in her old age she soured toward Percy, the man who would never measure up to her beloved Frank.

Nancy appears in the Record Books in her own right early in 1921, with a drawing, by which time Ruby was living in a house named 'St Yves' — the name that Frank had chosen.

What, one wonders, did Percy feel about that? As she grew up, Nancy came to stay with her grandparents at Sunnyside. Garry and Berta talked to her about the man she came to call 'daddy Frank'. By 1929, on the eleventh anniversary of her father's death, Nancy was old enough to write on her own account. She wrote to her Grandpa and Grandma that 1 September of how she was 'thinking of you today particularly and also daddy Frank'. Garry and Berta encouraged Nancy to think of Frank. In November 1929, Robert Croll published a eulogy about Frank ('Hated War but not Afraid to Fight'), but refused to take a fee for it. Garry used the fee to buy books for Nancy, including *The Sentimental Bloke* by C.J. Dennis, 'who esteemed and loved your father'. Garry wanted Nancy to 'feel proud of your father with his brave, loving and intellectual nature'.[41] The book, with photographs, clippings, and eulogies pasted in, is now owned by Nancy's daughter, Jilba. It represents how Ruby, Nancy, and Jilba remained conscious of the literary and artistic heritage they owed to the Robertses, and through them to the Sunnyside set.

Nancy left school in her teens, obliged to work as a secretary. She married in 1942, but the marriage did not last. Barbara, who became engaged to an airman shot down over Berlin in 1943, never married. She died young, of cancer, in 1967. Ruby, who herself had lost so much in the Great War, saw a second war rob one daughter of a husband and another of happiness. It seemed that the two great tragedies of twentieth-century Australia conspired to blight the lives of the Roberts women.

'LET'S BE COBBERS EVERYONE': THE 21ST BATTALION ASSOCIATION

Like many units, the 21st had formed a battalion association before the war's end. Bill Power, a Gallipoli man, called a meeting to form an association, in the Equitable Building in Collins Street on 28 October 1918—presumably before news of the 21st's demise reached Melbourne. Bill was to become the single most influential figure in the association: it and he were to live as long as the other. Its patrons were its colonels Frederick Forbes and Bernard Duggan (two of its three wartime commanders). One of the association's first tasks was to produce a battalion history. Captain Alexander MacNeil, its vice-president, began work soon after returning home. He wrote and the association published what he called 'a short, crisp narrative' of 17,000 words. Charles Bean (whom they seemed to call 'Barrett' in all their letters to him) helped them out with maps, and it appeared in 1920.[42]

The association cultivated a strong sense of common experience and shared comradeship, in peace as in war. At reunions, men sang:

> Now we're back in civvy life
> The Companies dispersed
> No more wars and no more strife,
> But still the Twenty-first!
> Active service days are done,
> But let's be cobbers everyone
> And carry on as we've begun,
> Gallant Twenty-first

For many years, reunions were rowdy affairs. At a reunion of 6th Brigade men in Melbourne in 1922, the chaplain, asked to say a few words, had to demand silence, fighting vainly to make himself heard. 'The boys did not want speeches', men called out. 'We're back in France tonight, lads', another said, thinking of convivial nights in canteens and estaminets. The catcalls ended for only two tributes: one for 'Those we left on the other side', greeted with silence, and the other for 'the Dads', greeted with cheers. Garry naturally clipped that report.[43] Ex-servicemen celebrated 'the Dinkum Twenty First' in song:

> Douglas Haig to Monash said
> 'I really fear the worst'.
> Monash said 'Don't shake your head,
> We've got the Twenty-first!
> Promise every Mother's son
> A pot of beer to make Fritz run,
> The War is then as good as won
> By the Twenty-first!'[44]

A few years later, Godfrey Dobson went along to a battalion reunion. He described it as 'a very fine affair', though only 'up to a certain point'. He had been glad to see 'many of the pals of war days' and, as individuals and events were mentioned, 'recollections (some sad & others pleasant) returned'. Godfrey thought that parents of men killed in the war could be invited to reunions—something that most fellow Twenty-firsters would surely have deprecated: they wanted to escape convention, not embrace it. If Dobson passed Garry's address to the committee, nothing happened.[45]

Not until 1934 did the association publish *The Red and Black Diamond*, 'the official organ of the 21st Battalion'. For a time, the *Diamond* appeared twice a year, a few weeks before the two annual reunions, on the eve of Anzac Day and in Royal Melbourne Show Week. The association held reunions at halls and ballrooms around Melbourne, at The Palms, Alexandra Avenue, cafés in the city, the Prahran Drill Hall, and for many years at the Albert Hall in Ascot Vale. Many men saw reunions as chances to renew the comradeship of wartime in a convivial atmosphere of beer and tobacco, recapturing a time when they were young and—except for the possibility of death or mutilation—carefree. The organisers' attempts to foster a festive atmosphere by hiring musicians or a comedian failed in the face of a fierce desire to talk about the war and sing its songs.

But by no means did all former battalion members join. While the battalion had drawn men from all over Victoria, the association was essentially a metropolitan body. In 1940, of its 988 members, 621 lived in greater Melbourne, with about 280 in country Victoria. About seventy-seven lived in New South Wales (thirty-nine in Sydney), with two or three in South and Western Australia and Britain. One man lived in Rabaul, and one (possibly Vic Edwards, unless he had let his subs lapse) in Tasmania. Of the Melbourne members of Nine Platoon, only Tom Wignall became active in the association, so much so that the *Diamond*'s editor noticed his presence or absence at reunions. Tom had a gift for singing, and for several years he organised a glee club, mainly of men of his old company. ' "C" Company made as much noise as usual', the editor reported in 1935, 'only more so'. By the mid-1930s, Tom had become the butt of good-natured jokes in successive issues about his 19-stone bulk.

Other members of Nine Platoon made occasional appearances in *Diamond*'s 'Where Are They Now' column. Vic Edwards sent in a report in 1937—he was a master baker now, in Tasmania, doing well enough to send along a donation of a pound, which was twenty times the annual subscription of a shilling. (As a member of the Railton sub-branch of the RSL, Vic marched on Anzac Day in Tasmania until foot trouble prevented him.) Godfrey Dobson contributed some reminiscences that the editor skilfully spread over several columns in 1935. Jack Castle joined—he showed up in a nominal roll of members in 1936—but seems to have taken no active interest in the association. He was not alone. 'Why don't you footsloggers fill in those forms and send them along?' the *Diamond*'s editor complained in 1935, and not for the first or last time. Like many social groups, the association's formal records made a lot of a small coterie of active members. Tom Wignall, also rotund and jolly, with his pleasing baritone, was one of these leaders. Others remained on the periphery, marching on Anzac Day but perhaps not even turning up for reunions.

The events of 1 September 1918 did not figure strongly in the *Diamond*'s columns of cheerful reminiscence and matey banter. On the magazine's masthead, the battle honour 'Mont St Quentin' sat among the 21st Battalion's other battlefield triumphs. In 1936, it published a story 'Hallowed Ground', illustrated with a photograph of the Mont St Quentin crosses, and the following year a story about Gilbert's memorial. But most men seemed to want to leave the battle and what it meant unexamined. The battalion had other important experiences — notably the sinking of the *Southland* and the protest against disbandment in 1918. A proposal in 1930 that Fred Sale, who, as brigade-major, had hastily written the orders for the 1 September attack, produce a more detailed history, came to nothing — though Sale collected records and hoped to begin 'at an early date'. (The records he collected seem to be lost, perhaps a victim of the Depression.)

Surprising as it may seem — or, on reflection, perhaps not so surprisingly — the effects of the Great Depression did not figure strongly in the *Diamond*'s cheerful badinage. The association's committee appealed for contributions to its welfare fund for 'Distressed Diggers', and the *Diamond*'s columns contained occasional hints of the hardships imposed by drought. These clues were invariably passed off as a joke: one man explained that he could not leave his wheat farm at Chinka Chinka because he had 'paraded before my banker the other day', but that when he sat down to his cold mutton he would think of his old friends.[46]

Their members' apathy baffled the editor and the association committee. Most men were happy to turn up for a boozy reunion once or twice a year, but saw little value in the association otherwise. The committee threatened that 'no liquid nourishment' would be offered until after the perfunctory annual general meeting. Many were not interested in the magazine (it was 'not wanted by the majority', the editor wrote with hurt bemusement). Not very many turned out for the annual remembrance ceremony—thirty-or-so members out of more than a thousand, more than half of whom lived in Melbourne. But surely every man remembered the war. Every time Charlie Tognella or Norrie Norwood took off their shirts, they saw the scars of their wounds. Others were tormented daily by the physical effects of wounds. In time, all of them dealt with 'the Repat'.

'KNOCKING AT THE REPAT DOOR': APPEALS

This book offers an example of what historical jargon calls a 'discontinuous narrative': that is, there are holes in the story that I can't fill. With some exceptions, the holes in the survivors' life stories run from the mid-1930s to the late 1950s. Around about then, as they entered old age, the platoon's stories pick up again, because they each of its former members began to apply to the Repat.

The Repat was more than a department; it became a state of mind, and an insistent fact of life for tens of thousands of returned men and their families. As Stephen Garton, one of its most perceptive historians, has shown, it presented a paradoxical face to the 'members' it served. Its proponents praised it as humane and generous; its detractors condemned it as heartless and mean-spirited. It was arguably more generous than any other nation's system, but by its essence turned those it served into supplicants and dependents.[47] Striving to comprehend the experience of all those who returned, and resisting the attraction of the 'troubled veteran' documented abundantly in the Repat's files, Garton asked how war experiences had affected the lives of those it touched. He acknowledged that returned men were more likely to suffer illness, unemployment, disability, and marital discord. Still, he wondered whether a true accounting of war's effects lay 'beyond our statistical reach' because of the character of the sources he drew on—the files of those driven to seek the Repat's aid. The experience of Nine Platoon therefore offers a different (albeit tiny and subjective) basis for further speculation. As Nine Platoon's survivors entered middle and old age (and at chronological ages decades earlier than we might expect today), they began to encounter the Repat as a stronger presence in their lives.

Over the decades, the Repat attracted bitter criticism, as its historians show.[48] John Whiting, who became a doctor after gaining a DFC flying with Bomber Command, used the disgust he came to feel while working as a Repat doctor to fuel a satirical novel, *Be In It, Mate!* Whiting's novel portrayed the system as a trough in which cynical veterans sank their snouts, rorting free treatment and benefits for conditions that could not possibly be attributable to war service. The experience of the Nine Platoon survivors does not accord closely with this satirical fiction. Even if Repat doctors deployed little psychological insight into the reasons for 'members' (as ex-servicemen were called) presenting with conditions that might have been caused or exacerbated by war service, their hospitals did a decent job in treating what they saw. While Godfrey Dobson tried it on, none of the Mont St Quentin men received undue consideration. But it remained their only recourse. 'Keep knocking at the Repat door', the

Diamond's editor counselled vaguely in 1945. Almost all of the survivors' files show that as they reached their sixties, they again sought Repat's help.

'A WASTED MAN': LES BAKER

Les and Agnes Baker and their six children lived in poverty through the Great Depression and a second world war. By the late 1940s, Les, who had just applied for the aged pension, found that his persistent cough had worsened. His doctor referred him to the Repatriation General Hospital at Caulfield. There, a specialist found that he had more than just a troublesome cough. His sputum was, in fact, mostly pus—he had advanced pulmonary tuberculosis (TB). He stayed in hospital, where further examination found a duodenal ulcer. No wonder he presented as a 'thin, small man'. Les's nurses reported that he had shockingly bad breath, and the hospital's dentist found his mouth to be in a 'deplorable condition'. His molars were worn down to the gums, which exuded pus when pressed. The dentist extracted all of his teeth. By the time he received dentures, several months later, Les's doctors and nurses thought he 'understands personal hygiene fairly well'. They found Les a 'sober, cheerful patient', stoic in the face of the pretty poor hand that life had dealt him.

Although Les's tuberculosis was not improving, he wanted to go home. Les and Agnes shared their weatherboard house, which he had built thirty years before, with one of his sons, his wife, and their two daughters, aged seven and nine. But neither Agnes nor the family wanted Les back while he was infectious. On weekend visits, Agnes told the medical social worker, Les became 'irritable and difficult', and he was careless with cutlery and 'scornful of supervision'. Agnes (who 'seemed fairly sensible') had an extension built so he could live separately, even though they had to share a kitchen. Les did not accept that he was 'a potential menace'—'he has taken a lot of convincing that his sputum contains tubercle bacilli', the social worker noted. Eventually, his son's family moved out to eliminate the danger of infection.

Then, in January 1951, Agnes, 'a stout, middle-aged woman' who herself suffered from high blood-pressure, had a heart attack. She could no longer care for Les, and he returned to Caulfield, where he died of TB a fortnight later, on 16 January 1951, aged sixty-seven. Agnes died in 1963, aged seventy-six. In a life dogged by unemployment and poverty, and ended by a wasting disease, Les Baker's war wounds—a bout of shell-shock on the Somme in 1916, a gun-shot wound at Ypres, and a shrapnel gash at Mont St Quentin—seem not to be the worst thing that happened to him. Les was, as the Repat doctors noted, 'a wasted man': wasted by poverty and its accompaniments.

'AS THE YEARS ADVANCED': CHARLIE TOGNELLA

For 45 years, Charlie Tognella worked as a woodcutter in the bush of north-eastern Victoria, broken only by his trip away to war, from which he returned with a chest wound that made his life increasingly difficult and, perhaps, denied him the comfort and satisfaction that he might have expected. Though regarded as 'permanently unfit' by the army doctors who had put him aboard the transport *Somerset* late in 1918, Charlie's war pension was cancelled in 1921. Between then and the late 1930s, his life is summarised by two sentences that he had a literate friend write to the Repat: 'had no medical treatment of any kind ... employed as a farm labourer by various employers—seasonal work'.

By the late 1930s, Charlie could no longer support himself

by manual labour. He experienced increasingly severe chest pains when he chopped wood or worked in the paddocks. A Repat doctor described him at the age of forty as a 'dark haired, dark skinned man, somewhat unkempt appearance', with teeth 'deficient and unhealthy'. The doctor found that Charlie suffered from ankylosing spondylitis—a chronic inflammation of the spine, calcifying and eventually fusing the vertebrae. Painful and debilitating, it was no condition for a labouring man but, the doctor declared, 'there is no incapacity resulting from this wound'. Charlie's 'slight cough' was 'doubtless due to smoking'—he admitted to using 2½ ounces of tobacco a week—and the Repat declined to restore his war pension. Charlie appealed. A friend summed up his case: 'pains in chest, worse when he works, becoming worse, much broken time', but he was told brusquely 'appeal disallowed'.[49] Charlie worked on in all weathers, an ageing, single, unskilled labourer, living in rural poverty and obscurity. The Repat system clearly had no room and little sympathy for a man who could not press his own case.

In 1954—still a self-employed wood-cutter, and now aged nearly sixty—Charlie was diagnosed with tuberculosis. It was not attributable to war service either, but the Repatriation Act allowed him to be treated anyway, and he briefly entered Heidelberg Repat Hospital (apparently for the first time). Just before Christmas 1954, Charlie shifted to Canberra to live with his brother and sister-in-law in their house in Ainslie, leaving his beloved horses, but perhaps taking his dogs with him. He was treated as an out-patient at the Canberra Community Hospital, the doctors judging him to have 'sufficient knowledge of his condition not to be a menace to the public'.[50]

While drugs kept the TB at bay, Charlie's final decade was dominated by the advance of the bony ankylosis of his spine. His lungs deteriorated—perhaps a consequence of the chest wound he suffered on Mont St Quentin in 1918—and, like several survivors, he began to lose his sight. Charlie was admitted to the Canberra Community Hospital on 9 August 1968 and died four days later, of a heart attack and pulmonary embolism.[51] Charlie lies beneath a brilliant white headstone, paid for by Repat, in the Woden cemetery in Canberra.

'RIGHT UP AGAINST IT': GODFREY DOBSON

The thickest, and in many ways the most perplexing, of Nine Platoon's Repat files is Godfrey Dobson's. The sources bearing upon his life present a conundrum, because of the different faces they reveal. The ratepayers of western Melbourne knew him as councillor George Dobson, while to the Repat he was Godfrey. Privately, he became a vexatious serial appellant, an attitude encouraged by the Repatriation system. Godfrey had had a sickly war. He contracted enteric fever on Gallipoli, so severely that he was repatriated, but went back in 1916. On the Western Front, he had trench fever twice, and rheumatism. On his discharge, the examining doctors found a 'slight irregularity' in his heartbeat, and he was discharged with a pension for 25 per cent incapacity.

To the doctors, he presented as a 'well nourished florid man in good condition'. But he kept going off sick, imperilling his position as a tram motorman. A sheaf of sick notes on his file reflects a great range of illnesses: bronchitis, influenza, nerve strain, and debility [he had knocked over a woman crossing in front of his tram and worried over it], acute neuritis, septic tonsillitis, neuritis, musculo-neuritis, and gastric ulcer. He was 'unable to follow any occupation'. In 1927, aged 35, he asked to be admitted to Caulfield hospital, complaining of 'bad turns'—shortness of breath, dizziness, headaches. He had recently collapsed at home and had become 'very afraid of his general health'. The Caulfield doctors could find nothing organically wrong ('Looks alright', one noted unsympathetically), but a year later accepted 'Toxaemia Post Trench Fever', though declining to diagnose 'anxiety neurosis'. From this point, Godfrey was off work for months at a time, living on a combination of pension and sick pay, and lodging a series of appeals and claims for acceptance of various conditions as 'war caused'.

Eventually, Dobson's Repat file bore a note detailing the conditions it accepted as attributable or not to war service:

Due to War Service	*Not Due to War Service*
Rheumatism	Defective vision
Toxaemia post trench fever	Astigmatism
Anxiety state and arterial hypertension	Umbilical hernia
Duodenal ulcer	Allergic sinusitis
Cholecystitis	Emphysema (not present)
Diabetes	

Each of these determinations involved an exhaustive series of clinical examinations, referrals, and reports. [52] It would be tedious to detail each. By the mid-1930s, Godfrey had pains all over his body and constant wind (relieved by powders and a light diet), with 'headaches practically continuous', and seeming 'very nervy, excitable'. He called for help from his federal MHR, James Fenton, whom he had met through his service on the Braybrook shire council. Mr Fenton testified that Godfrey was 'a very deserving man ... in daily danger of losing his war service home'. Godfrey, he wrote, was 'a splendid type who would not apply for further assistance if he could avoid it. He is right up against it.'

Godfrey was 'up against' the Repat system and the dependency it created. When declining a claim, it invited the 'member' to appeal. Godfrey Dobson was almost always preparing for, lodging, or awaiting the results of one appeal or another. The system was in the main unsympathetic, but he was undeterred, and by the late 1930s had become seen as a nuisance. In 1937, for example, he had another 'nervous collapse', but refused to attend a doctor accredited to Repat because he was 'disgusted with last decision of Tribunal'. This doctor unhelpfully found his heart 'clear' and pulse 'normal'. His troubles, he decided, were 'anxiety neurosis'. When Godfrey did see a Repat doctor, he decided his patient was a 'most insolent man: impertinent'. Godfrey took offence when the doctor suggested he looked well: he walked out, telling the doctor he was going home to bed. The doctor minuted that Godfrey was 'Antagonistic to whole Repatriation Commission'. Godfrey had some actual and serious complaints—he suffered agonies from calculus in his ureter, hypertension, and a duodenal ulcer, but his 'main trouble', a doctor noted, was 'due to non-accepted disabilities'.

By 1944, when he lodged yet another 'Appeal by a member of Forces to War Pensions Entitlement Appeal Tribunal', the typed summary of his medical history took over thirty pages. By the end of the Second World War, when he was working at the Munitions Department at Maribyrnong, he was 'very obese', often going sick with 'nervous prostration', a condition he thought 'definitely due to war service'. By 1950, he could 'describe his symptoms with practical ease' using medical jargon. At the age of 58, he said that he 'knows he can only have a few years to go before he is "snuffed out" and he won't be sorry'. The doctor—the first psychiatrist Godfrey had seen—found him to be 'intelligent' and able to appreciate that his symptoms had a nervous basis, but it was too late; Godfrey 'tells me he has heard it all before from various doctors'. The psychiatrist summed it up in one word: 'Diagnosis: hysteria'.

The rest of Godfrey's Repat file, between a diagnosis of diabetes in 1952 and his death in 1964, is missing. It presents a conundrum. Of all of Nine Platoon, Godfrey achieved the most public success. He was a successful member of the Braybrook and Sunshine councils—president of one and mayor of the other, between 1926 and 1962. When he died in 1964, the *Sunshine Advocate* published a warm eulogy, praising him as 'one of the greatest councillors ever', a man who 'put his life at the people's beck and call'.[53] He and Janet worked tirelessly for their community, remembered by a kindergarten named after her and a reserve after him. And yet Godfrey's Repat file portrays him as a self-centred hypochondriac, a man who would never be satisfied with a firm answer as long as it was no. Still, in 1958 there is a telling snippet, when G.E. 'Dobbie' Dobson dropped the editor a line to genially say how much he enjoyed reading the *Diamond*, 'especially the bits and pieces about old cobbers'.[54]

'JOVES!': JACK CASTLE

By contrast, some former members of Nine Platoon enjoyed longer and happier lives than either Les Baker or Charlie Tognella. Jack Castle's Repat file is a serious disappointment. As thick as your thumb, it seems to promise something; but, besides Jack's medical record from the Great War, it consists largely of change-of-address letters and the paperwork involved in advising local medical officers of the various shifts that the Castles made between the 1950s and the late 1960s. Fortunately, his family fill the silences in the official file.

Jack Castle's start in life had been unpromising. When he was just five his mother died, and soon after his father abandoned the family. Jack and his younger brother William were brought up in an orphanage and fostered out. When Jack turned eighteen he left the orphanage, his sixteen-year-old brother William 'escaping' to be with him. The two knocked around Victoria together, labouring and making do. That the two brothers were all the family that each had explains William's attempts to find Jack after they had both enlisted: his letters are on Jack's AIF file, but the reason for his search is not apparent.[55]

Jack and Ethel had four children. His son, Gordon, has fond memories of his father, who expressed his love for his family by providing for them. Jack was an easygoing man, quiet but good humoured, taking a lively interest in the world (his favourite expression was 'Joves!'—meaning 'By Jove, that's interesting!'). Like many returned men, Jack did not talk about the war much, though his son Gordon remembers Jack telling him that his sons would never have to go to war. 'I went to war so you'll never have to', he told Gordon. Gordon later reflected that no one thought much about what Jack had gone through in the war, or at least, 'we didn't talk about it'. But Gordon also remembers his father saying of the attack on the Mont that 'we were not taking prisoners'.

Garry Roberts had also helped Jack to get a job on the trams, and he kept it until he retired at sixty-five, taking pride in his work as a machinist at the Preston workshops. Jack was a good provider—unusually for a semi-skilled worker at the time, he even bought and ran a Fiat 501 Torpedo car. Good with his hands, Jack brought odd bits of material home and pottered handily about the garden of the various houses he and Ethel bought. Their life was not idyllic—he and Ethel experienced the rough passages that all marriages encounter. In the mid-1930s, Ethel even took the children on a year-long visit to Smethwick. Restless in retirement, Jack worked for Johns and Weygood, repairing hydraulic lifts around Melbourne for years before heart disease claimed him, aged seventy-nine, in 1968.

'FOOT TROUBLE': VIC EDWARDS

By the early 1930s, Vic Edwards had made the transition from casual timber-worker to small businessman. He followed several of his six brothers into the baking business in northern Tasmania, describing himself on the electoral roll as a 'master baker', though he seems not to have obtained any formal qualification. Vic and Anne (known as Nan, who never lost her Scots accent) later lived in Launceston, and then from 1941 at Squeaking Point, on the beautiful Rubicon estuary. Childless, they lived in a modest shack, sustained by the bakery they owned at nearby Railton and by Vic's fishing. Two of his nieces and nephews (he was one of ten children) recall Vic as a gregarious man, one who never concealed his opinions. By the early years of the Second World War, Vic had given up marching on Anzac Day, as a painful foot gave him trouble.

In the later 1950s, Nan became ill and died, and by the early 1960s Vic had moved into the Meercroft Home in Devonport. There, official documentation caught up with him when, in 1962, he applied for a war pension at the age of seventy-seven—the most advanced age at which any of the survivors sought assistance. By then he suffered from cataracts and diabetes, and from peripheral vascular disease—poor circulation in the extremities—which was to bring him into conflict with Repat. Still, he was, as a doctor noted on his file, a 'fit looking active old man', who, even though he still smoked heavily, was 'slow on hills but not stopped by them—not bad for his age'. But, by the mid-1960s, Vic was having greater difficulty getting about, hampered by a persistent foot infection.

But what had caused the infection? The doctors assumed it was a consequence of the vascular disease, but Vic made a claim that they found hard to accept. Vic lodged a claim for 'disability left foot', stating 'piece of steel came out of toe 2 years ago'. This piece of steel, he said, had 'been in since 1st World War'. Vic's doctors found this hard to believe. 'We only have his word for it', one noted, asking the nursing staff at the home whether they remembered a fragment coming to light. 'I don't think this patient is deliberately trying to mislead us', the doctor decided, 'but he is old and apt to get confused at times'.

But Vic was having none of it: he refused to be patronised, insisted on his story, and in July 1968 lodged an appeal to have his 'disability left foot' regarded as a disability attributable to war service. It made no difference to how it was treated or how the treatment was paid for: Vic merely stuck to his story. Repat, lacking any evidence (including any reference to a wound at any time during his war service), swiftly rejected the claim.

Vic appealed, writing a statement that, while uncertain in its spelling and punctuation, was vigorous in its claim. It is a statement that deserves to be quoted in full:

> I am an exserviceman enlisted in Victoria 2nd February 1915 discharged from Victoria in 1919 after 4 years and 4 months service torp[ed]oed going to Galopie [sic] which I have the Galope star served in France won the Military Medal in Mont Saint Quinton ... in 1918 therefore I consider I am entitled to some help for my service I have had a piece of shell in my foot since Posozieres [sic] 50 years which come out 22 months ago and is the still running pus and is being dressed every day by a sister in the home, if you know of anybody that has a better service please let me know his name I don't think you have don't you [think you] or yours are entitled to grant me something for my service. If you or yours would like to see my Medal and Certificates and can send you 5 pay books and all other necessary [proof].

Three weeks later, the Repat replied simply: 'appeal disallowed'. Three weeks after that, perhaps urged on by the pensions adviser at the Devonport sub-branch of the RSL, Vic appealed again, explaining in detail what had occurred:

> Two years and six months ago while barthing [sic] I fell and kicked my foot on a tap and out came a piece of metal which went through the toe of my Boot in Pozyiers [sic] fifty years ago and has been running every since I have had the toe taken off with two operations and the foot is still making puss. If you know of anybody with a better service I would like to here [sic] of his name

Here is an echo of the voices that Charles Bean had heard in the yard of Brewery Farm at Querrieu exactly fifty years before. We hear again the voice of 'strong, independent, determined individuals', men whose 'every statement is downright, unhesitating, ripped out without the slightest doubt'. Vic had not the slightest doubt that for what he had done at 'Mont Saint Quinton ... I consider I am entitled to some help for my service'. 'If you know of anybody with a better service', he demanded, 'I would like to here of his name'. Coincidentally, Bean himself died a couple of days later, released from several years of a terrible senility, at Concord Repat.

Regardless of what caused Vic's 'foot trouble', the intractable infection worsened. In October 1968, surgeons at the Mersey General Hospital amputated the third toe on Vic's left foot and cut away the associated metatarsal bones and tendons, though the wound took a long time to heal. Two years later, Vic, now aged 81, tried again. He went down to the Repat office in Devonport and had a talk to a man at the desk. There, he learned that he could ask for his case to be reviewed. The desk clerk's superior tried to head Vic off, explaining that 'a case can sometimes be re-opened even after an unsuccessful appeal', but only 'if you are able to produce further evidence ... of some weight'. Vic merely told them that he had 'foot trouble'. The department, sensing it had no option but to comply, asked Vic to complete form MF9A. Vic did so, though his description of his 'foot trouble' hardly constituted new evidence: 'difficulty walking; cold feet at all times ... piece of shell lodged in left foot during an explosion in 1916'. This last appeal was 'disallowed' in October 1971.

Soon after, Vic was taken to the Mersey General again, suffering from a large perianal abcess, and in December 1971 died of a tumour in the lung: his heavy smoking rather than his foot trouble did for him in the end. His surviving brothers and sisters (Harry, Brightie, Alex, and Tas) buried him at Devonport. Forthright to the last, Vic asked for neither flowers nor condolences.

'INTELLIGENT, ELDERLY MAN': NOBLE NORWOOD

Noble Norwood's case is one of the most poignant. Like Charlie, Norrie never married, but lived with his brother in a house in Como, by the Swan River. He had been active in amateur theatre in Perth, and had taken up painting. (Did he remember how, in Edith Alston's flat in the Latin Quarter in 1918, Frank had teased Norrie that 'he kids himself he's an artist'?[56]) But Annelle Perotti, daughter of a neighbour, has a painting he did, of a sea scene reminiscent of the Dutch school. It is tempting to suppose that, as a single man living with his brother, active in amateur theatricals and inclined to the artistic, Noble was gay. The subject was never discussed, and we will never know. But we should at least acknowledge how different Noble was from the conventional stereotype of the Great War 'Digger'.

Late in 1959, Noble saw his doctor, complaining of a 'nervous condition and pain from left shoulder'—where he had been wounded on 1 September 1918. Repat easily accepted his claim for 'incapacity as due to war service'. A regular reader—he had been a bookseller for forty years—he now feared that his eyesight was deteriorating. A doctor found him 'restless and introspective ... very nervy'. So depressed did Norrie seem that the doctor advised him to enter hospital immediately. Norrie 'presented', as doctors say, as an 'intelligent, elderly man', but also as a severely depressed insomniac. An operation for glaucoma had failed, and now Norrie—formerly a reader and an artist—saw the world through a grey mist. Though bearing the physical scar of his war wound, it seemed that his failing sight caused his depression.

In his last years, Norrie enjoyed visits and conversation with his niece Joyce Wilson, and his neighbours Eva Stewart and Annelle Perotti. Annelle remembers him fondly as a courteous, gentle man. 'He was a gentleman', his niece Joyce recalled. Norrie moved to a Salvation Army hostel, where he died in May 1973 of bowel cancer. He donated his body to the Department of Anatomy at the University of Western Australia, and was finally buried only in June 1974.

'A DIAGNOSTIC PROBLEM!': TOM WIGNALL

Tom Wignall worked for the Red Cross from soon after the Great War to the early 1960s. In 1960, now retired at Rosebud, he applied for a Repat pension, a decision that seemed to bring him disquiet rather than ease. The Repat doctor's examination described Tom as a 'very heavily built', florid man, whose twenty-a-day cigarette habit did not help his 'wheezy breathing' (soon diagnosed as emphysema). He had suffered 'pains where I was wounded'—in the stomach—for over forty years, and still had to watch his diet for fear of agonising constipation. He now suffered arthritis, especially in his wounded hand. Tom's life had been ruled by the consequences of that grenade exploding on the afternoon of 1 September 1918. Repat did not regard either his arthritis or emphysema as attributable to war service, but his wounds qualified him as 100 per cent eligible for pension regardless.

Like Vic Edwards, Tom appealed anyway, claiming that a whiff of gas in 1918 explained the emphysema, even though his medical record made no mention of gas. Tom enlisted the aid of his former officers, friends from the association. Captain Alfred Brown, formerly the 21st's adjutant, who testified that the Germans used gas at Warlancourt, Ploigsheet Wood [sic], Dernancourt, and 'forward of Viller's Bretenaux [sic]'. Spelling aside, the 21st did not fight at Ploegstreet Wood or Dernancourt. Bernard Duggan also weighed in, stating 'with confidence that any member of the 21st Battalion who had served on any of the fronts mentioned ... must have had contact with enemy gas, to a more or less serious degree'.

While one Repat doctor dismissed these general statements ('I do not consider this evidence is material'—he had probably read similarly vague claims before), members of the review panel accepted that Tom probably had been exposed to 'considerable gas' in 1918, even if his medical record made no reference to it.

By the early 1960s, now in his late sixties and retired, Tom Wignall fell into a pattern of declining health. It is hard to dismiss the suggestion that the Repat system encouraged him to mention every symptom, but also that a man who had accepted his disabilities stoically for years quite suddenly began to feel the consequences of war service fifty years before. A Repat doctor examining him in 1962 found that he suffered from listlessness, continual headache, a cough (that had never cleared up since the war), 'intermittent giddy turns', joint pain, and such severe indigestion that he 'has to eat slops'. Tom, the doctor noted, was 'inclined to be garrulous', but he suspected that there was more than hypochondria at work. He noticed 'obvious anxiety features with depression', and referred Tom to a psychiatrist.

The psychiatrist documented the same list of vague symptoms, and listened to Tom describe how 'his nerves' made him 'totally and permanently incapacitated'. For the first and only time among the survivors of his platoon, a psychiatrist decided that it would be 'reasonable to infer that he has had persisted [sic] symptoms of anxiety from at least the time he was wounded'. His anxiety state was, of course, 'due to War Service'. Here, in a Melbourne psychiatrist's consulting room, someone who bothered to ask Tom questions connected what he was feeling to what had happened on Mont St Quentin. The effects of this event were still apparent.

If anything, acknowledging that Tom's health problems could be attributed to the war seemed to aggravate them, and brought him firmly into dependency upon the Repat system. In 1963, acting on advice, possibly from another Twenty-firster, he claimed a monthly bottle of brandy. The doctor challenged this 'entitlement', but 'he seemed to know his rights', he conceded grumpily. 'One would like to know from whom these people find out about there [sic] "entitlements"', he minuted. But for Tom, an occasional brandy would not compensate for the wretched state into which he fell.

In 1966, his doctors observed that psoriasis—an intractable, itching, painful skin condition—began to spread rapidly on his hands, body, and face. In 1968, he collapsed and was admitted to Heidelberg Repatriation Hospital with jaundice, fever, and colic so severe that it required pethidine to relieve it. The psoriasis returned, even more severely. Tom became, as his doctors noted, 'a diagnostic problem!' He claimed that his skin condition was a 'nervous condition, related to combat fatigue'. The Repat doctors disagreed: '"Anxiety State" is not a cause of "Psoriasis"', they ruled. By 1972 he suffered from 'gross psoriatic eruptions', and was 'slowly deteriorating', often admitted to try another chemical or diet remedy, beta methasone cream, Alpha-keri baths, Ultra-violet light, and soybean lecithin. But nothing eased a debilitating and demeaning complaint. The Heidelberg nurses' clinical notes trace a losing battle with his painful and distressing complaint—'rash looks angry … rash slow to respond'.

Eadie Wignall died in 1977, and within a year Tom had followed her. He did not die from psoriasis—though he may often have wished for it—but it made his life miserable for a decade before his death. Perhaps the Repat was right: a skin condition contracted at seventy-five was not caused directly by his war service, but one can't help feeling that it might have been. Acknowledging that he had been wounded in his mind as well as in his stomach and hand seems to have freed Tom from the stoicism he had maintained since 1918. Perhaps treatment which followed that diagnosis might have spared him some of the discomfort and indignity he suffered.

'DISABILITIES DUE TO WAR SERVICE—NIL': BILL RABLING

Bill Rabling survived the war unwounded. He returned to Melbourne in 1919 to work in the London Stores in Elizabeth Street as a clerk. In 1923, he married Elsie, whom he had met at a neighbouring Methodist church. They had three children: Gwen, Douglas, and Eveline. The Depression hit the Rablings hard. He lost work, and for a time worked on the Great Ocean Road, a huge relief effort on which many unemployed returned men laboured. In the 1930s, Bill found work on the trams—first as a conductor, then as a driver, and later as an inspector, responsible for the trams running through the busy St Kilda Junction. Eveline remembers that when she was a child, her father 'just didn't talk about the war', but also that he was 'never really well'.

Bill went to some battalion reunions—'it was nice to see Bill Rabling at the Reunion', the *Diamond* reported in 1962, which was his first for six years because of the shifts he worked.[57] Bill's Repat file contains nothing until 1954, when he made an 'application for acceptance of "Stomach Trouble"' as the basis of a war pension.[58] He relied upon the doctors' assessments, declining 'at this juncture to make a written statement in support of my claim'. Bill had suffered from stomach ulcers for the previous six years, more severely since 1948, when he suffered a ruptured ulcer and a partial gastrectomy. The anxiety of running a busy tram junction could not have helped. The Repat doctors were not moved. They found him a 'garrulous, friendly, likeable type', but their decision was unsympathetic: 'NO—onset of symptoms about 1923'.

Bill appealed in a brief statement. He explained that he had had stomach trouble which gradually got worse 'ever since I returned from the war'; 'I believe it was caused by the conditions we had to live under', he wrote. It was the only explanation he ever gave. He probably did not mean that a diet of bully beef and biscuit caused his dyspepsia; rather, that the tension of facing death or wounds was expressed by a visceral derangement. The Repat doctors did not read between the lines; instead, they took a literal view of Bill's case. But while he may have first consulted a doctor for 'acute dyspepsia' in 1923, he had clearly suffered from indigestion since 1918. It seems reasonable to conclude that the tension of war experience might be expressed as digestive disturbance. Once again, the doctors' failure of imagination seemed opposed to common sense, but they noted 'appeal disallowed'.

Due to war service or not, Bill's stomach trouble persisted. Over the next twenty years he also became blind and hard of hearing, and developed heart disease. By the early 1970s, he moved between his daughters, Gwen in Mitcham and Eveline in Pascoe Vale South. Occasionally, his son-in-law Ken sat with him, and Bill would talk about the war — the only time he shared his memories of it. The family treasures a story that he told (recorded by Ken) of an encounter in a muddy trench near Warneton in the winter of 1917–18:

> A party of top brass was going up to the trenches so I get off the duckboards to let them go past. A young officer told me to keep going and they would get off. The rule was that people going out always had right of way. When I looked up one of them was the King.

The Royal Archives confirms that while George V did not formally inspect AIF troops, he did indeed tour BEF formations on the Franco–Belgian border in March 1918.

His family's care softened the discomfort of Bill's final years. Until deafness cut him off, he listened to the radio and books on cassettes. Eveline would read to him annual issues of the *Red and Black Diamond*. Soon he became 'very deaf and difficult to communicate with ... blind and very frail', with 'so many pills he'd pour them into his hands'. The final years of Bill's hospital files remain closed under the Archives Act, but his daughter Eveline and son-in-law Ken describe how Bill moved permanently into a home near Heidelberg Repat Hospital. 'He knew he wouldn't be able to come home', Eveline and Ken recalled, 'and lost the will to carry on'. Bill, the last survivor of Nine Platoon, died on 1 February 1980. Among the final entries on his medical file is the annotation 'disabilities due to war service — nil'.

Bill might be said to have had a better war than some: he was not wounded, and returned seemingly whole. He was reserved even with his family and did not talk about the war. The files cannot reveal what the war did to him. We must accept that there are limits to what a document can disclose, and we will never know how he, a retiring, private man, remembered the danger he had faced and the horror he had witnessed. He may not have realised this at the time, or been able to articulate it, even if he had been given the chance. But it seems at least likely that the trauma of Mont St Quentin and the remainder of his service affected his digestion for the rest of his life. By the time Bill Rabling died, a new memorial had been erected on the Mont.

'NOSTALGIC RETURN': THE 1971 PILGRIMAGE

The thought of another war had haunted the men of the 21st, even before the Great War had ended. Frank had told Ruby exactly a year before he was buried on Mont St Quentin that Germany had to be decisively defeated so that 'you and I won't have to send our laddies to war in years to come to fix them again'.[59] As the 1930s advanced, it seemed that this was exactly what would occur. Already, in April 1935, the *Diamond* was publishing sombre articles speculating on 'The Next War'. In 1937, Charles Bean, in an article written for a conference of the International Peace Campaign, conceded that his war had ended in a '"settlement" that could only be ... a cause of further strife'.[60] As indeed it was.

In May 1940, the Germans returned to Péronne. Affronted by the triumphant vengeance of Gilbert's statue showing a Digger bayoneting a Prussian eagle, the Germans soon tore the statue down, and cast it and May Butler-George's panels into the Third Reich's crucibles. Gilbert's figure, with or without

Frank Roberts's face and Corporal Roy Guest's stocky body, had been destroyed. Occasionally, rumours surfaced that fragments of the statue had been spotted in junk shops, but the reality was that it had gone. In the aftermath of war in a new Europe, not everyone was sorry. The Australian military historical writer John Laffin, whose father had fought at Mont St Quentin, thought that Gilbert's figure had been 'in poor taste'. He agreed with the secretary of the Mont St Quentin Memorial Association (composed of 2nd Division veterans), who did not blame the Germans for destroying a 'to them, offensive statue', and recognised that, 'as a new image and relationship now exists between the Western [European] Countries', simply replacing Gilbert's bellicose figure was untenable.[61]

The RSL's lobbying (including playing the card that the empty plinth embarrassed Australia in France) persuaded the Australian government in 1966 to fund replicas of May Butler-George's panels (complete with a misspelled 'Moquet Farm') and a new statue. The sculptor Stanley Hammond at first proposed a stiff pair of steel-helmeted Diggers advancing up a slight slope. Sir William Dargie, doyen of the Commonwealth Art Advisory Board, irked at not being consulted over Hammond's commission, damned the pair as 'appalling'. (Even a bureaucrat, the mandarin-in-training Keith Pearson, wrote a note for file for his boss, Sir Geoffrey Yeend, wondering 'whether bombs and bayonets are necessary' on such a sculpture.) Eventually, Dargie approved Hammond's second go—a 3-metre-tall reflective standing figure, reminiscent of the archetypal suburban or country war memorial, but on a grander scale—as 'good enough'.[62] In 1970, John Gorton disallowed a proposal that a replica be erected on Anzac Parade in Canberra, on the advice of the National Capital Development Commission, which recommended that the desired spot be reserved for a sculpture of broader interest. The site is now earmarked for a memorial to Australian peacekeepers.⁶³

Completed too late for the 50th anniversary, Hammond's figure would be dedicated in the presence of a group of Mont St Quentin veterans. They travelled to France, not as government guests, but as part of a holiday-cum-pilgrimage. In 1971, 47 former members of the 2nd Division and some of their wives made a 38-day 'nostalgic return to our haunts of fifty three years previously'.⁶⁴ The group, led by Donald Coutts, now a retired doctor, who in 1918 had worked unceasingly in the dugout in Lost Ravine as a medical officer, paid $1400 each for a journey that traversed the modern world as well as taking them back to their past.

They flew by Qantas jet to Honolulu via Nadi on 6 August. 'Billeted' at 'the Palatial Reefs Hotel', they visited a 'native village' and took a tour of Battleship Row in Pearl Harbor. On the United Airlines flight to New York, they had the novel experience of watching colour films on the plane, but from a 'second rate' hotel in New York saw sights that both thrilled and appalled them. They saw what one pilgrim called the 'League of Nations' building, and the statue of Liberty, but were disgusted that 'drug addicts lay openly in the gutter' in filthy streets.

Relieved to be back in the hands of Qantas again, they landed in London on 9 August, though 'the hippy element' was visible even when they placed a wreath on the Cenotaph in Whitehall. In London, as well as touring historical and cultural sites, they met Lady Sarah Rosenthal, widow of their old divisional commander, at a reception at Australia House. While sightseeing, they came across other Australians. At the Old Curiosity Shop, they met 'Australian girls from Bondi' and (appropriately at the Changing of the Guard) 'several young lads and lasses on working holidays'. During a ten-day bus tour of the beauty spots of England and Scotland, they marvelled at the changes visible all over Britain. 'Gone were the cobble stone roads and country lanes' they remembered from their leaves in 1917–18, finding that 'freeways with under and overpasses' had taken their place. On farms, they noticed 'superphosphate instead of the midden heaps of the early twentieth century'.

The awareness of change persisted when they arrived in Europe. They visited a dozen memorials or cemeteries, including the Arc de Triomphe, the Menin Gate, and the Australian national memorial at Villers-Bretonneux, where they were given a booklet and a souvenir ballpoint pen. At a reception at Amiens, they mixed with other veterans, from Britain, France, Belgium — and Germany. 'Blessed by springlike weather', they enjoyed a visit to Péronne, which made much of the visit, offering the party a vin d'honneur. The commune had long pressed for the restoration of the Australian monument, in 1965 re-naming the road that many of them had crossed under fire as the 'Avenue des Australiens'.

On the 53rd anniversary of the battle, they took part in the unveiling and dedication of the new statue in a 'most solemn and religious ceremony'. Representing France was M. Boinet, who had fought with the French army in front of Mont St Quentin when it formed part of the front line through 1917, and representing the Australian delegation was Donald Coutts. At the official ceremony on the Mont, a French military band played the Marseillaise and the Australian national anthem (still 'God Save the Queen'); but when local officials dedicated the road over the Mont, it played 'Waltzing Matilda'.

Early in September, they returned to Australia with 'happy memories of a happy band'. As often happens when old people survive a demanding journey, they lost two members of the party in the following months. Still, as Mr Jones wrote, they were 'most fortunate to be able to undertake such an exciting journey'.

'MONT ST QUENTIN CHANGED HIM':
THE EFFECTS OF A BATTLE

As we have seen, almost all of Nine Platoon's survivors lived with the consequences of their war. I cannot prove it absolutely, but it seems that Bill Rabling's poor digestion, Tom Wignall's psoriasis, Charlie Tognella's bad chest, and even Vic Edwards's infected toe were in one way or another attributable to the effects of living through that war. Neither the survivors nor their families were very communicative in reflecting on the more profound consequences of the war; but, as in pondering why they enlisted, a broader view might suggest ways in which the war might have affected them.

A surprising number of veterans' families grew up in homes or properties called 'Mont St Quentin'. Lieutenant Edwin Edmondson of the 28th Battalion was killed on Mont St Quentin's eastern slopes a day later and a few hundred yards from where the bodies of Roy, Alf, Frank, and the other 21st Battalion dead lay. Edwin's death cast a pall over the family—particularly his mother, Louise—ever after. When the Edmondsons moved from Collie to Palmyra, a suburb of Fremantle, a year later, Louise named the house 'St Quentin'. A niece, Isabel McBride, recalled that her grief, unspoken but obvious, hung over Louise for almost thirty years. She was reminded of the place where her Edwin had died every time she walked through the gateway. Nuggett Allen of the 21st named his house in Balmoral in Melbourne 'Mont St Quentin', as did William White's father when naming his property near Streatham in central Victoria; perhaps there were more who did the same.[65]

Some value their connections with the battle for the Mont. After 1918, the Department of Defence distributed 'trophies'—usually guns—to communities to place by (or even constitute) their war memorial. Larger communities received field guns; little places got machine-guns. The size of Mallee Plains, near West Wyalong in the central west of New South Wales, may be gauged by the fact that it was presented with a German 08/15 machine-gun—the smallest of the trophies distributed. Men from Mallee Plains had enlisted in the 20th Battalion, and had taken the gun in the first assault on the Mont on 31 August. The gun hung in the township's corrugated-iron hall for thirty-or-so years. In the 1950s, as the hall fell into disuse, William McLachlan, the president of the local RSL sub-branch, took the gun home to his property, 'Betweenvale', for safekeeping. His son, Gil, played Cowboys and Indians with the gun (not Diggers and Germans), but the gun went missing after William died. In 1994, Gil tracked the gun down, recovered it from a neighbouring property, and still holds it, under the requisite 'Heirlooms Permit'. Gil's son, Mat, is a journalist and author, and in the preface to *Walking with the Anzacs*, his 2007 guide to the Australian battles on the Western Front, he described the gun as his personal connection with the Western Front in general and the taking of Mont St Quentin in particular. He attributes his passionate interest in understanding and explaining the Great War to that connection.

For other families, the name Mont St Quentin had a darker colouring. Michael McKernan, once deputy director of the Australian War Memorial, tells the story of what happened one day in 1994 when he was escorting a Second World War veteran around the memorial's galleries. The old man—he would have been in his eighties—seemed a bit shaky, so Michael invited the man to use a wheelchair. The offer was refused, with what Michael recalled as 'a look of contempt'. Knowing veterans as he did, Michael knew better than to insist; but a couple of galleries further on, the man asked if he could sit down for a while. Michael was inclined to feel vindicated, until he realised that the man was looking intently at the diorama of the taking of Mont St Quentin, depicting the moment at which Frank Roberts and the other men of Nine Platoon headed up the hill to take the Mont. Then the man spoke. 'That was the whole damn trouble', he said. 'What?' Michael replied, thinking he'd missed something. 'What was the trouble?'

'My dad fought there', the man explained. Then he revealed a fragment of his own history that had meant trauma for his family. People who had known his father before the war described him as a 'a good man, a kind man', a man ready for 'a few beers and a laugh'. But, he went on, with Michael listening just as intently as he stared at the diorama, 'The war changed him; Mont St Quentin changed him.' Like many returned men, 'he came back morose; he had moods of black depression that rarely seemed to lift'. In a few words that summarised decades of abuse and unhappiness, the man described how his father had 'few good words for my mother and even fewer for me … We lived in fear of him', he remembered. Only in the last years of his life—he had died just twenty years after coming home—did the blackness seem to ease. 'His war had scarred us all', he said.[66] The veteran's wretched story may stand for the generations blighted by that war. Mont St Quentin, the AIF's greatest single triumph, here stood for a childhood and a marriage ruined by depression and anger.

In other families, Mont St Quentin did not live on, even as a name. In May 1918, the Murrayville Progress Association decided to plant trees in honour of the sixty men who had enlisted from the district. The Smerdons were represented by two trees beside each other along the southern side of McKenzie Street, now the Ouyen Highway. The trees did not distinguish between the living and the dead: when they were planted, Cliff was dead and Roy had just over three months to live. Their father, John, initiated a Soldiers' X-Ray Memorial

Ward for the Murrayville Cottage Hospital. It has since been demolished and the hospital closed—but what happened to the foundation stone? Ann and John Smerdon retired to Ballarat, where they died in 1932 and 1940 respectively. With them, the memory of a Smerdon connection with Mont St Quentin also died. A great nephew, Don Smerdon, a history teacher for his entire career, only recently learned that he had two cousins in the AIF, both killed—one at Mont St Quentin. 'What amazes me', he later wrote, 'is that these fellows were cousins of my father and the fact that they were involved in the war was never mentioned to me', despite his obvious interest in history.[67]

RED AND BLACK DIAMOND: THE ASSOCIATION'S FINAL YEARS

Alby Lowerson accepted the Victoria Cross from his sovereign on 1 March 1919, exactly six months to the day after his 'deed' on the summit of the Mont. Then he went back to Victoria to the dairy and tobacco farm near Myrtleford. He became the only one among those connected to Nine Platoon to die in uniform, of illness, as a militiaman in 1945. Lowerson's death introduced a new element in the 21st Battalion's Association's annual calendar. At his graveside, members of the association made a solemn pledge to return each November to pay their respects. From 1949, when his headstone was installed in the cemetery at Myrtleford, the association made an annual pilgrimage, coinciding with the sub-branch's own annual reunion. Over the years, firm friendships developed between the two groups. By the 1950s the event had become a fixture among its active members, who sorted themselves into half-a-dozen carloads and, bearing fresh crayfish, made their way up the Hume Highway.

Mont St Quentin had, of course, a special place in the

Twenty-firsters' 'tremendous bond of friendship' with the Myrtleford sub-branch.[68] In December 1971, Bill Oliver, who had returned to Mont St Quentin with the pilgrimage, presented the Myrtleford sub-branch with a fragment of stone from 'an ancient abbey at Mont St Quentin'. Exactly where he found this stone is hard to say: there is no 'ancient abbey' on the Mont. Perhaps it came from the parish church, itself re-built after 1918. Perhaps a parishioner gave him a piece from the rubble left over after its reconstruction. The stone, mounted on a polished pine board bearing a 21st Battalion colour patch, had been brought from Mont St Quentin 'on the unveiling of a new Second Division Memorial to replace the one destroyed by German troops'. The inscription went on to quote the by-now customary accolade from Rawlinson that the capture of the Mont was 'the finest single feat of the war'. It was to have 'a treasured place of honour' in the sub-branch's club-rooms, and it still does.

Except for Tom Wignall, Nine Platoon's members had never been active in the association. But every so often, one connected to its story would pop up, sometimes in the most surprising way. In 1962, the *Diamond* mentioned that Frank's friend Alf Fox, who had missed the battle by being gassed, had published a book, *Answer to Omar*. It seems that Alf had been nursing a hitherto-unsuspected interest in esoteric poetry. He privately published a little book—actually called *Reply to Omar*—opposing the *Rubaiyat of Omar Khayyám*. Taking exception to Edward FitzGerald's celebrated translation of the eleventh-century Persian poet's philosophy, Alf urged upon his readers, in a couple of dozen elegant quatrains, 'a more hopeful message' than 'the gloomy and godless philosophy of Omar'.[69]

The association's final decades might seem like a sad chronicle of illness, infirmity, and the inevitable deaths of its members. But running through the pages of the *Diamond* is a touching strain of cheerfulness and good humour in the face of the infirmities that Nine Platoon's members embodied. While the number attending the reunion fell (and while it became a sedate afternoon function), a feeling of fellowship intensified. The *Diamond* often referred to those present as 'one big happy family'. Its visible weakening impelled Bill Power, a mainstay of the committee for sixty years, to assert that the association, and the battalion, would endure for as long as it had a member. 'Only when the last of us has passed on will the 21st Battalion become a memory', he wrote. Part of that memory came from the increasing involvement of members' widows—'our staunch lady correspondents', as the editor coyly described them. Their messages, of thanks for condolences offered, and of friendly enquiries after health and happiness, are profoundly moving. Widows' names appear for several years and then they, too, begin to disappear. Sometimes, daughters and sons explained the absence, but more often they simply stopped corresponding.

Astonishingly, the 'Association' survived, even though only three members attended the 1981 reunion at the Caulfield RSL, the association's home for its final decade. Allan Gregerson called for nominations for three positions, and the three solemnly proposed and seconded each other. 'I take it the motion is carried unanimously', Bob Burns, the secretary, observed drolly. Although there was a five-year gap in the appearance of the *Diamond*, Mr Gregerson produced one further, final edition in April 1986. He addressed the handful of surviving members, widows, and families who received the newsletter, now typed and photocopied. 'Our Battalion ... inspired us and gave us memories that will never fade', he wrote; 'we will never forget'. Even though Nine Platoon's last member had died five years before, a member of it was to appear in the very last paragraph that Mr Gregerson typed before the *Diamond*'s demise. On its last page, he published an appeal from a relative of Godfrey Dobson, who wanted confirmation that he had been 'one of the 7 men who took a particular part with Sgt A. Lowerson when he won the V.C.'. Nine Platoon was with the *Diamond* to the end.

'THE DREAM ON THE WIND': NANCY'S LIFE

Nancy eventually married again. She adopted and named Jilba, the daughter of a teenaged neighbour who fell pregnant. (Nancy found her name, Jilba patiently explains, and not for the first time, in a book of baby names. Supposedly meaning 'spring time', it expressed the growing Australian awareness of Aboriginal culture.) Jilba found her mother a trial. Nancy had been indulged as a child, and she tended to be wilful and rather selfish. She found it difficult to stick at anything—she changed jobs often, lived fecklessly, and mostly relied on the long-suffering Ruby to bail her out financially. (She not only sold the last of the land in the Dandenongs that Frank had wanted to call 'St Yves', but which Ruby called 'Nankby'—formed from pairs of letters from Nancy, Frank, and Ruby—but did so without telling Jilba.) But Jilba remains grateful for the love of learning instilled by her Roberts forebears, and followed that lead herself, reading to her eldest son, Evan, from a book given to her by Nancy.

Influenced by her literary Roberts grandparents, Nancy saw herself as a writer, and in 1977 she published a novel, *The Wine of Courage*, through a vanity publisher in Britain. It dramatised the life of her Barratt grandmother, Mary Ann, called Polly. The novel, telling 'Polly's story', began with her courtship by George Barratt in Melbourne in 1880. Though infused with a stilted jollity ('Let us call it Warwick Farm, dear one', Polly says to George on their arrival at Olinda), it seems to have been based closely on memories and stories circulating within the Barratt family. A homage to her pioneering forebears, it describes George and Polly settling in the Dandenongs and raising their seven children, and ends with the wedding of Ruby and Frank, which she describes in detail, presumably based on her mother's memories. Sadly, the projected trilogy remained incomplete.

The 'blurb' she wrote for the back cover of her novel reveals how she saw herself. Thanks to her Roberts grandparents, she grew up 'in a world of Books, Art, Music, and Theatre'. Although 'plagued by ill-health', Nancy was 'a dedicated writer on various subjects including travel, fairy stories and a play, quite apart from the other two novels in this trilogy', and, following her grandfather perhaps, 'an intended book on old goldfields'. She planned to write a musical comedy and 'perhaps a ballet'. Of this output, only one part of the projected trilogy was ever published. 'Keen on travel', she visited Europe and the Pacific islands. In France, she saw 'the old battlefields' and 'visited the Australian War Graves, including that of her own father, killed in September 1918'. In fact, her daughter corrected, she travelled abroad only twice, once to Fiji for a week's holiday and once in 1958 to Britain and Europe, when she was at last able to visit the grave of the father she never knew.

Though the trilogy remained incomplete, Nancy did have 'The Dream on the Wind', the second part, typed—the title taken from a letter that Frank had written to Ruby just over a month before his death. In fact, the entire 430-page typescript comprised Frank's letters and diary, dictated into a cassette recorder and typed phonetically by a typing service (and paid for by Ruby). Except for a few explanatory notes by Nancy, the 'novel' was entirely Frank's words. At least it preserved his letters and diaries that were not pasted into Garry's Record Books.

Sensible and good-humoured, Ruby lived to be ninety-four. She died in March 1989, living in her own home and retaining her faculties until the end. At the age of fourteen, on her grandfather's seventy-first birthday, Nancy had wondered if she would live to be seventy-one, in 1988. In fact, she lived well beyond, dying at the age of seventy-nine in 1997.

'THE FINEST SINGLE FEAT OF THE WAR'?: RE-THINKING MONT ST QUENTIN

Account after account represents the taking of the Mont as a great Australian feat of arms—the archaic language seems inescapable. Are we to accept that an Australian force barely as strong as a battalion captured the position, defended by parts of five German divisions—at least one of them comprising élite troops—and that, the next day, a similarly weakened force finished the job? It seems hard to believe, so how should we think of this battle's reputation?

We can read the battle of Mont St Quentin in at least two ways. First, we can accept that a weak Australian force—by dint of greater vigour, skill, and courage—defeated a larger, élite force. Or we might accept that a weak but very skilful and determined Australian force defeated the Mont's exhausted and demoralised defenders. No one would argue that the effort was not prodigious or that the fight was not costly. The question is whether the capture of the Mont really ought to be regarded as the AIF's 'finest single feat of the war'.

The more closely we investigate what happened at and after Mont St Quentin, we find that, for nine decades, we have been the unwitting victims of a confidence trick. It began with hasty wartime correspondents' reports. Submitted within hours of the battle and subject to a rigorous censorship, they wrote about the taking of the Mont as a triumph. Congratulatory messages and especially Monash's self-serving memoir cemented the reputation—one hardly ever subjected to a thorough analysis. Charles Bean's account in his official history, detailed but unclear, added to the battle's standing, though his judgement was qualified. Most subsequent accounts, unwilling to investigate Monash's boosting, confirmed his judgement. Like most confidence tricks, it has succeeded because the victims entered willingly into their deception.

A mature consideration drawing on all of the available sources and a careful dissection of the events of August–September 1918 denies us the comfort of simply quoting Rawlinson's easy, premature praise as 'the finest single feat of the war'. The seizure of Mont St Quentin was an important part of the continuing advance toward ultimate Allied victory. It was achieved by Australian troops directed by Australian commanders, and entailed both rapid, decisive leadership and hard fighting by a weak, tired force against defenders who, though just as exhausted, were also skilful and motivated. The battle cost both sides dearly. So why does it not deserve the reputation it has acquired?

Mont St Quentin's reputation has been distorted by the easy acceptance of Monash's inflated account, by an unjustified description of the defenders' numbers and attitude, and by author after author becoming confused over the chronology of the battle and describing it as a rapid triumph rather than as the mismanaged, messy success that it was.

Monash efficiently channelled brigades across the Somme and directed them towards the key objectives of Mont St Quentin and Péronne. He was no mere methodical, bite-and-hold general: he was able to keep on top of a fast-paced advance over a wide front. But he did not order their attacks in detail or even keep in touch with what they were doing. Instead, he anticipated success by passing on to Rawlinson on the morning of 31 August the misleading news that an Australian flag few from the summit of the Mont, a full thirty hours before the hill finally fell. Then he lost interest in the action, and not until Charles Rosenthal resumed control on the morning of 1 September did the final Australian attacks begin. Even then, it took a further two attacks—the final one reinforced by the 21st Battalion—before the Australians prevailed. By that time, the Mont's élite, volunteer defenders had largely withdrawn. The final attack, in which Nine Platoon took part, was against a different, weaker, reluctant force of defenders who gave up the hill, if not without a fight, then at least without contesting it as fiercely as its first defenders had. Even taking into account their members' modesty, Nine Platoon's first-hand accounts—effectively constituting new evidence—do not describe the fight for the Mont as a desperate battle against a determined élite enemy: the defenders did not counter-attack, but were evicted with relative ease.

Mont St Quentin was indeed a triumph, but we need to say exactly why. It was a battle won in spite of slipshod command, fought by battalions, companies, and platoons who were determined to press on—a battle taken on by tired men near the end of a long and exhausting war. We should still admire men whose qualities of comradeship, skill, and courage got them to rise yet again from a trench and walk forward toward machine-gun fire and death. But we need to be clear why we admire them. Above all, we must recognise that, even if it was not a triumphant feat of arms, as it has traditionally been represented, men died and were wounded in taking that hill. This battle took and, as we have seen, changed lives.

EPILOGUE

The Sound of a Voice So Still

In 1918, the editor of *The Red and White Diamond*, the newsletter of the merged 21st/24th Battalion, noticed how many streets in deserted French villages had been named 'Digger Street', or 'Little Lonsdale Street'. He wondered whether 'these Aussie signs will be retained when the French people rebuild'. As it happened, with the exception of Villers-Bretonneux, which cultivated a special relationship with Victoria, most would not. In 1997, though, the commune of Péronne restored the name of 'Roo de Kanga' to the stretch of the rue de St Savour by the Hôtel de Ville. You have to look for the sign, high on the building's side wall, but reminders exist of those whose lives were ended or changed by the fight for Mont St Quentin.

In his eulogy—published in the *Sun News Pictorial* on Anzac Day 1929 as 'Hated War but not Afraid to Fight'—Robert Croll described Frank Roberts as a 'typical member of the AIF'. Of course, he was no such thing. The representative Great War digger was actually a single, urban Anglican labourer in his early twenties who enlisted in 1915—and who returned, though probably wounded. (Vic Edwards is perhaps more representative, even if no one but him knew of the shrapnel fragment in his foot.) Frank was older, married, better educated, and middle class rather than working class. He enlisted later in the war and arguably from a rural community rather than a city. He died, rather than survived. But while Frank Roberts may have been unrepresentative in not conforming to the social markers of the representative digger, he was emblematic in another way: he represents the bonds of comradeship, the effects a soldier's death had on loved ones far away, and the long and complex legacy of remembrance that is such a powerful expression of the impact of the Great War, even to this day.

Some reminders of this story have long since disappeared. Gilbert's Mont St Quentin memorial and May Butler-George's bronze panels disappeared into the Third Reich's smelters over sixty years ago. On the slopes of Mont St Quentin, Elsa Trench can just be traced by a smear of chalk among the beet fields, but only with a detailed map. Of Sunnyside, nothing now exists besides some foundations half-concealed by a private garden off a road bearing its name. In Kallista, the only Roberts publicly acknowledged is Garry and Berta's friend and neighbour Tom—the artist who lived there briefly in the 1920s.

But reminders of the story exist. In the State Library of Victoria's warehouse in Ballarat lie piles of shrink-wrapped Record Books, literally a truckload of them. Page after page of clippings and letters and cuttings and photographs, all closely annotated by Garry Roberts, testify to his exhaustive search for solace. In Canberra, the exhibition galleries of the Australian War Memorial once again feature the Mont St Quentin diorama. Though quite different to the plaster model that an appalled Gilbert saw spinning on the platform at Péronne, and though much changed by many hands, the diorama still shows the attackers rising from Elsa Trench at 1.30 p.m. on Sunday 1 September 1918. And the cross raised over the grave of the 21st Battalion's dead of that afternoon, once regarded as 'too sad and personal' to be worth preserving, is now seen by visitors leaving the exhibition galleries on the way to the Roll of Honour, where the names of Roy, Ted, Albert, and Frank are cast on bronze panels.

Of the men of Nine Platoon, little remains physically but the files that document their lives so unevenly: the AIF files that describe posting, training, trials, and treatments; the accounts that they wrote as a favour to Robbie's poor grieving father that describe their part in the battle minute-by-minute; and the Repat files that detail their final painful years. Some of these men, such as Alf Crawford, remain shadowy figures even in a book that tells Nine Platoon's story in unprecedented detail. Others remain as characters in family memory, preserved strongly in some (such as the Castles or the Rablings); in others, just a photograph in an album.

Then there are the war cemeteries. Nine Platoon's war dead lie in two cemeteries. Frank, Albert Kelly, and Roy Smerdon lie in the Péronne Communal Cemetery Extension, and Ted Heath in St Sever Cemetery at Rouen.

Péronne's cemetery lies on a quiet residential street off the main Bapaume-Péronne road containing 1,494 British and Empire graves, and (unusually) some 97 German graves. As the fighting flowed over the town, both sides interred their dead in plots beside the municipal cemetery; after the Armistice, war graves units brought remains in from smaller outlying grave plots. Most of the dead are British, but they include 500-odd Australians, mainly killed in the battle for the Mont and for the town in a few days of fighting in August and September 1918. Nine Platoon's graves lie in a row of twelve 21st Battalion dead from the battle, with Alf, Frank, and Roy beside each other in the centre of the row, near to the customary memorial stone inscribed 'Their Names Liveth For Evermore'. Like all those looked after by the Commonwealth War Graves Commission, the cemetery is beautifully kept. Beer bottles lying about its porch suggest that it is used by bored teenagers looking for a quiet place to drink, but the Visitors' Book testifies to a steady stream of visitors, casual and purposeful, moved by the poignancy of this place, and by the dozens of cemeteries like it that dot the country that was the Western Front.

Ted Heath was buried in what became the St Sever Cemetery Extension, one of over 8,300 men, including 782 Australians, who died in the more than a dozen hospitals established at Rouen during the war. The cemetery, a large one even by the profligate standards of the Great War, is even sadder than the graveyards on the battlefields. It lies in a nondescript part of Rouen, virtually invisible within a warren of suburban streets, unvisited by all but the most dedicated pilgrim: it took me nearly an hour to find it, and I had a GPS unit in my car. In the six months before I visited, fewer than thirty others had signed the visitors' book—two of them War Graves Commission staff making routine inspections. Only two of the visitors were Australians, though there are more Australian-named headstones here than at Pozières, Villers-Bretonneux, or at any single cemetery on Gallipoli. By late 1918 the dead were being buried more or less in the order in which they died, usually more than a dozen each day. Sixteen other ranks died on 13 October (in the British way, officers were interred in separate plots). All were British, except for Ted and Corporal Albert Thom, also of the 21st Battalion, who came from Portarlington, close to Ted's home at Curdies River.

Like all other bereaved families, Ted's was asked to compose an epitaph. It expresses the additional pain that distance added to loss: 'Oh for a touch of a vanished hand and the sound of a voice so still'. I don't know if any of the Heaths visited Ted's grave in the ninety years between his death from infection in

12 General Hospital and the unseasonably cold and showery day in July that I visited his grave.

Some of the members of the Mont St Quentin families have odd souvenirs of the war distributed about grandchildren or great nieces or nephews: medals; a commemorative medallion; a pair of binoculars acquired in circumstances and a place now forgotten. Vivienne Lewis, Bert Roberts's daughter, cherishes a copy of C.J. Dennis's *The Glugs of Gosh*, which Dennis dedicated to her father after his shooting accident early in 1918. Her family is also proud of caring for a marble statuette of Mabel, Web Gilbert's wife, which was a gift from Gilbert to Garry. Jilba Georgalis, Nancy's daughter, treasures one of the red-and-black enamelled remembrance brooches that Garry commissioned in the week after his most awful day. Indeed, perhaps the most poignant reminders of the story of Mont St Quentin are Jilba's.

Ruby and then Nancy kept an assortment of mementos. They are now Jilba's. They include framed photographs of Frank and Ruby, and one of Garry's surviving federation Record Books, and Ruby's autograph book from the happy years at Sunnyside before the war — with not only C.J. Dennis's autograph, but what seems to be an original verse by Dennis in his own hand. The treasures also include the copy of C.J. Dennis's *Songs of a Sentimental Bloke*, bought with Robert Croll's fee from the *Sun News Pictorial* in 1929. Like Vivienne Lewis's *Glugs of Gosh*, it has been annotated, with clippings and photographs pasted in — additions that help to answer questions about Garry and Berta and their children, and to conclude their story. (Creating scrapbooks seems to have been something of a Roberts habit: thank goodness.)

Jilba also has a shoe box holding medals, badges, and odds and ends in which, as a museum historian, I take a particular interest. Some were collected during the Second World War when Ruby and Percy entertained servicemen at Orrong Road. American Marines at liberty in Melbourne left their badges, as did airmen, like the young man whom Barbara loved and lost. But the box also contains Frank's two service medals—the Victory Medal and the War Medal, and the Female Relative Badges sent to both Ruby and Berta as the widow and mother of a dead soldier. There is the membership badge of the Sailors and Soldiers' Fathers' Association, the organisation in which Garry 'carried on'—although this particular badge belonged to Percy Minter's father, also a member. Perhaps that was how Garry came to meet Percy.

And there is a small cotton bag, hand-sewn and covered with a name and address in thick black ink:

No. 6874
F.W. Roberts
C Company
21st Battalion
Australian Imperial Force
ABROAD

Opening the bag, you find a small fold of paper bearing a lock of fine golden-blonde hair—it is Frank's, cut and preserved by Garry and Berta some time in 1888. And there are two bootees, or rather, baby shoes, made of soft, burgundy-coloured leather. These were Nancy's first shoes, in which she took her first steps. Ruby sent one of the shoes to her Frank: the other she kept, to be reunited when Frank's lucky star brought him safely home as he promised. She posted the parcel on 11 September; ten days after Frank's death and two days before she learned she was a widow. The bag was among the last items to be returned to Ruby among Frank's effects, months later. The booties are 'the sound of a voice so still': a final, poignant reminder of what the Great War did to this family. Ruby kept them in a shoebox, symbols of the marriage she had lost, and of the little girl robbed of a father a little after 2.30 on the afternoon of 1 September 1918, on the slopes of Mont St Quentin.

Acknowledgements

My principal debt is to the families and friends of the men of Nine Platoon: Mr Gordon Castle, Mr Greg Castle, Mrs Anita Comran, Ms Anne Eastaugh, Mrs Lorraine Eastaugh, Mr Jim Edwards, Mrs Jan Fraser, Mrs Kaye Hurcum, Mrs Ruth Lennie, Ms Vivienne Lewis, Mrs Margaret Maloney, Mr & Mrs Ken and Eveline McLeod, Mrs Annelle Perotti, Mr Don Smerdon, Mrs Ollie Tognulla, Mr Murray Williams, Mrs Joyce Wilson, Mr John Yard, Ms Margaret Young, and, above all, Mrs Jilba Georgalis. Thanks to all for their generous co-operation.

In that it began as war history and ended as Australian social history, this book is a fitting symbol of the transition I made in the course of researching and writing it, from the Australian War Memorial to the National Museum of Australia. I am deeply appreciative of the support of Mr Craddock Morton, director of the National Museum of Australia, who has not only established my new and very congenial workplace, the Centre for Historical Research, but has greatly encouraged and eased my work, notably by accepting this project as part of my research at the museum.

My colleagues at the National Museum of Australia, and especially in its Centre for Historical Research, while not always understanding why a museum historian was 'doing military history', nevertheless welcomed and supported me in this enterprise. It has become one of the first products of our Centre's 'Material Histories' project. I am particularly grateful to the Centre's grants and administration officer, Ms Anne Faris, who assisted in locating sources, shared the ups and downs of the search for Nine Platoon families, and read and commented on the manuscript.

The museum's librarian, Ms Julie Philips, assisted the project greatly by acquiring the Inglis collection of books dealing largely with the remembrance of the Great War. (Naturally, I am also grateful to Professor Ken Inglis for his generosity in donating his collection to the museum.)

Members of the Museum's Friends, notably Mr Tom Campbell, also read and made valuable comments on the manuscript. I am grateful to the leaders and participants of the community, U3A, and Probus groups who've stimulated my research, and especially to Ms Ann Moyal, Mr Ian Stagoll, and Mr Barrie Virtue.

Many friends and colleagues have helped me along the way: Ms Victoria D'Alton, Dr Nial Barr, Ms Michele Bomford (a future historian of Mont St Quentin), Mr Mike Cecil, Ms Anne-Marie Condé; Dr John Connor, Prof. Bill Gammage, Ms Margaret Hutchison, Prof. Jeff Grey, Prof. Ken Inglis, Prof. Pat Jalland, Dr Mark Johnston, Dr John Lack, Dr Isabel McBride, Mr Gil McLachlan, Mr Mat McLachlan, Dr Ann Mitchell, Dr Richard Reid, Ms Di Rutherford, Lt Col Neil Smith, Mr Anthony Staunton, Mr Nigel Steel, and especially Ms Sharon Pereira of Births, Deaths and Marriages, Victoria, whose responsiveness enabled me to trace Frank and Ruby's granddaughter, enabling the fruitful meeting that followed.

Mr Roger Lee and his Army History Unit once again assisted my work in a highly practical manner. An army research grant for 2007 enabled me to make the first of two field trips to Mont St Quentin. I am also grateful to the Research School of Humanities at the Australian National University which, through a visiting fellowship in 2008, enabled me to complete the manuscript.

Many curators, librarians, and archivists have helped, some more than they knew. At the State Library of Victoria (as the endnotes show, the key repository for this book), I thank Ms Anne-Marie Schwirtlich and the staff of the Australiana reading room in the La Trobe Library, particularly Mr Greg Gerrard, the librarian responsible for the manuscripts collection. The staff of the National Archives of Australia, at its Canberra, Melbourne, Perth, and Sydney repositories, provided invaluable help, particularly Ms Kim Burrell and Mr Simeon Barlow. The staff of the National Library of Australia, particularly the librarians in the Petherick Reading Room, provided an efficient and congenial place to read and write. At the Department of Veterans' Affairs, Mr Anthony Staunton and Mr Norman Kalagayan assisted me to identify and obtain the vital Repat files. At the Australian War Memorial, I thank Mr Craig Tibbetts and his colleagues in the memorial's research centre and Ms Laura Webster of the art section. Thanks, too, to David Hurlston of the National Gallery of Victoria, Olwen Ford of the Sunshine and District Historical Society, Kate Prinsley and Geradine Horgan of the Royal Historical Society of Victoria ,and the staff of the Mitchell Library, Sydney. In Britain, I again appreciate the expert assistance of Miss Pamela Clark and her colleagues at the Royal Archives, and the staff of the National Library of Scotland, the National Army Museum, and the National Archives at Kew.

I especially thank Miss Gretel Ayre, my volunteer researcher, whose painstaking research contributed greatly to my understanding of the detail of Nine Platoon and the 21st Battalion's men's lives.

I acknowledge the fine work of cartographer Keith Mitchell who produced the location maps for the book.

I am grateful to Dr Carly Millar, Dave Altheim and Miriam Rosenbloom for their creative co-operation in producing the book.

I thank my publisher, Mr Henry Rosenbloom of Scribe, for his patient support of a project that continued for longer than I had planned. The book I delivered is very different to the 'battle book' I sketched out to him in 2005, but I believe that it is all the better for concentrating on Nine Platoon.

I am grateful to Kairen Harris and Mike Puleston, and to Gordon Cruickshank, whose hospitality greatly eased the burden of research in distant places.

As ever, I acknowledge the forbearance of Claire, and Claire and Jane, who for the first time were able to travel with me to the scene of this book: the fields, the cemetery, and the memorial in and around Péronne.

Notes

Prologue

1 The main source for reconstructing Garry Roberts's most awful day is his 1918 diary, held at 265/4, Ms 9949 in the State Library of Victoria (SLV).

Introduction

1 Charles Bean, *The Australian Imperial Force in France: during the main German offensive, 1918*, Angus & Robertson, Sydney, 1942, p. 873.
2 *Quinn's Post: Anzac, Gallipoli*, Allen & Unwin, Sydney, 2005.
3 Joy Damousi, *Labour of Loss: mourning, memory, and wartime bereavement*, Cambridge University Press, Cambridge, 1999; Tanja Luckins, *The Gates of Memory: Australian people's experience and memories of loss and the Great War*, Curtin University Books, Perth, 2004; Pat Jalland, *Changing Ways of Death in Twentieth Century Australia*, Oxford University Press, Oxford, 2002; Bruce Scates, 'Soldiers' journeys: returning to the battlefields of the Great War', *Journal of the Australian War Memorial*, No. 40, http://:www.awm.gov.au/journal/j40/scates.asp

Part I: Belonging

1 2/10, *Herald*, 20 December 1913, Roberts Record Books, 2/10, Ms 8 505, SLV.
2 Robert Croll, *I Recall: Collections and Recollections*, Robertson & Mullens, Melbourne, 1939, p. 44.
3 Alec Reid, Betty Hotchin & Yvonne DeLacy, *A Village in the Forest: the story of Kallista*, Kallista Centenary 1993 Association, Kallista, 1993, p. 31.

4   Ian McLaren, *C.J. Dennis: his life and work*, Hall's Book Store, Melbourne, 1961, p. 12.
5   'Uncle Jim', in C.J. Dennis, *The Songs of a Sentimental Bloke*, Angus & Robertson, Sydney, 1915.
6   2/10, *Herald*, 20 December 1913, Roberts Record Books, Ms 8505, SLV.
7   24/365, Frank Roberts to Garry Roberts, 5 May 1915, Roberts Record Books, Ms 8508, SLV.
8   Frank Roberts to Ruby Roberts, 22 May 1917, 'The Dream on the Wind', p. 6.
9   Frank Roberts to Garry Roberts, 9 October 1917, 'The Dream on the Wind', p. 187.
10 Diary, Frank Roberts, 20 August 1917 & 8 September 1917, 'The Dream on the Wind', pp. 120; 148.
11 Frank Roberts to Ruby Roberts, 25 December 1917, 'The Dream on the Wind', p. 209.
12 Frank Roberts to Garry Roberts, 5 January 1918, 'The Dream on the Wind', p. 214.
13 4/83, Frank Roberts to Garry Roberts, 27 December 1917, Roberts Record Books, MS 8508, SLV.
14 Frank Roberts to Ruby Roberts, 3 September 1917, 'The Dream on the Wind', p. 140.
15 Frank Roberts to Ruby Roberts, 23 August & 1 September 1917, 'The Dream on the Wind', p. 131.
16 Diary, Frank Roberts, 18 August 1917, 'The Dream on the Wind', p. 119.
17 Frank Roberts to Bert Roberts, 8 January 1918, 'The Dream on the Wind', p. 229.
18 Frank Roberts to Ruby Roberts, 31 July 1918, 'The Dream on the Wind', p. 392.
19 4/88, Bert Roberts, 'My Niece', 4 November 1917, Roberts Record Books, Ms 8508, SLV.
20 4/94, Frank Roberts to Nancy Roberts, 9 January 1918, Roberts Record Books, Ms 8508, SLV.
21 5/35, Frank Roberts to Edith Alston, 5 May 1918, Roberts Record Books, Ms 8508, SLV.
22 J.N.I. Dawes & L.L. Robson, *Citizen to Soldier: Australia before the Great War — recollections of the First A.I.F.*, Melbourne University Press, Melbourne, 1977; throughout.
23 Jocelyn Linder (ed.), *Murrayville 1910–2007*, Murrayville Liaison Committee, Murrayville, 2007.

24 DCM, Pte G.E. Dobson, 21st Battalion' A471, 19783, NAA.
25 Baker, Arthur Leslie, M7618, B73, NAA.
26 5/38, Frank Roberts to Garry Roberts, 3 May 1918, Roberts Record Books, Ms 8508, SLV.
27 Frank Roberts to Ruby Roberts, c. 5 February 1918, 'The Dream on the Wind', p. 248.
28 Frank Roberts to Ruby Roberts, 2 June 1918, 'The Dream on the Wind', p. 345.
29 6/42, Frank Roberts to Edith Alston, 10 July 1918, Roberts Record Books, Ms 8508, SLV.
30 Frank Roberts to Garry Roberts, 26 February 1918, 'The Dream on the Wind', p. 260.
31 Frank Roberts to Garry Roberts, 27 December 1917, 'The Dream on the Wind', p. 213.
32 Frank Roberts to Ruby Roberts, 9 January 1918, 'The Dream on the Wind', p. 235.
33 Diary, Charles Bean, c. 15 April 1918, 3 DRL 606, item 107 [2], AWM 38.
34 Diary, Frank Roberts, 23 June 1918, 'The Dream on the Wind', p. 343.
35 Diary, Charles Bean, 8 September 1918, 3 DRL 606, item 116, AWM 38.
36 Diary, Frank Roberts, 26 July 1918, 27/494, Roberts Record Books, Ms 8508, SLV.
37 Diary, Frank Roberts, 29 August 1917, 'The Dream on the Wind', p. 104.
38 385/21, Lewis gun tactics in trenches, AWM 25.
39 385/4, Lectures ... Machine-guns including Lewis guns, AWM 25.
40 Diary, Frank Brewer, 2 & 14 July 1918, ML MSS 1536/2, ML.
41 John Monash to Thomas Dodds, 7 September 1918, and associated papers, Monash papers, Series 1, Correspondence B, Box 73, Folder 504, MS 1884, NLA.
42 Diary, Garry Roberts, 28 October 1916, Box 265/3, Ms 9949, SLV.
43 Diary, Garry Roberts, 28 February 1917, Box 265/3, Ms 9949, SLV.
44 Diary, Garry Roberts, 21 December 1917, Box 265/3, Ms 9949, SLV.
45 4/83, Frank Roberts to Garry Roberts, 27 December 1917, Roberts Record Books, Ms 8508, SLV.
46 C.J. Dennis to Garry Roberts, 16 September 1918, J.G. Roberts diary, 1918, Box 265/4, Ms 9949, SLV.
47 6/57, *Age*, 28 September 1918, Roberts Record Books, Ms 8508, SLV.

48 6/57, 'Carry On!', by 'Oriel', *Our Empire*, May 1918, Roberts Record Books, Ms 8508, SLV.
49 6/53, Frank Roberts to Ruby Roberts, 21 August 1918, Roberts Record Books, Ms 8508, SLV.
50 Frank Roberts to Ruby Roberts, 4 February 1918, 'The Dream on the Wind', p. 243.
51 Diary, Charles Bean, 22 August 1918, 3 DRL 606, items 116, AWM 38.
52 Charles Bean, 'The beginnings of the AWM', 3 DRL 6673, item 619, p. 10, AWM 38.
53 *The Times*, 12 June 1920, 11a.
54 5/35, Frank Roberts to Edith Alston, 5 May 1918, Roberts Record Books, Ms 8508, SLV.
55 6/25, Frank Roberts to Berta Roberts, 24 June 1918, Roberts Record Books, Ms 8508, SLV.
56 Postcard, Roy Smerdon to his sister Emily, 14 May 1918, courtesy of Mrs Jan Fraser.
57 Diary, Charles Bean, 29 August 1918, 3 DRL 606, item 116, AWM 38.
58 5/63, Frank Roberts to Ruby Roberts, 2 June 1918, Roberts Record Books, Ms 8508, SLV.
59 Notebook, Charles Bean, May 1918, 3 DRL 606, item 112, AWM 38.
60 6/37, Frank Roberts to Ruby Roberts, 9 July 1918, Roberts Record Books, Ms 8508, SLV.
61 Diary, Frank Roberts, 28 July 1918, ML DOC 1361, ML.
62 Erich Ludendorff, *My War Memories*, 1914–1918, Vol. II, pp. 679; 684.
63 4/61–65, Frank Robert to Garry Roberts, 27 December 1917, Roberts Record Books, Ms 8508, SLV.
64 6/61, Frank Roberts to Ruby Roberts, 23 August 1918, Roberts Record Books, Ms 8508, SLV.
65 6/73, Frank Roberts, Diary, 30 August 1918, Roberts Record Books, Ms 8508, SLV.
66 John Monash, *The Australian Victories in France in 1918*, Hutchinson and Co., London, 1920, p. 181.
67 Diary, Charles Bean, 20 August 1918, 3 DRL 606, item 116, AWM 38.
68 Diary, Charles Rosenthal, 29 August 1918, ML MSS 2739/1, CY2465, ML.

69 Diary, Charles Bean, 23 August 1918, 3 DRL 606, item 116, AWM 38.
70 Frank Roberts to Ruby Roberts, 23 August 1918, J.G. Roberts diary, 1918, 265/4, Ms 9949, SLV.
71 Diary, Charles Bean, 4 September 1918, 3 DRL 606, item 116, AWM 38.
72 Frank Roberts to Ruby Roberts, 23 August 1918, 'The Dream on the Wind', p. 429.
73 Lieutenant William Emlyn Hardwick, 21st Battalion, B2455, NAA.
74 Bean notebook, interview with McColl (23rd Battalion), 3 DRL 606, item 228, AWM 38.
75 Tom Wignall statement, 3 DRL 6673, item 91, AWM 38.

Part II: Fighting

1 *The Times*, 30 September 1914, 7a.
2 Robert Graves, *Goodbye to All That*, Jonathan Cape, London, 1929, p. 297.
3 *The Times*, 26 March 1917, 8c.
4 *The Times*, 20 March 1917, 6c.
5 W.A. Somerset, 'The Greatest Feat of the War', *Life*, 1 June 1921, p. 467.
6 Diary, Charles Bean, 29 August 1918, 3 DRL 606, item 116, AWM 38.
7 John Monash, *The Australian Victories in France in 1918*, Hutchinson and Co., London, 1920, p. 184.
8 'Report on operations of Second Australian Division', 1/45/34, part 3, War diary, 2nd Australian Division, AWM 4.
9 Frank Brewer, 'Report on the Battle of Mont St Quentin', ML MSS1536/2, ML.
10 Les Carlyon, *The Great War*, Macmillan, Sydney, 2006, p. 686.
11 1/44/37, part 1, War diary, 2nd Australian Division, 31 August 1918, AWM 4.
12 Richard Travers, *Diggers in France: Australian soldiers on the Western Front*, ABC Books, Sydney, 2008, p. 309.
13 'Message of appreciation from Gen Rawlinson to Aust Corps on capture of Mont St Quentin Sept 1918', 'Papers 1918; twelve files of miscellaneous records …', 3 DRL 6673/57, AWM 38. Curiously, records of the 'flag' message do not seem to appear in the war diaries of either the Australian Corps (1/35, AWM 4) or of Fourth Army (1/14, AWM 4).

14 'Operations 6th Infantry Brigade, August 31st–September 4th', 526/2, Period 12, Final Offensive 27 August–5 September 1918, Fourth Army, Australian Corps, 2nd Australian Division, 6th Australian Brigade, AWM 26.
15 21st Battalion reports, orders and signals, Box 526, item 3, AWM 26.
16 John Monash, *The Australian Victories in France in 1918*, Hutchinson and Co., London, 1920, pp. 182–83.
17 Diary, Charles Bean, 29 August 1918, 3 DRL 606, item 116, AWM 38.
18 Entries on German divisions on the Mont St Quentin sector in Terry Cave, (ed.), *Histories of Two Hundred and Fifty-one Divisions of the German Army*, London Stamp Exchange, London, 1989.
19 'Fourth Army 1918, German order of battle on Fourth Army front', WO153/576, NAUK.
20 Diary, Charles Bean, 6 May 1918, 3 DRL 606, item 109, AWM 38.
21 21st Battalion war diary, Sep 1918, 23/38/37, AWM 4.
22 James Edmonds, *Military Operations in France and Belgium 1918*, Vol. IV, HMSO, London, 1947, p. 386.
23 Jillian Durance, *Still Going Strong: the story of the Moyarra Honor Roll*, Moyarra, 2006, p. 131.
24 Jack Castle statement, 3 DRL 6673/91, AWM 38.
25 Charles Bean to John Gellibrand, 18 March 1918, 3 DRL 6673, item 419/8/1, AWM 38, cited in Dale Blair, *No Quarter: unlawful killing and surrender in the Australian experience 1915–18*, Ginninderra Press, Canberra, p. 2005, p. 9.
26 *Ibid*, pp. 15–16.
27 Memorandum, 21st Battalion, 1 Sep 1918, War diary, 23/37, AWM 4.
28 Tom Wignall statement, 3 DRL 6673/91, AWM 38.
29 Second Lieutenant Alfred Sennitt, 21st Battalion, B2455, NAA.
30 Bean notebook, interview with McColl (23rd Battalion), 3 DRL 606, item 228, AWM 38.
31 Noble Norwood statement, 3 DRL 6673/91, AWM 38.
32 385/4, Lectures … machine-guns including Lewis guns', AWM 25.
33 Tom Wignall statement, 3 DRL 6673/91, AWM 38.
34 Noble Norwood statement, 3 DRL 6673/91, AWM 38.
35 Tom Wignall statement, 3 DRL 6673/91, AWM 38.
36 Vic Edwards statement, 3 DRL 6733/91, AWM 38.
37 385/4, Lectures … Machine-guns including Lewis guns, AWM 25.
38 Alf Crawford statement, 3 DRL 6673, item 91, AWM 38.
39 Phil Starr statement, 3 DRL 6673/91, AWM 38.
40 Jack Castle statement, 3 DRL 6673/91, AWM 38.

41 Review of Photographic volume in *Evening Sun* (Melbourne) 16 November 1923, 3 DRL 6673, item 204B, AWM 38.
42 Phil Starr statement, 3 DRL 6673/91, AWM 38.
43 Diary, Charles Bean, 2 September 1918, 3 DRL 606, item 116, AWM 38.
44 *Op. cit.*
45 Bean notebook (21st Battalion informant), 3 DRL 606, item 228, AWM 38.
46 Clipping, *Age*, 28 December 1918, Roberts papers, Diary, Garry Roberts, December 1918, 265/4, Ms 9949, SLV.
47 A.G. Butler, *The Official History of the Australian Army Medical Services in the War of 1914–1918*, Vol. II, *The Western Front*, AWM, Canberra, 1940, p. 689.
48 Wignall, Thomas Henry, HX51337, B73, NAA.
49 6518, Edward Oliver Heath, 21st Battalion, B2455, NAA.
50 Roll of Honour circulars, Edward Oliver Heath & Leslie Toulmin Heath, AWM 131.
51 Frank Roberts to Garry Roberts, 13 May 1918, 'The Dream on the Wind', p. 335.
52 Roll of Honour circular, Edward Oliver Heath, AWM 131.
53 Diary, Donald Coutts, 4 September 1918, PR83/155, AWM.
54 W.H. Downing, *To the Last Ridge*, H.H. Chapman, Melbourne, 1920, p. 165.
55 Diary, Charles Bean, 2 September 1918, 3 DRL 606, item 116, AWM 38.
56 Diary, Norman Nicolson, 5 September 1918, 3DRL 2715, AWM.
57 *Sydney Morning Herald*, 17 December 1918, p. 7.
58 C.E.W. Bean, *The Australian Imperial Force in France: during the Allied offensive, 1918*, Vol. VI, Sydney, 1942, pp. 883–84.
59 Disbandment of 21st Battalion, 344/6, AWM 27.
60 Diary, Lawrence Polinelli, 23 September 1918, PR86/072, AWM.
61 *The Red and Black Diamond*, Vol I, No. 4, April 1936, p. 6.
62 Document dated 20 September 1918, Papers of William Montgomery, 'Acting Adjutant of the 21st', PR00093, AWM.
63 Disbandment of 21st Battalion, 344/6, AWM 27.
64 Bean notebook (22nd Battalion officer), 3 DRL 606, item 228, AWM 38.
65 Vic Edwards statement, 3 DRL 6673/91, AWM 38.
66 Diary, Charles Bean, 9 October 1918 and annotation 1954, 3 DRL 606, item 117, AWM 38.

67 21st Battalion war diary, October 1918, WO95/3329, NAUK.
68 'The Break Up of the Battalion', *The Red and Black Diamond*, Vol. I, No. 4, April 1936, p. 7.
69 Diary, Donald Coutts, 14 October 1918, PR83/155, AWM.
70 John Monash to Charles Rosenthal, 4 September 1918, Monash papers, Series 1, Correspondence B, Box 73, folder 504, MS 1884, NLA.
71 John Monash to John McCay, 6 September 1918, Monash papers, Series 1, Correspondence B, Box 73, folder 504, MS 1884, NLA.
72 John Monash to John Longstaff, 3 September 1918, Monash papers, Series 1, Correspondence B, Box 73, folder 504, MS 1884, NLA.
73 War Office communiqué, 6.20 p.m., 1 September 1918, Hughes papers, Series 23, Box 119, MS 1538, NLA.
74 Bean extract book, Mont St Quentin–Péronne, 3 DRL 1722/35, 116/120, AWM 38.
75 *The Times*, 2 September 1918, 9f.
76 *The Times*, 2 September 1918, 8b.
77 'Record of Part of the Work Done in 1918', Hughes Papers, Series 23, Box 121, MS 1538, NLA.
78 H.C. Smart to Monash, 3 September 1918, Monash papers, Series 1A, Box 16, Folder 140, NLA.
79 *The Times*, 2 September 1918, 10b.
80 *Aussie: the Australian Soldiers' Magazine*, No. 7, September 1918.
81 *Sydney Morning Herald*, 9 September 1918.
82 Charles Bean, 'The West Front Tours of Billy Hughes, 1916–18', 3 DRL 6673, item 220, AWM 38.
83 *Op. cit.*
84 'Taking of Mont St Quentin', *Argus*, 23 November 1918.
85 *Herald*, 4 January 1919.
86 Diary, Charles Bean, 18 September 19183 DRL 606, item 116, AWM 38.
87 *Age*, 12 March 1921, Diary, Garry Roberts, Box 266/1, Ms 9949, SLV.
88 Louis McCubbin, *The battle of Mont St Quentin in progress as seen from a ridge near Clery and painted between 2 am and 4 am on the day of the battle*, ART03051, AWM.
89 Arthur Streeton to Nora Streeton, 26 October 1918, Ann Galbally & Anne Gray, (eds), *Letters from Smike: the letters of Arthur Streeton*, Oxford University Press, Melbourne, 1989, p. 154.
90 Frank Brewer, 'Report on the Battle of Mont St Quentin, ML MSS1536/2, ML.

91 Anne Gray, *Streeton in France*, AWM, Canberra, 1982, p. 17.
92 *The British Australasian*, 12 June 1919, p. 11.
93 *Age*, 14 July 1926.
94 Diary, Lawrence Polinelli, 22 October, 6 November and 11 November 1918, PR86/72, AWM.

Part III: Grieving

1 Frank Roberts to Ruby Roberts, 9 July 1918, Diary, Garry Roberts, September 1918, 265/4, Ms 9949, SLV.
2 8/49, N. Lloyd to Garry Roberts, nd, Roberts Record Books, Ms 8508, SLV.
3 8/100, C.J. Dennis to Garry Roberts, 21 Sep 1918, Roberts Record Books, Ms 8508, SLV.
4 Diary, Garry Roberts, 16 September 1918, 265/4, Ms 9949, SLV.
5 7/23–24, Phil Starr to Garry Roberts, 6 Sep 1918, Roberts Record Books, Ms 8508, SLV.
6 7/44, Percy Barratt to Ruby Roberts, 11 Oct 1918, Roberts Record Books, Ms 8508, SLV.
7 7/34–35, Noble Norwood to Ruby Roberts, 19 September 1918, Roberts Record Books, Ms 8508, SLV.
8 7/45, Edward Edwards to Ruby Roberts, 13 December 1918, Roberts Record Books, Ms 8508, SLV.
9 *Daily Express*, 2 Sep 1918, 7/225, Roberts Record Books, MS 8508, SLV.
10 7/33, Sydney Buckley to Ruby Roberts, 12 Sep 1918, Roberts Record Books, Ms 8508, SLV.
11 7/45, Edward Edwards to Ruby Roberts, 13 December 1918; 7/67, Red Cross to Garry, 3 June 1919, Roberts Record Books, Ms 8508, SLV.
12 7/48, Red Cross Inquiry Office to Garry Roberts, 11 January 1919, Roberts Record Books, Ms 8508, SLV.
13 7/66, Red Cross to Garry Roberts, 6 May 1919, Roberts Record Books, Ms 8508, SLV.
14 Diary, Garry Roberts, 25 January 1919, 266/1, Ms 9949, SLV.
15 7/69, Base Records to Ruby Roberts, 16 October 1919, Roberts Record Books, Ms 8508, SLV.
16 J. Beacham Kiddle to Garry Roberts, 14 April 1919, copy in Roberts Papers, ML.
17 7/40–41, Edward Barratt to Ruby Roberts, 23 September 1918, Roberts Record Books, Ms 8508, SLV.
18 7/127, John Blackmore to Garry Roberts, 30 November 1918, Roberts Record Books, Ms 8508, SLV.

19 7/135, Dave Chandler to Garry Roberts, Roberts Record Books, Ms 8508, SLV.
20 Alexander Walker, 6398, 21st Battalion, B2455, NAA; 7/160–161, Bella Walker to Garry Roberts, 2 May, 5 July, 1 and 20 Sep 1920, Roberts Record Books, Ms 8508, SLV.
21 7/129, Isabel Kelly to Garry Roberts, 12 Nov 1918 and 10 Feb 1920, Roberts Record Books, Ms 8508, SLV.
22 7/71, Circular from Imperial War Graves Commission, 18 January 1920, Roberts Record Books, Ms 8508, SLV.
23 7/71–74, Imperial War Graves Commission to Roberts family, 1920, Roberts Record Books, Ms 8508, SLV.
24 'Shed thou no tears', MSS 1297, Harry Barrett, 21st Battalion, AWM.
25 7/51, Note by Garry Roberts, May 1919, Roberts Record Books, Ms 8508, SLV.
26 7/51, Note by Garry Roberts, May 1919, Roberts Record Books, Ms 8508, SLV.
27 7/66, Note by Garry Roberts, c. March 1919, Roberts Record Books, Ms 8508, SLV.
28 11/102, Noble Norwood to Garry Roberts, 31 Dec 1919, Roberts Record Books, Ms 8508, SLV.
29 10/103 Alf Fox to Garry Roberts, 18 May 1919, Roberts Record Books, Ms 8508, SLV.
30 12/54, Les Baker to Garry Roberts, 22 February 1920, Roberts Record Books, Ms 8508, SLV.
31 12/64–65, Alby Lowerson to Garry Roberts, 6 April 1920, Roberts Record Books, Ms 8508, SLV.
32 10/116, Phil Starr to Garry Roberts, 1 June 1919, Roberts Record Books, Ms 8508, SLV.
33 11/121, Phil Starr to Garry Roberts, 14 January 1920, Roberts Record Books, Ms 8508, SLV.
34 11/115, Guy Innes to Garry Roberts, 12 Jan 1919, Roberts Record Books, Ms 8508, SLV.
35 12/59, Jeannie Gunn to Garry Roberts, 6 March 1920, Roberts Record Books, Ms 8508, SLV.
36 12/112, Noble Norwood to Garry Roberts, 6 September 1920, Roberts Record Books, Ms 8508, SLV.
37 11/126, Vic Edwards to Garry Roberts, 19 Jan 1920, Roberts Record Books, Ms 8508, SLV.
38 Garry Roberts to Charles Bean, 8 September 1921, 3 DRL 6673/91, AWM 38.

39 14/224, Phil Starr to Garry Roberts, 28 Aug 1922, Roberts Record Books, Ms 8508, SLV.
40 Diary, 6 & 7 Sep 1918, Charles Rosenthal, ML MSS 2739/1, CY 2465, ML.
41 *Argus*, 10 January 1920.
42 J.G. Roberts, diary, 8 January 1919, 266/1, Ms 9949, SLV.
43 7/72–53, Web Gilbert to Garry Roberts, 20 November 1918, Roberts Record Books, Ms 8508, SLV.
44 J.G. Roberts, diary, 7 February 1919, 266/1, Ms 9949, SLV.
45 *The Red and White Diamond*, in Donald Coutts's diary, PR83/155, AWM.
46 25/488, *Table Talk*, 9 April 1920, Roberts Record Books, Ms 8508, SLV.
47 13/106, Noble Norwood to Garry Roberts, 5 November 1920, Roberts Record Books, Ms 8508, SLV.
48 Garry Roberts to John Treloar, 14 September 1921, 12/11/4144, J.G. Roberts, Esq ... Request for the donation of private records of Private Francis William Roberts, AWM 93.
49 F.M. Cutlack, *The Australians: their final campaign, 1918*, Sampson Low, Marston, London, 1919, p. 275.
50 F.M. Cutlack, *The Australians: their final campaign, 1918*, Sampson Low, Marston, London, 1919, p. 294.
51 15/123, Jack Castle to Garry Roberts, 4 Sep 1922, Roberts Record Books, Ms 8508, SLV.
52 *Herald* (Melbourne), 1 September 1919.
53 Frederick Maurice, *The Last Four Months: the end of the war in the west*, Cassell, London, 1919, p. 116.
54 Extract book 'Mont St Péronne–Péronne Aug 27, 1918–Sep 6', 3 DRL 1722/35, AWM 38.
55 25/446, 'The Australian Victories in France', No. VIII, *Sydney Mail*, March 1920, Roberts Record Books, Ms 8508, SLV.
56 John Monash, *The Australian Victories in France in 1918*, Hutchinson and Co., London, 1920, p. 178 (emphasis added).
57 John Monash, *The Australian Victories in France in 1918*, Hutchinson and Co., London, 1920, p. 191.
58 27/428, Note by Garry Roberts, 8 September 1921, Roberts Record Books, Ms 8508, SLV.
59 12/28, *Argus*, nd, Roberts Record Books, Ms 8508, SLV.
60 'My Trip with Dad to France', Monash papers, Series 4, Box 130, Folder 965, MS 1884, NLA.

61 7/170, *Our Empire*, 19 January 1920, Roberts Record Books, Ms 8508, SLV.
62 21/402, Clippings relating to Monash's death, October 1931, Roberts Record Books, MS 8508, SLV.
63 War Trophies – 21st Battalion, 4386/42/21, AWM 16.
64 13/79, Roberts Record Books, Ms 8508, SLV.
65 7/59, Red Cross to Garry Roberts, 3 February 1919, Roberts Record Books, Ms 8508, SLV.
66 15/123, Jack Castle to Garry Roberts, 4 Sep 1922, Roberts Record Books, Ms 8508, SLV.
67 7/165, Web Gilbert to Garry Roberts, 15 June 1919, Roberts Record Books, Ms 8508, SLV.
68 Photograph of the cross erected over the graves of men of the 21st Battalion AIF at Mont St Quentin, 17/1/11/110, AWM 93.
69 Models of Battlefields, 4372/21/4, AWM 16
70 7/245, Charles Bean to John Treloar, 5 September 1921, Roberts Record Books, Ms 8508, SLV.
71 Charles Bean to John Treloar, 14 May 1918, Proposal re. scheme of models required for Australian War Museum, 4372/21/3, AWM 16.
72 *Age*, 12 March 1921, Diary, Garry Roberts, 1921, Box 266/3, Ms 9949, SLV.
73 *Sunday Times*, 9 January 1921, Diary, Garry Roberts, 1921, Box 266/3, Ms 9949, SLV.
74 *Herald*, 4 June 1921, Diary, Garry Roberts, 1921, Box 266/3, Ms 9949, SLV.
75 *Age*, 12 March 1921, Diary, Garry Roberts, 1921, Box 266/3, Ms 9949, SLV.
76 Gilbert, C. Web—Staff, 22/2/273, AWM 93.
77 Purchase of stores from Mrs C. Web Gilbert, 23/5/5, AWM 93.
78 Mont St Quentin picture model, 13/1/33, AWM 93.

Part IV: Remembering

1 C.H.M. Clark, *A History of Australia*, Vol. VI, Melbourne University Press, Melbourne, 1987, p. 117.
2 11/91–92, Noble Norwood to Garry Roberts, 21 November 1919, Roberts Record Books, Ms 8508, SLV.
3 11/125, Edith Alston to Garry Roberts, 14 Jan 1920, Roberts Record Books, Ms 8508, SLV.
4 13/141, Noble Norwood to Garry Roberts, 5 March 1921, Roberts Record Books, Ms 8508, SLV.

5 *The Hundred Best Photographs of the World War*, Windsor, nd, np.
6 Record of Evidence, 19 August 1919, C138/3, C122956, 'Charles Tognella', NAA.
7 Noble Joseph Norwood, R1151, PP889/1, NAA.
8 15/132, Noble Norwood to Garry Roberts, 16 Sep 1922; 15/170–71, Noble Norwood to Garry Roberts, 30 Dec 1922, Roberts Record Books, Ms 8508, SLV.
9 11/72–73, Noble Norwood to Garry Roberts, 15 Oct 1919, Roberts Record Books, Ms 8508, SLV.
10 Victor James Edwards, P107/38, M5789, NAA.
11 13/194, Vic Edwards to Garry Roberts, 23 May 1921, Roberts Record Books, Ms 8508, SLV.
12 12/60, Vic Edwards to Garry Roberts, c. 19 February 1920, Roberts Record Books, Ms 8508, SLV.
13 13/248, Vic Edwards to Garry Roberts, 19 October 1921, Roberts Record Books, Ms 8508, SLV.
14 14/169, Vic Edwards to Garry Roberts, 16 May 1922, Roberts Record Books, Ms 8508, SLV.
15 12/110, Tom Wignall to Garry Roberts, 8 Sep 1920, Roberts Record Books, Ms 8508, SLV.
16 Frank Brewer, *All About the War Gratuity*, Melbourne, 1920, p. 10 and Table '1915'.
17 12/84, Godfrey Dobson to Garry Roberts, 28 June 1920, Roberts Record Books, Ms 8508, SLV.
18 14.193, Godfrey Dobson to Garry Roberts, c. 5 July 1922, Roberts Record Books, Ms 8508, SLV.
19 17/172–73, Godfrey Dobson to Garry Roberts, 9 Sep 1925, Roberts Record Books, Ms 8508, SLV.
20 17/297, Godfrey Dobson to Garry Roberts, 9 Sep 1926, Roberts Record Books, Ms 8508, SLV.
21 13/110, Jack Castle to Garry Roberts, c. 26 Nov 1920, Roberts Record Books, Ms 8508, SLV.
22 13/251, Tom Wignall to Garry Roberts, 24 Oct 1921, Roberts Record Books, Ms 8508, SLV.
23 13/252, Alf Fox to Garry Roberts, 30 Oct 1921, Roberts Record Books, Ms 8508, SLV.
24 15/282, Jack Castle to Garry Roberts, 28 June 1923, Roberts Record Books, Ms 8508, SLV.
25 18/236, Noble Norwood to Garry Roberts, c. 14 June 1928, Roberts Record Books, Ms 8508, SLV.

26 19/7, Jack Castle to Garry Roberts, 26 January 1930, Roberts Record Books, Ms 8508, SLV.
27 K.S. Inglis, *Sacred Places: war memorials in the Australian landscape*, Melbourne University Publishing, Melbourne, 2008, p. 248.
28 *The Times*, 4 June 1919, 11a.
29 *The Times*, 2 October 1923, 13g.
30 *The Times*, 7 June 1920, 13g.
31 13/133, Noble Norwood to Garry Roberts, 21 January 1921, Roberts Record Books, Ms 8508, SLV.
32 17/390, W.J. Roberts to Garry Roberts, 8 December 1926, Roberts Record Books, Ms 8508, SLV.
33 Garry Roberts to Charles Bean, 8 Sep 1921, 3 DRL 6673/91, AWM 38.
34 7/245, Charles Bean to Garry Roberts, nd [circa August 1922?], Roberts Record Books, Ms 8508, SLV.
35 C.E.W. Bean, *The Australian Imperial Force in France: during the Allied offensive, 1918*, Vol. VI, Sydney, 1942, p. 873.
36 4/484, clipping, April 1920, Roberts Record Books, Ms 8508, SLV.
37 Catalogue of works executed by Arthur Streeton, 18/1/22, AWM 93.
38 Humphrey McQueen, *Tom Roberts*, Macmillan, Sydney, 1996, p. 673.
39 J.G. Roberts Esq, Upper Hawthorn, Vic, 12/11/4144, AWM 93.
40 19/152, Ruby Minter to Garry Roberts, 8 Nov 1928, Roberts Record Books, Ms 8508, SLV.
41 19/239, Garry Roberts to Nancy Roberts, c. 2 Nov 1929, Roberts Record Books, Ms 8508, SLV.
42 Capt A.R. MacNeil to Charles Barrett, 10 March 1920, Unit histories—21st Battalion, 56, AWM 184.
43 7/434, *Herald*, 9 May 1922, Roberts Record Books, Ms 8508, SLV.
44 Anonymous, 'The Dinkum Twenty-first', PR84/125, AWM.
45 17/305, Godfrey Dobson to Garry Roberts, 20 Sep 1926, Roberts Record Books, Ms 8508, SLV.
46 *The Red and Black Diamond*, Vol. I, No.3, August 1935, p. 5.
47 Stephen Garton, *The Cost of War: Australians return*, Melbourne, Oxford University Press, 1996, pp. 29–30, 86–7, 97.
48 Clem Lloyd and Jacqui Rees, *The Last Shilling: a history of repatriation in Australia*, Melbourne University Press, Melbourne, 1994; Stephen Garton, *The Cost of War: Australians return*, Oxford University Press, Melbourne, 1996, Chapter 3 'Repatriation'.
49 Charles Tognella, C138/3, C122956, NAA.
50 *Op. cit.*

51 *Op. cit.*
52 Godfrey Dobson, M57778, B73, NAA.
53 *Sunshine Advocate*, 20 February 1964.
54 *The Red and Black Diamond*, April 1958, p. 5.
55 I am grateful to Greg and his father Gordon Castle for their help in clarifying Jack's family history, based largely on Greg's careful family history research.
56 Frank Roberts to Ruby Roberts, nd, c. March 1918, 'The Dream on the Wind', p. 286.
57 *The Red and Black Diamond*, April 1962.
58 Rabling, William T., M114991, B73, NAA.
59 Frank Roberts to Ruby Roberts, 3 September 1917, 'A Dream on the Wind', p. 139.
60 Charles Bean, 'A Lesson of 1914–18', *Peace*, Melbourne, 1937, p. 13.
61 Report by W.F. Anderson to Doug Anthony, Minister for the Interior, 1966, 1964/4940, Restoration of 2nd Division Memorial at Mont St Quentin, France (Somme), A463, NAA.
62 William Dargie to W.R. Cumming, 22 December 1969, 1964/4940, Restoration of 2nd Division Memorial at Mont St Quentin, France (Somme), A463, NAA.
63 1970/2448, Mont St Quentin Memorial—Proposal for Duplicate to be erected in Anzac Parade, A431, NAA.
64 W.S. Jones, Account of 1971 pilgrimage, 3 DRL 6034, AWM.
65 Interview with William White, Tape 3, 1470, Australians at War Film Archive.
66 Michael McKernan, *This War Never Ends: the pain of separation and return*, University of Queensland Press, Brisbane, 2001, pp. xiii–xiv. I am grateful to Niall Barr for drawing my attention to this anecdote.
67 Don Smerdon to Peter Stanley, 7 January 2008.
68 *The Red and Black Diamond*, April 1972.
69 Alf Fox, *Reply to Omar*, privately published, Melbourne, c. 1962.

Epilogue
1 *The Red and White Diamond*, No. 2, October 1918.
2 27/401, *Sun News Pictorial*, 25 April 1929, Roberts Record Books, Ms 8508, SLV.

Bibliography

Australian War Memorial, Canberra
AWM 4 AIF unit war diaries, 1914–18 War
   23/38, 21st Infantry Battalion, AIF,
   23/6, 6th Infantry Brigade, AIF
   1/44, 1/45, 2nd Infantry Division, AIF
   1/35, Australian Corps
   1/14, Fourth Army
AWM 8 Unit embarkation nominal rolls, 1914–18 War
AWM 9 Unit roll books, 1914–18 War
   18/1, Nominal roll, 21st Battalion, 1917–18
AWM 10 AIF Administrative Headquarters Registry "A"
   4309/3/53, Reduction in establishment: Infantry Battalion and Platoon
AWM 16 Australian War Records Section files and register of titles
   4386/42/21, War Trophies—21st Battalion
   4372/21/4, Models of Battlefields
   4372/21/3, Mont St Quentin memorials
   4372/21/3, Proposal re scheme of models required for Australian War Museum
AWM 25 Written Records, 1914–18 War
   519/22, Report on operations of 2nd Australian Division, Aug–Sep 1918
   385/21, Lewis Gun tactics in trenches
   385/4, Lectures ... Machine-guns including Lewis Guns
   911/9, Strength returns, 21st Battalion, 1918

Bibliography 283

AWM 26 Operations files, 1914–18 War
    550/5, Period 12
    526/3, Period 12
AWM 27 Records arranged according to AWM Library classification
    310/98, Tactical employment of Lewis guns
    344/6, Disbandment of 21st Battalion
AWM 38 Papers of Charles Bean
    3 DRL 606
        228, notebooks, 1918
    3 DRL 6673/
        42, Notes for Volume VI
        57, Papers 1918; twelve files of miscellaneous records
        91, Historical Notes—Mont St Quentin Aug/Sep 1918
        204B, The War History
        308, Work of official and other artists, including Will Longstaff
        309, Work of official and other war artists, including McCubbin
        322, Work of official and other artists, including Streeton
        619, The beginnings of the Australian War Memorial
    3 DRL 1722/
        35, Extract Book Mont St Quentin Péronne 27 Aug–6 Sep 1918
AWM 93 AWM Registry files—First Series
    12/11/4144, J.G. Roberts, Esq ... Request for the donation of private records of Private Francis William Roberts
    12/1/63, History of 21st Battalion, AIF
    13/1/33, Mont St Quentin picture model
    17/1/110, Photograph of the cross erected over the graves of men of the 21st Battalion AIF at Mont St Quentin'
    18/1/6, Mr J. Longstaff, Artist
    18/1/22, Catalogue of works by Mr Arthur Streeton
    18/1/177, Mont St Quentin picture by Leist'
    18/7/9, Australian artists sent to the front: Mr J. Longstaff
    18/7/12, Australian artists sent to the front—Mr A. Streeton
    22/2/273, Gilbert, C. Web—Staff
    23/5/5, Purchase of modelling stores
AWM 131 Roll of Honour circulars
AWM 224 Unit manuscript histories
    MSS 149, 21st Battalion

Private Records
PR84/125, Anonymous, 21st Battalion, AIF

MSS 1297, Pte Harry Barrett, 21st Battalion, AIF
PR85/39, Cpl Robert Graham, 21st Battalion, AIF
PR86/072, Pte Lawrence Polinelli, 21st Battalion, AIF
1 DRL 474 Sgt James Makin, 21st Battalion, AIF
3 DRL 7004, Maj Ernest Mason, 21st Battalion, AIF
PR00093, Sgt William Montgomery, 21st Battalion, AIF
3 DRL 2715, Captain Norman Nicolson, Australian Field Artillery, AIF
PR84/20, Pte Charles Skinner, 17th Battalion, AIF
PR91/113, Cpl Ivor Williams, 21st Battalion, AIF

Troopship Serials
Homeward Bound (Ulysses 1919)
Our Homeward Stunt (Port Macquarie, 1919)
The Red and White Diamond, 1918–19

Works of Art
ART03000 Will Longstaff, *Mt St Quentin*, drawing, 1918
ART03001 Will Longstaff *Mont St Quentin*, drawing, 1918
ART03524 Arthur Streeton, *Mont St Quentin*, drawing, 1918
ART03105 Louis McCubbin, *Mont St Quentin road*, drawing, 1918
ART03051 Louis McCubbin *The battle of Mont St Quentin … drawing, 1918
ART03290 Cecil Percival *Mopping up Péronne, after taking of Mont St Quentin*, drawing, 1920
ART03520 Arthur Streeton, *Péronne, looking towards Mont St Quentin*, drawing, 1918
ART11435.001 Louis McCubbin, *The wall, Mont St Quentin*, first section, painting, 1919
ART12632 Arthur Streeton *Mt St Quentin from Péronne*, drawing, 1918
ART12635 Arthur Streeton, *Road to Mont St Quentin*, drawing, 1918
ART13319 Louis McCubbin, *Mont St Quentin*, drawing, c. 1919
ART41018 C. Web Gilbert, Louis McCubbin and Modelling Sub-section, *Mont St Quentin*, diorama, 1920–23

Australians at War Film Archive
Interview 1470 William White
Interview 1916 Norman Tims

Mitchell Library
ML1536, Pte Francis Joseph Campbell Brewer, 20th Battalion, AIF

ML MSS 1164, J.I. Marshall 'My story of the Big War', 53rd Battalion, AIF
ML DOC 1361, Pte Francis William Roberts, 21st Battalion, AIF
ML MSS 1688, James Ray Lewis, 17th Battalion, AIF
ML MSS 2739/1 CY2465, Maj Gen Charles Rosenthal, 2nd Division, AIF

National Archives of Australia

Canberra
A431 Department of the Interior
    1970/2448 Mont St Quentin Memorial—Proposal for Duplicate to be erected in Anzac Parade
A463 Prime Minister and Cabinet
    1964/4940 Restoration of 2nd Division memorial at Mont St Quentin, France (Somme)
A471 Attorney General's Department, courts martial
    19783 Court martial, Private G.E. Dobson, 21st Battalion
A3211 Correspondence files, Australian High Commission, United Kingdom
    1971/1087 Memorial to the 2nd Australian Division, Mont St Quentin
B2455 First AIF Personnel Dossiers, 1914–1920
    Personnel files of members of Nine Platoon and other soldiers

Melbourne
B73 Repatriation Department—medical files
    HX51337 Wignall, Thomas Henry
    MX51337 Wignall, Thomas H.
    M114991 Rabling, W.T.
    M114991 Rabling, William Thomas
    M57778 Dobson, Godfrey
    M7618 Baker, Arthur Leslie
    M85589 Castle, John
    M52782 Starr, Phillip Henry

Sydney
C138/3 Repatriation Department—medical files
    C122956 'Charles Tognella'
P107/38 Repatriation Department—medical files
    M5789 'Victor James Edwards'

Perth
PP889/1 Repatriation Department
   R11511, Noble Joseph Norwood

National Archives (United Kingdom)
WO95 British Expeditionary Force War diaries
   /437 Fourth Army GS War Diary, August 1918
   /438 Fourth Army War Diary, September 1918
   /3328–3329 21st Battalion, AIF, August–October 1918
WO153 War Office, maps and plans, First World War
   /576 German order of battle on Fourth Army front
WO157 War Office, Intelligence summaries, First World War
   /197 Fourth Army Intelligence summaries
WO158 War Office, Military headquarters, First World War
   /241 Headquarters, Fourth Army

National Army Museum, London
5201–33, Gen Sir Henry Rawlinson

National Gallery of Victoria
Arthur Streeton, *Mont St Quentin*, oil on canvas, 1919

National Library of Australia, Canberra
MS 1538 W.M. Hughes
   Series 23 (Imperial Conference, 1918)
MS 1884 John Monash
   Series 1 (General Correspondence)
   Series 4 (Correspondence)
   Series 14 (Newspaper cuttings)

State Library of Victoria, Melbourne
MS 8508, J.G. Roberts, Record books 1–27
Ms 9949, J.G. Roberts, Diaries 1915–21

Documents in private hands
Roberts papers in the possession of Mrs Jilba Georgalis, Melbourne, including Nancy May Roberts's 'The Dream on the Wind', comprising the diary and letters of Frank Roberts, 1917–18, and Roy Smerdon's postcards in the possession of Mrs Jan Fraser, Shorncliffe, Queensland.

Published sources

Joelle & Didier Arisio, *Memoire en Images Péronne*, Editions Alan Sutton, Saint Cyr-sur-Loire, 1998

Robert Asprey, *The German High Command at War: Hindenburg and Ludendorff conduct World War I*, William Morrow, New York, 1991

C.E.W. Bean, *The Official History of Australia in the War of 1914–18*
    Vol. I *The Story of Anzac*, Angus & Robertson, Sydney, 1921
    Vol. II *The Story of Anzac*, Angus & Robertson, Sydney, 1924
    Vol. III *The Australian Imperial Force in France 1916*, Angus & Robertson, Sydney, 1936
    Vol. IV *The Australian Imperial Force in France, 1917*, Angus & Robertson, Sydney, 1940
    Vol. V *The Australian Imperial Force in France: during the main German offensive, 1918*, Angus & Robertson, Sydney, 1938
    Vol. VI *The Australian Imperial Force in France: during the Allied offensive, 1918*, Angus & Robertson, Sydney, 1942

Frank Brewer, *All About War Gratuity*, privately published, Melbourne, 1920

A.G. Butler, *The Official History of the Australian Army Medical Services in the War of 1914–1918*, Vol. II, *The Western Front*, Australian War Memorial, Canberra, 1940

Les Carlyon, *The Great War*, Macmillan, Sydney, 2006

Terry Cave, (ed.), *Histories of Two Hundred and Fifty-one Divisions of the German Army*, London Stamp Exchange, London, 1989

Alec Chisholm, *C.J. Dennis: His Remarkable Career*, Angus & Robertson, Sydney, 1976

Hugh Clout, *After the Ruins: restoring the countryside of northern France after the great war*, University of Exeter Press, Exeter, 1996

Commonwealth War Graves Commission, *Péronne Communal Cemetery Extension*

Rose Coombs, *Before Endeavours Fade: a guide to the battlefields of the First World War*, After the Battle, London, 1983

Robert Cowley, (ed.), *The Great War: perspectives on the First World War*, Pimlico, London, 2004

Robert Croll, *I Recall: collections and recollections*, Robertson & Mullens, Melbourne, 1939

——, (ed.), *Smike to Bulldog: letters from Sir Arthur Streeton to Tom Roberts*, Ure Smith, Sydney, 1946

F.M. Cutlack, *The Australians: their final campaign, 1918*, Sampson Low, Marston & Co., London, 1919

——, (ed.), *War Letters of General Monash*, Angus & Robertson, Sydney, 1935

Joy Damousi, *Labour of Loss: mourning, memory, and wartime bereavement*, Cambridge University Press, Cambridge, 1999

J.N.I. Dawes & L.L. Robson, *Citizen to Soldier: Australia before the Great War—recollections of the First A.I.F.*, Melbourne University Press, Melbourne, 1977

C.J. Dennis, *The Songs of a Sentimental Bloke*, Angus & Robertson, Sydney, 1915

W.H. Downing, *To the Last Ridge*, H.H. Champion, Melbourne, 1920

Arthur Conan Doyle, *The British Campaign in France and Flanders: July to November 1918*, Hodder and Stoughton, London, nd

James Edmonds, *Military Operations France and Belgium 1918*, Vol. IV, HMSO, London, 1947

J.E. Evans, Battle for Mont St Quentin, *Reveille*, 1 September 1932

L.F. Fitzhardinge, *The Little Digger 1914–1952: William Morris Hughes: a political biography*, Volume II, Angus & Robertson, Sydney, 1979

Anne Galbally, *Arthur Streeton*, Landsdowne Press, Melbourne, 1971

—— & Anne Gray, (eds), *Letters from Smike: the letters of Arthur Streeton 1890–1943*, Oxford University Press, Melbourne, 1989

Stephen Garton, *The Cost of War: Australians return*, Melbourne, Oxford University Press, 1996

General Staff, *The Tactical Employment of Lewis Guns*, London, 1918

J.P. Harris (with Niall Barr), *Amiens to the Armistice: the BEF in the Hundred Days Campaign, 8 August–11 November 1918*, Brassey's London, 1998

Betty Hotchin, *The Bus Camp at Beagley's Bridge*, Monbulk Historical Society, Monbulk, 1989

Ken Inglis, *Sacred Places: war memorials in the Australian landscape*, Melbourne University Publishing, Melbourne, 2008

Pat Jalland, *Australian Ways of Death*, Oxford University Press, Oxford, 2002

J.H. Johnson, *1918: the unexpected victory*, Cassell, London, 1997

Vivienne Lewis, *A Pretty Kettle of Fish: a history of some Australian pioneers*, privately printed, Bellbowrie, 2008

B.H. Liddell Hart, *The Real War 1914–1918*, Faber & Faber, London, 1930

Jocelyn Linder (ed.), *Murrayville 1910–2007*, Murrayville Liaison Committee, Murrayville, 2007

Norman Lindsay, *Norman Lindsay's Book No. II*, Bookstall, Sydney, 1915

Clem Lloyd and Jacqui Rees, *The Last Shilling: a history of repatriation in Australia*, Melbourne University Press, Melbourne, 1994

Tanja Luckins, *The Gates of Memory: Australian peoples' experience and memories of loss and the Great War*, Curtin University Books, Perth, 2004

Erich Ludendorff, *My War Memories 1914–1918*, Vol. II, Hutchinson & Co., London, 1919

A.R. MacNeil, *The Story of the Twenty-First, being the official history of the 21st Battalion, A.I.F.*, 21st Battalion Association, Melbourne, 1920

Kathleen Mangan, *Autumn Memories: a McCubbin family album*, Georgian House, Melbourne, 1988

Frederick Maurice, *The Last Four Months: the end of the war in the west*, Cassell, London, 1919

Ian McLaren, *C.J. Dennis: His Life and Work*, Hall's Book Store, Melbourne, 1961

Ross McMullin, *Pompey Elliott*, Scribe Publications, Melbourne, 2002

Humphrey McQueen, *Tom Roberts*, Macmillan, Sydney, 1996

John Monash, *The Australian Victories in France in 1918*, Hutchinson & Co., London, 1920

David Nash (ed.), *German Army Handbook April 1918*, Arms & Armour Press, London, 1977

Simon Nasht, *The Last Explorer: Sir Hubert Wilkins, unknown Australian hero*, Hodder Australia, Sydney, 2006

Robin Neillands, *The Great War Generals on the Western Front 1914–18*, Robinson, London, 1999

Ian Passingham, *All the Kaiser's Men: the life and death of the German Army on the Western Front 1914–1918*, Sutton, Stroud, 2003

Peter Pedersen, *Monash as Military Commander*, Melbourne University Press, Melbourne, 1985

Victoria Peel, Deborah Zion and Jane Yule, *A History of Hawthorn*, Melbourne University Press and the City of Hawthorn, 1993

Roland Perry, *Monash: the outsider who won a war*, Random House, Melbourne, 2007

Alec Reid and others, *A Village in the Forest: the story of Kallista*, Kallista Centenary 1993 Association, Kallista, 1993

Simon Robbins, *British Generalship on the Western Front 1914–18: defeat into victory*, Frank Cass, London, 2005

J.G. Roberts, *Chronicles of the Scarsdale "Old Boys" Reunion*, privately published, Melbourne, 1927

N.M. Roberts, *The Wine of Courage*, Arthur Stockwell, Ilfracombe, 1977

Geoffrey Serle, *John Monash: a biography*, Melbourne University Press, Melbourne, 1982

Gary Sheffield & John Bourne (eds), *Douglas Haig: war diaries and letters 1914–1918*, Phoenix, London, 2006

Neil Smith, *The Red and Black Diamond: the history of the 21st Battalion 1915–198*, Mostly Unsung Military History, Melbourne, 1997

C.C. Thurlow, *Murrayville Reminiscences*, Sunnyland Press, Red Cliffs, 1996

Richard Travers, *Diggers in France: Australian soldiers on the Western Front*, ABC Books, Sydney, 2008

Jeffrey Verhey, *The Spirit of 1914: militarism, myth and mobilization in Germany*, Cambridge University Press, Cambridge, 2000

Alexander Watson, 'Junior Officership in the German Army during the Great War, 1914 1918, *War in History*, 200714 (4)

H.R. Williams, *Comrades of the Great Adventure*, Angus & Robertson, Sydney, 1935

Bart Ziino, *A Distant Grief: Australians, war graves and the Great War*, University of Western Australia Press, Perth, 2006

Newspapers and magazines

Age (Melbourne); *Argus* (Melbourne); *Aussie*; *The British Australasian* (London); *Herald* (Melbourne); *Mufti*; *The Red and Black Diamond*; *Reveille*; *The Times* (London); *Sydney Morning Herald*

Film

Dick Dennison, *Mutiny on the Western Front*, Mingara Films, Sydney, 1979

Field work, 2007–2008

France: Péronne Cemetery Extension, St Savour Cemetery, Rouen and the Mont St Quentin battlefield

Melbourne: houses in which Nine Platoon lived c. 1914–80

Interviews and meetings with members of the families of the men of Nine Platoon, 2007–08

Index

Allen, 'Nugget' 244
Alston, Edith 48, 53, 151, 191, 233
Americans in France 56–7
Amiens (battle) 46, 57
Anderson, Stanley 27
Anderson, Wallace 187
Anthon, Daniel 79
Anzac legend 51
Armistice 145, 146, 154
Ascanius (ship) 26, 151, 152
Aussie: the Australian Soldiers' Magazine 140
Australian Imperial Force
  contribution to victory 7, 136, 252–4
  repatriation of 160–1
  units and formations
    Australian Corps 42
      stress, 1918 45, 46, 64
      confusion 125
    2nd Division 41–2, 76, 81–2, 87
    3rd Division 97, 101
    5th Division 41
    5th Brigade 76, 77–8, 81, 88, 96, 131, 142, 134, 171
    6th Brigade 40–1, 61, 66, 68, 83, 87, 97, 103, 123, 134, 142, 171, 184, 216
    7th Brigade 120, 123, 131, 134
    14th Brigade 125, 139
    15th Brigade 125
    17th Battalion 80
    19th Battalion 80
    20th Battalion 45, 78, 80, 137
    21st Battalion 26, 39–41, 83
      Association 215–20, 235, 247–50
      at Amiens 57–8
      at Mont St Quentin 65, 88–96, 184–5
      at Querrieu 51–5
      in diorama 184–5
      'mutiny' 129–33
      relics of 180
      Ten Platoon 101–02, 104, 107
      see also Nine Platoon
    22nd Battalion 27, 41, 82, 131
    23rd Battalion 41, 83, 93,

103, 185
24th Battalion 41, 83, 93, 117, 133
43rd Battalion 97
54th Battalion 125
57th Battalion 125
Australian War Museum/Memorial 51, 92, 150, 169, 177, 180–3, 213, 245–6, 256
  origins of dioramas 51–2
  Roll of Honour 257
Australian War Records Section 51, 119

Baker, Agnes 37, 198, 222–3
Baker, Les 9, 10, 33, 120, 197
  at Mont St Quentin 58–9, 68, 69
  background 36–7
  post-war life 198–200, 222–3
  return to Australia 163
Barrett, George 4
Barrett, Percy 24, 152
Barrett, Ted 24, 155, 156
Battle of Mont St Quentin, The (McCubbin) 143–4
Bean, Charles 12, 56, 65, 91, 125, 132, 171, 216, 240
  account of Mont St Quentin 85, 87, 92
  and Arthur Streeton 211
  and artists 144
  and diorama 183–5
  as journalist, 1918 50–5, 61, 139, 143
  criticises Gilbert's memorial 203
  first sees Mont St Quentin 76
  idolises Gellibrand 41
  intrigues against Monash 51
  official history 42, 78, 118–19, 127, 207–10, 253
  records life at Brewery Farm 53–5, 58, 232
  view of and opinions on battle 96–102, 121, 173, 210
Bentwitch, Lizzie 175
Berryman, Frank 206
Bevern, Henry 162
Blackmore, Albert 157
Blackmore, John 157
Blair, Dale 88
Boddy, Herbert 96, 99
Bouchavesnes Spur 97, 101, 144
Bowles, Leslie 187
Brand, Charles 46
Brewer, Frank 45, 78–81, 137–9, 144, 184, 198
Brewery Farm, Querrieu 50–5, 232
Brissenden, Edwin 52–3
British Expeditionary Force 46
  Fifth Army 76
  Fourth Army 60, 75, 76
Broadmeadows camp 14, 25
Broken Years, The 78
Buckley, Sydney 154, 159
Bullecourt 14, 42, 66, 127
Bullus, Bert 112
Burns, Bob 249
Butler-George, May 166–7, 203, 206, 240, 256

Cable, Boyd 204–05
Campbell, Alec 13
Cappy 127, 129–33
Carlyon, Les 14, 81
Carlyon's Hotel, Melbourne 161
Casey, Richard 140
Castle, Ethel 164, 192, 229
Castle, Gordon 229
Castle, Jack 31, 33, 154, 155, 198, 206
  account of Mont St Quentin

INDEX 293

158, 159, 164, 168, 171, 181, 192, 208
at Mont St Quentin 58, 68, 88, 90, 102–18, 123, 124
marries Ethel 164, 192
post-war life 201–02, 218, 228–29
return to Australia 161
supports Lowerson 128
visits War Memorial 183, 186
Cathie, Harry 178
Cemeteries
  Péronne 178, 257–8
  Rouen 258
Chandler family 157
Clark, Manning 191
Cléry 63, 66, 74, 96, 97, 99, 120
Colour patches 40
Conscription 39, 47, 158
Cook, Joseph 141
Coutts, Donald 67, 69, 124, 133, 242–3
Crawford, Alf 11, 33, 193
  account of Mont St Quentin 164
  at Mont St Quentin 58, 102–18
Croll, Robert 22, 25, 28, 170, 206, 210, 215, 255, 259
Cross, Mont St Quentin 156
Cutlack, Fred 169, 171

Damousi, Joy 10
Dargie, William 241
Dearden, George 66, 95, 100, 101, 117
Dennis, C.J. 21–3, 25, 28, 39, 48, 58, 150, 158, 215, 259
Dickson, Selwyn 88, 96, 153
Diorama, Mont St Quentin 51–2, 103–04, 144, 183–87, 256
Dobson, Godfrey 32, 133, 155, 250

account of Mont St Quentin 165
at Mont St Quentin 58, 69, 88, 89, 91, 102–18, 124, 128
background 36–7
post-war life 200–01, 217, 218, 221, 225–8
return to Australia 161
Dobson, Janet 201
Downing, Walter 125
Doyle, Arthur Conan 141
Duggan, Bernard 39, 65, 84, 89, 119, 127, 129, 130, 132, 216, 235
view of attack 93–6, 110, 208
Dyson, Edward 21
Dyson, Will 12, 21, 50, 56, 85, 96, 143, 183, 185

Eastaugh, Edie 4, 21, 212
Edmonds, James 87
Edmondson, Edmund 244
Edwards, Nan 192, 196, 230
Edwards, Vic 10, 32, 132, 133, 155, 162, 244
  at Mont St Quentin 58–9, 102, 102–18
  post-war life 196–7, 218, 230–33, 234
  representative digger 255–6
  return to Australia 161
  supports Lowerson 128
Elliott, Pompey 42, 152
Elsa Trench 81, 83, 91, 103, 109, 118, 167, 177

Fenton, James 226
Fox, Alf 26, 38, 58, 154, 161, 163
  Reply to Omar 248
Fromelles 14
Fullwood, A. Henry 50, 52
Gammage, Bill 78

Garton, Stephen 220–1
Gellibrand, John 41, 96
Georgalis, Jilba 215, 250, 259
George V, King 192, 239
German army 80, 82–4, 84–8
  Bavarian Alpine Corps 85
  2nd Guard Division 78, 84, 86, 87, 172
  14th Division 86
  21st Division 86
  38th Division 86, 87
  41st Division 86
  185th Division 86
  232nd Division 86
Gilbert, Charles Web 12, 22, 25, 27, 76, 103, 152, 181, 207
memorial on Mont 166–8, 203, 206
diorama 183–7
death 186

Gilbert, Mabel 27–8, 167, 186, 207, 259
Gilmore, Alex 109, 133
Gilmour, Gordon 50, 96, 98, 140–1
Glasgow, Will 88
Gorton, John 241
Graves, Robert 74, 85
Great War
  memory of 9–15, 59–60, 220, 244–7
Green, Arch 64, 114, 124, 133, 156, 180, 181
Green, Oswald 38, 48, 58
Gregerson, Allan 249
Guest, Roy 203, 241
Gunn, Jeanie 22, 28, 164
Gye, Hal 21

Hague Convention 89
Haig, Douglas 46, 60, 176, 217
Hamel (battle) 46, 56

Hammond, Stanley 241
Hardwick, William 66, 95, 96, 104, 132
Heath, Mary 123
Heath, Ted 33, 39, 55, 257
  at Mont St Quentin 58–9, 88, 102–18
  death of 122–3
  wounded 112, 122–3
Heath, William 123
Hindenburg Line 85, 131
Historial de la Grande Guerre 125
Hobbs, Talbot 41
Holt, Norman 91, 95, 96, 124
Hughes, Billy 136, 141–2
Hurley, Frank 50

Imperial (Commonwealth) War Graves Commission 159–60
Innes, Guy 2, 149, 164

Jackson, Stonewall 134
Jalland, Pat 11
Jones, Joe 164

Kelly, Albert 33, 257
  at Mont St Quentin 58, 102–18
  shared grave 156, 159
  supports Lowerson 128
  wounded and killed 113, 117
Kelly, Isabel 158

Laffin, John 241
Lambert, George 187
Lawrence, D.H. 181
Lewis guns 43–5, 105
Lewis, Vivienne 259
Lindsay, Norman 2
Longstaff, Will 50, 135, 144
Lost Ravine 67–8, 88, 93, 114, 121, 242
Low, David 21, 25

Lowerson, Alby 101–02, 104, 112, 121, 163
　awarded Victoria Cross 126–7
　death and commemoration 247–8
　return to Australia 161
　wounded 114
Luckins, Tanja 11
Ludendorff, Erich 57, 75

Mactier, Robert 126
Manual of Military Law 89
Martin, Edward 77, 81
Material culture 12, 40, 153, 181, 180–7, 192, 259–61
Maurice, Frederick 172
McBride, Isabel 244
McColl, John 68
McConochie, Willie 66
McCubbin, Louis 143–4, 186
McKernan, Michael 245–6
McLachlans, William, Gil and Mat 245
McLeod, Eveline 237, 239
McLeod, Ken 239
McNeil, Alexander 216
Memorials, War, *see* War memorials
Mendelsohn, Harris 68, 121, 124
Minter, Percy 214
Mitchell Library 78, 212
Monash, Bertha 175–80, 205
Monash, John 41, 96, 217
　account of battle 77, 81, 134, 187, 253
　and Australian Corps 42, 60
　and mutinies of 1918 131
　and stress on Corps 46, 64
　and plans for attack 63, 82
　Australian Victories in France 42, 61, 169, 173–4
　inspects 21st Battalion 43
　records contributions to victory 136, 140, 172–4
　reputation of 7, 42
　supposed friend of Robertses 28
　visits Mont St Quentin, 1919 175–80, 205
Montbrehain 132
Montgomery, William 130, 131, 132
Mont St Quentin
　1971 pilgrimage 242–3
　after the war 203–06
　artists and 143–5
　burial of dead 123–4
　'crater'/'quarry' 100, 110–18
　diorama 183–7, 245–6
　fame of the battle 7–8, 252–4
　'finest feat of the war' 142, 134, 187, 248, 253
　first (31 August) attack 77–82
　'flag' report, 31 August 80–1, 172, 254
　genesis of battle 60–1, 63
　Gilbert's memorial on Mont 166–8, 205–06, 219, 240–1, 256
　Hammond's memorial on Mont 241, 243, 248
　history to 1918 73–5
　judgement on the battle 61–3, 82–3, 151, 170–5, 252–4
　material culture 12, 40, 153, 181, 180–7, 192, 259–61
　medical arrangements 121–2
　memorial cross 181–2
　memorials on 166–8, 205–06, 219, 240–1, 241, 243, 248, 256
　Monashes' visit, 1919 175–80
　press delegation visits 140–1
　press reports on 133–6, 139–43
　properties named after 244
　second (1 September) attack 82–4

sources about battle 77, 84, 88–9, 92–3, 94–5, 208
state rivalry over 142–3, 174–5
third (1 September) attack 102–18
Victoria Crosses and 126–8
'worthy of the highest praise' 82
Mont St Quentin (Streeton) 145, 211
Morris, 'Doc' 79
Mouquet Farm 42, 127
Murdoch, Keith 50, 61

Nicolson, Norman 126
Nine Platoon, 21st Battalion
at Mont St Quentin 67, 91, 101–02, 102–18
composition, 1918 31–4
enlistment 32–4
individuals' backgrounds 35–9
leadership in battle 66
reorganised, June 1918 43
significance of 93, 254
No Quarter 89
Norwood, Noble 33, 38, 162, 192
account of Mont St Quentin 165, 208
at Mont St Quentin 58–9, 89, 102–18
meets Edith Alston 191
Paris leave, 1918 48, 150
post-war life 194–5, 220, 233–4
return to Australia 161
wounded 109, 122
writes to Robertses 152, 169, 192, 202, 205

Osterley (ship) 101

Peacock, Edward 142, 172
Pearson, Keith 241
Pedersen, Peter 82

Péronne 60, 125–26, 177
'Roo de Kanga' 126, 177, 255
Perotti, Annelle 234
Peterson, Daniel 80
Picture models, *see* Dioramas
Ploegsteert Wood 29
Polinelli, Lawrence 130, 145, 146
Power, Bill 249
Pozières 14, 42, 184, 232
Prisoners of war 87, 88–9, 108, 120

Querrieu 50–5
Quinn, James 144

Rabling, Bill 33, 133, 244
at Mont St Quentin 58–9, 102–18
marries Elsie 237
post-war life 237–40
return to Australia 161
Rawlinson, Henry 60–1, 76, 81–2, 96, 248
Red and Black Diamond, The 217, 219, 228, 238, 248–50, 255
Red Cross 3, 156, 181, 197, 234
'Red Zone' 204–5
Reed, Alfred 130
Repatriation Department ('the Repat') 193–4, 194–5, 199, 220–2, 223–5, 225–8, 230–3, 234–7, 238
Road to Querrieu (Fullwood) 52
Roberts family
and Frank's death 1–5
and Sunnyside circle 20–3
introduced 1–2
patronage of C.J. Dennis 22–4
Roberts, Berta 1–5, 53, 191, 213
Roberts, Frank
as 'souvenir king' 56, 88, 124

INDEX 297

at Mont St Quentin 58, 64–5, 68, 102–18, 127
at Querrieu 54
burial places 154, 155–6, 178, 258
childhood 20
Croll's eulogy 215, 255–6
death 3, 8–9, 111, 112, 114, 154–5, 161–2
embarkation for war 26–7
friendship with C.J. Dennis 23, 215
in memoriam notices 150, 206
interest in slang 39, 47–8, 58
letters to Ruby 29–31, 49–50, 55–6, 59, 64, 65, 150, 251
marriage to Ruby 25
model for memorial figure 167, 205
Monashes visit grave 178
orchardist in Dandenongs 24–5
Paris leave, 1918 48, 150
relationships with comrades 38
shared grave 156, 159
supports Lowerson 128
training in Australia and Britain 27–9
Roberts, Garry
and Frank's death 1–5, 149–51, 153
and Frank's memorial book 168–70
and memorial on Mont 167
and shared grave 156–60
attitude to war 47, 49, 179
contact with Frank's comrades 161–6, 195, 196, 200–02, 208
diary 1–5, 149
does not travel to France 205
farewells Frank 26
final years 210–14
meets Edith Alston 191

Record Books 2, 8–9, 59, 152–3, 209, 251, 256
relationship with AWM 180–3
views of Mont St Quentin 153, 171–5
sends Bean accounts of battle 208
Roberts, Gwen
and Frank's death 1–5, 212, 213
Roberts, Johnny/Bert 1, 29, 213–14
and Frank's death 1, 5
injured 31
verse 30
Roberts, Lennard 4, 25
Roberts, Nancy
birth 30
childhood 214–15
Frank's feelings toward 49–50
keepsakes 259–61
life 250–2
Roberts, Ruby 4
courtship and marriage 24–5
keepsakes 259–61
life and death 250, 252
photographs in Record Book 170
reactions to Frank's death 149, 260
re-marries 214
Roberts, Tom 210–12, 256
Roberts, Will 4
Robertson, James 40, 61, 68, 83, 84, 129, 131
Robson, Lloyd 34
Rosenthal, Charles 41–2, 76, 78, 82, 94, 140, 130, 131, 132, 144, 166, 181, 203, 211, 254

Sailors and Soldiers' Fathers' Association 2, 48–9, 179, 260
Sale, Fred 83, 84, 219

Scates, Bruce 11
Scott, Walter 169
Sennitt, Alfred 66, 91, 96, 100
Shirlow, John 21, 206
Simmie, Jock 187
Smart, H. Casimir 137
Smedley, Harold 156
Smerdon family 35, 159, 246–7
Smerdon, Cliff 33, 36
Smerdon, Don 247
Smerdon, Roy 33, 53, 193, 257
  at Mont St Quentin 58–9, 68, 102–18, 168
  background 35–6
  death 113
  shared grave 156, 159
  supports Lowerson 128
Smith, Hugh 111, 115–16, 133
Somme (battle, 1916) 14, 42, 45, 87
Somme, River 60, 66
Southland (ship) 32, 40
Staaf family 205
Starr, Phil 38, 64–5, 102, 104, 116, 119, 151–2, 163, 166
State Library of Victoria 168, 213, 256
Streeton, Arthur 12, 50, 144–5, 211–12
Sullivan, James 94, 95, 118–19, 185
Tognella, Charlie 33, 192, 197, 244
  at Mont St Quentin 58–9, 102–18
  background 36
  post-war life 193–4, 220, 223–5
  return to Australia 161
  wounded 121, 122
Towner, Edgar 126
Treloar, John 51, 91, 145, 169, 183–5, 203, 207–8, 211

Trevascus, Bill 129, 130, 131, 132, 133
Trophies 124
Tuchman, Barbara 12

Verdun 87
Victoria Cross 126
Villers-Bretonneux 14, 176
Ville-sur-Ancre 55–6
von der Marwitz, Georg 86

Walker, Alex 115, 124, 157
Walker, Bella 157
Walker, George 157, 182
Walker, Janet 157, 182
Walking with the Anzacs 245
War memorials 13–14
Watt, James 93–4
Wellington, Duke of 77
White and Red Diamond, The 133
White, William 244
Whiting, John 221
Wignall, Tom 33, 55, 133, 206, 244, 248
  at Mont St Quentin 58, 66, 67, 69, 88, 90, 94, 102, 102–18
  contact with Robertses 170
  post-war life 197–8, 218, 234–7
  return to Australia 161
  wounded 110–11, 121, 122
Wilkins, Hubert 12, 50–1, 54, 64, 126, 132, 181
  and diorama 184–5, 207
  photographs, 1 September 1918 118–19
Winnett, George 112
Woolcock, Len 176–80

Yeend, Geoffrey 241
Ypres (Passchendaele) 42, 127, 184